I0879299

almanac

association for welsh writing in english

PARTHIAN

almanac

a yearbook

of

welsh writing

in english

critical
essays

edited by Katie Gramich

association for welsh writing
in english

PARTHIAN

almanac – a yearbook of welsh writing in english: critical essays is supported by the Association for Welsh Writing in English

and is published by
Parthian
The Old Surgery
Napier Street
Cardigan
SA43 1ED
www.parthianbooks.co.uk

First published in 2010

ISBN 978-190699-831-8

The publisher acknowledges the financial
support of the Welsh Books Council.
Cover image: The Dream Approaches © Salvador Dalí, Gala-Salvador Dalí Foundation, DACS, London
Cover design: Marc Jennings www.theundercard.co.uk

Printed and bound by www.lightningsource.com

British Library Cataloguing in Publication Data

A cataloguing record for this book is available from the British Library.

almanac

a yearbook of welsh writing in english: critical essays

vol 14 | 2009–10

Contents:

Civilizing the Natives:

Henry M. Stanley's and Joseph Conrad's Narratives of Identity

Steve Hendon
Cardiff University

On 30 May 1890, The American Testimonial Banquet, organised by the US Consul General, was held in London to honour Henry Morton Stanley's 'Heroic Achievements in the cause of Humanity, Science & Civilization'.[1] Stanley's reputation had been made through his leadership of the expedition to search for Livingstone in Africa, and subsequent intrepid ventures which opened up unknown regions of that continent. By the time of the banquet, Stanley had become one of the most representative figures of 'successful' nineteenth-century imperialism, yet his origins were marginal. Born into poverty in the north Wales town of Denbigh, he left Britain for the USA when he was seventeen years old and made his name as an Anglo-American, only being re-naturalized in 1892, at the age of fifty-one. Stanley's income derived largely from his writing career. His accounts of his life and his expeditions played a vital role in the self-fashioning of a 'civilized', centred identity which became particularly important as his adventuring days ended, and he based himself at his Westminster and Surrey homes.

As the Testimonial Banquet was taking place, Joseph Conrad was travelling to the Congo; as an employee of a Belgian trading company, he would see first-hand the effects of imperialism's perceived 'success'. Conrad's 'legend', as Allan H. Simmons puts it, is 'well known'; a Polish émigré who learned to speak English while working in the British Merchant Service for much of the period between 1878 and 1890, he became 'one of the country's most celebrated authors'.[2] Conrad settled in England and, in 1886, was naturalized as British, as Stanley had been re-naturalized. His most famous text, *Heart of Darkness* (1899), illuminates the problematic issues of dual identity that resulted from his alienating experience in the Congo, where the 'civilizing' work went hand-in-hand with commercial rapacity. In his writings, images of marginalization co-exist with a complicity with central ideas of European imperialism. Through earlier texts, however, Conrad was keen to establish not only a literary career, but also a place in his adopted English homeland.

The purpose of this essay is to compare texts by Stanley and Conrad, as, respectively, Welsh and Polish exiles, in relation to what Homi K. Bhabha terms the 'double narrative movement'[3] of cultural identity. Bhabha suggests that in 'the production of the nation as narration there is a split between the continuist, accumulative temporality of the pedagogical, and the repetitious, recursive strategy of the performative'.[4] A cultural complex is generated in the interaction of an organizing principle with something more elusive and challenging. Such a complex provides fertile ground in respect of the way in which Conrad's texts shed light on his own hybridized identity; however, his novella *The Nigger of the 'Narcissus'* (1897) suggests the formation of more fixed ideals. In that context, this essay takes Stanley's *Autobiography* (1909) and *Through the Dark Continent* (1878) as exemplars of pedagogical writing, and compares their narrative strategies with those deployed in Conrad's novella, with regard to notions of 'civilized' Englishness.

Henry Morton Stanley

Stanley was born John Rowlands on 28 January 1841, the illegitimate son of a butcher's daughter, and a father whose identity was somewhat undecided. He was cared for by his extended family until 1847, when, because of financial difficulties, he was sent to the workhouse at St Asaph. The *Autobiography* describes his experience there in the language of oppression. The inmates are 'made slaves',[5] but his escape, in 1856, after repelling a supposed attack by a teacher, has been exposed by recent biographers as 'a fantasy':[6] as Stanley recalls, '[I] possessed myself of his [cane] and struck him at random', before running away (*A*, 41–42). However dramatic this account, its notions of triumphing over adversity and classification as 'Other', the 'British outcast' (*A*, 20), are key to his public acceptance as a successful 'man of the Nineteenth Century' (*A*, 15).

In 1858, Rowlands emigrated to America, and was effectively adopted by a New Orleans merchant, Henry Hope Stanley, whose name he assumed. He subsequently became a journalist and, between 1869 and 1871, undertook the assignment for the *New York Herald* to search for Livingstone. This expedition made Stanley famous, and his book, *How I Found Livingstone* (1872), was a bestseller. In London, however, the English Establishment was sceptical. Members of the Royal Geographical Society were disbelieving of his achievements, and alleged that he 'lacked the credentials of either a gentleman or a scientist'.[7] Nevertheless, after other notable ventures, Stanley was popularized as a hero. He was later elected MP for North Lambeth in 1895 and knighted in 1899. Stanley had undergone a social metamorphosis from his humble Welsh origins, and Dorothy Stanley's Preface[9] to the *Autobiography* suggests that his re-positioning should be regarded pedagogically. She quotes Stanley:

> [i]magine yourself in personal view of all the poor boys in these islands, English, Scotch, Welsh and Irish, and ... our Colonies; regarding them as we regard those in schools we visit in Lambeth, or at Cadoxton, we should see ... thousands [to] whom [we] wish to say something that would encourage them in their careers.
>
> ... Not all who hear are influenced by precept, and not all who see change by example. But ... there must be a goodly number of boys who are penetrable, and it is for these ... that I would care to leave a truthful record of my life [so as] to teach some lessons. (*A*, 1–2)[10]

The Preface establishes Stanley's life as a 'precept' – a 'rule for conduct', as the *Oxford English Dictionary* defines the word. Dorothy Stanley notes that the young Stanley was himself governed by strong cultural forces. As she asserts: the 'denials of [his] early years ... were shaping [him for] great work'; he wished 'to obliterate the stigma of pauperism [so] that, when he had achieved fame', he would be recognized as someone of 'real nobility of character' (*A*, 2–3). That Dorothy Stanley emphasizes issues of cultural acceptance for the publication of the *Autobiography* in 1909 indicates that they were as important then as when Stanley was a Welsh workhouse boy over fifty years previously. His declared method of writing supports this principle:

> [m]y prospects now cannot be blasted by gibes. [Therefore] I can lay bare all [of my] circumstances ... Indeed, I wish to appear without disguise, as regards manners and opinions, habits and characteristics. (*A*, 7–8)

The assertion of appearing without disguise is questionable. I propose to show how Stanley constructs his narratives as 'precepts'.

After 'escaping' from the workhouse, Stanley travelled to his aunt's home in the nearby village of Tremeirchion. He remembers that its inhabitants were:

> all exceedingly proud ... they despised all foreigners [and had a] prejudice born of ignorance ... which knew nothing of the broad, sunny lands beyond the fog-damp Vale [of Clwyd]. (*A*, 59)

He then generalizes:

> [t]he North-Welsh are a compound of opposites ... sensible in business, but not enterprising; ... industrious and thrifty, but not rich; [they] waste their spare time in [the] malice, ill-nature, and filthy or idle gossip [of] vacuous minds. (*A*, 59–61)

Emyr Wyn Jones considers these remarks, not surprisingly,

'gratuitously offensive' and observes that the region was 'one of the most important cultural centres in Wales'.[11] However, Stanley recalls the community as 'a temporary visitor ... the last in the village' (*A*, 61), othered by his lowly upbringing. He thus represents it as alien and directionless, reflecting his own displacement. Nearby Liverpool, however, is presented through an outward-looking perspective as the place where Stanley's 'future [is] shaped' (*A*, 62). An uncle suggests that he might obtain work in the city. He is taken there, and 'Wales recede[s] from view' (*A*, 63).

As Stanley gets to know Liverpool, he is drawn towards the imperial romance of the 'magnificent ships' in the Docks:

> [s]uch broad and long-reaching extent of decks ... and dizzy height of masts! What an atmosphere of distant regions, suggestive of spicy Ind ... bales of silk ... barrels [rising] up as high as the shed-roof ... it was grand to see the gathered freight from all parts of the world under English roofs. (*A*, 71–72)

Stanley's exclamatory tone and accumulative language, 'long-reaching ... dizzy height', stresses a contrast with the oppressively 'fog-damp' Vale of Clwyd. Correspondingly, the people employed on the ships are the opposite of the indeterminate, 'vacuous' North–Welsh: positively engaged within a productive hierarchy,

> [t]here were real Liverpool boys ... prodigies of practical wisdom [who] pointed out to me certain stern-faced men, ... as the captains ... men of unlimited energy and potent voices as the mates, or officers, who [carried out] their superior's commands; and the jerseyed workmen in the rigging [displayed] strength, daring, and defiance. (*A*, 72)

The 1850s, during which Stanley began work, was, as E. J. Hobsbawm has observed, a period of 'unproblematic' imperialist expansion driven freely by market forces.[12] The qualities which Stanley sees represented in the workers in the Liverpool dockyards denote hard work, and a compliance with duty through a centralized command structure. They constitute a formative narrative of identity that suits the enterprising zeitgeist. Although his decision to leave Britain for America in 1858 at the age of seventeen[13] suggests a capacity for self-determination, Stanley was to adhere to such a progressive imperialist narrative throughout his life.

The contrast between Stanley's Welsh home and what is available to him in the wider imperial world, notably that represented 'under English roofs', sheds light on his later attitude towards any 'Other', including his own family, that does not conform to hegemonic ideas of progress. This feature of his writing is illustrated in his account of a brief visit to Wales, when he was twenty-one. After working in the commercial world of New Orleans, Stanley served on both sides in the American Civil War. In 1862, he was invalided out and returned to his mother. However, she had married, and had become more respectable; the illegitimate outsider was quickly asked to leave. Such 'rebuffs', nevertheless, produced in him a strong 'self-command', and a determination to 'rebound towards the world of vigorous action' (*A*, 225);[15] the Welsh world, by implication, appears to be unyieldingly static.

After working briefly in the merchant service, Stanley returned to America. He later took up the journalist's job that developed into exploration. The latter role fulfilled his destiny: to be 'a maker of events' (*A*, 226).[16] Stanley, in a letter written in 1869, emphasizes his active fashioning of an archetypal imperial identity; he explains how he is achieving success:

> [h]ow have I done this? By intense application to duty, by self-denial, which means I have denied myself all pleasures, so that I might do my duty thoroughly and exceed it ... I am so much my own master, that I am master over my own passions ... my future promotion to distinction hangs upon

> [doing my duty] ... I have nothing to fall back on but energy, and much hopefulness. (*A*, 254)

This is his defining declaration: there is no thought of a home to which he can return, only the repeated notion of succeeding by doing one's duty. In *Through the Dark Continent*, he projects this idea, in cultural and imperial terms, onto his account of his 1874–77 expedition to central Africa. The 1988 republication celebrates his 'major role' in 'assembling the fragmented ... geographical knowledge of [the territory] into a coherent picture'.[17] As Stanley, after leaving Wales, single-mindedly fashions his own life around central ideals, so the 'Other' of Africa is formalized through conventional modes of representation. However, Stanley was criticised for the force which he used to suppress native tribes during the expedition. The disapproval of his methods indicates that he thinks as the Welsh outsider who is seeking acceptance – the same outsider who, six years earlier, was considered by the English Establishment to be less than a gentleman. He prefaces *Through the Dark Continent* with an acknowledgement that his 'conduct [had] not been understood;' the book thus serves a corrective purpose, as a 'simple record of his daily actions' (*DC*, ix). Nevertheless, its original publication in 1878 places it in the era of influential imperialist texts.[18] As Andrea White comments, such narratives were 'shaping discourses'; they were pedagogical, not only for other explorers, but also for fiction writers, Conrad in particular, because of their 'idealizing power'.[19]

Stanley's narrative form declares itself in Chapter One's title, 'Explanation'. His mission is to fill the 'white blank' of Africa 'to the advantage of science, humanity, and civilisation' (*DC*, 2–3).[20] His method is to 'map, lay out, and describe' (*DC*, 2): illustrations and precise data suggest the organizing narrative of a report.[21] However, Stanley occasionally deviates into imaginative representation: at Zanzibar, a stopping-off point, he personifies the 'verdant shores' where '[p]alms raise their feathery heads [and] trees loom up [from] the warm heaving bosom of the island' (*DC*, 23). Such feminized language creates the sensation that the expedition members have encountered a complicating and alluring Mother Nature. However, this diversion serves only to prepare for a re-assertion of Stanley's shaping binary discourse: at the moment of the expedition's departure, '[t]hick shadows fall ... as we glide away through the dying light towards The Dark Continent' (*DC*, 54). The conventional diminishing light and increasing dark imagery marks boundaries between civilization and 'Other', the latter being subtly manoeuvred into place through the feminized narrative. Stanley, himself an 'Other', thus sets the foundations of a 'simple record' which will, in fact, persuasively support an ideological 'Sameness'.

Stanley recruited hundreds of indigenous bearers for the journey. He judges them to be 'fixed deeply in barbarism' (*DC*, 38). As the 'honourable white man', his 'sacred' duty is to 'help ... the negro' to understand his 'moral powers rightly' (*DC*, 38–39). He draws up a 'covenant' in which he undertakes to act like a 'father and mother' to the natives; this imperial exchange requires them to 'do their duty' and honour Stanley's instructions (*DC*, 51–52). To his sponsors, the *Daily Telegraph* and the *New York Herald*, he writes: '[w]hat a ... harvest ripe for the sickle of civilization!'; 'saviour[s] of Africa' such as he, should be 'practical Christian tutors' guiding the 'Other' towards the norm of the 'white race' (*DC*, 164).[22] However, as the expedition proceeds and is challenged by hostile tribes, Stanley becomes less the 'tutor' and more the wielder of the 'sickle'.

In his account of violent confrontations at Bumbireh Island on Lake Victoria, Stanley asserts a 'continuist precept' that civilizing the natives entails calculated prohibitive action. On the expedition's first visit to Bumbireh it had been attacked. Returning three months later,[23] Stanley plans an act of 'justice which, according to all laws human and divine, savage and civilised, demands that blood shall atone for blood' (*DC*, 226).[24] In his sub-section 'The Work of Punishment', he describes how 'a volley was fired into [the natives], which quite crushed their courage', and confirms his purpose as 'chastisement' (*DC*, 229).[25]

The punishment that Stanley meted out caused outrage in Britain. Felix Driver notes that Stanley's newspaper reports of the second Bumbireh incident, rather than justifying his actions, gloried in the 'entic[ing] of the natives' to their deaths: 'at least forty-two [were] slaughtered'. However, as Tim Jeal has argued, a more significant cause of outrage 'was that [Stanley] had written openly about killing Africans'; these things were done, but not 'advertised',[26] at least, not by 'gentlemen'. Here is the 'outcast', who publicizes his compulsion to excel so as to erase his marginalized status. However, Stanley's Welsh workhouse upbringing betrays him: in pursuit of cultural acceptance at the English centre, he ignores received wisdom in respect of 'proper' conduct.

As if the dispensing of fierce 'justice' were insufficient to prove his qualities, Stanley goes on to re-assert the Christian ethics which he had earlier espoused in his 'covenant' with the natives. He achieves this through a narrative strategy that appropriates African voices to his own paternalist discourse. For instance, when he meets Ungomirwa, the king of Ubagwé, the king reportedly asks Stanley's bearers why they are part of the expedition; 'they' reply in impossibly convenient language:

> [t]he white people know everything. They are better than the black people ... We carry his goods for him and he bestows a father's care on his black children. Let Ungomirwa make friends with the white man ... and it will be good for [his] land. (*DC*, 390)

In support of such pedagogical ideals of European morality, Stanley persistently presents the image of white men as bringers of light, even in death. One of his officers later drowns: the natives who find him are 'attracted by something gleaming on the water ... [the] face of a white man'.[27] His strategy exemplifies what Bhabha terms 'iteration'.[28] This is, in effect, a shaping device that Stanley uses to 'articulate' natives to the completeness of the white hegemony; however, Bhabha points out that this very 'repetition of ["Sameness"] can in fact be its own displacement'.[29]

Declan Kiberd has noted the way in which displacement occurs during the repetitious process of creating the 'gleaming' identity to which 'Others' should aspire. Although referring to the Irish colonial situation, Kiberd's analysis of the typical imperialist's persona establishes a telling principle: paradoxically, 'their polished surface [evidenced] their premature self-closure which left them at once incomplete and *finished*. [It] indicated a person immune to self-doubt and therefore incapable of development.'[30] The principle of displacement is well-illustrated by another instance of Stanley's appropriation of African voices. Almost at the end of the expedition, Stanley and his party are at the point of starvation, but he nevertheless guides everyone to the safety of the coastal region. The natives thank Stanley for his efforts: '[v]erily, our master has found the sea ... God be praised for ever [that] we shall see white people to-morrow, and our wars and troubles will be over.'[31] In the light of history, this iterative statement is, for Africans, cruelly ironic.

The complexities entailed in sustaining an image of perfect 'Sameness' have implications for Stanley's representation of himself as a 'precept' – a shaper of 'Others'. For those natives amenable to 'civilized' ways, he is a faith-inspiring teacher: the pedagogical face of imperialist received wisdom. Where resistance is encountered, he is the uncompromising imperialist enforcer: the performative reality of colonization. The civilizing mission integrated both approaches, but, in the late nineteenth century, public perception was that enforcement had all but obscured the moral dimension. This may account for the tone of Stanley's Preface to the

1899 edition of *Through the Dark Continent*, in which he strives to secure his status as a pioneer of 'remarkable progress' (*DC*, xi). The Preface describes advances made by King Leopold II of Belgium, assisted by Stanley as his chief agent, in exploiting the Congo, and, in the *Autobiography*, Dorothy Stanley supports this position by portraying her husband as the epitome of a dutiful imperialist. His purpose in the Congo was to further a grand shaping discourse: 'the betterment of mankind'; his aim was 'as *pure* ... as Livingstone's. But, as a means, he looked not alone to the efforts of isolated missionaries, but to the influx of great tides of beneficent activities' (*A*, 346).

Stanley's Preface is self-congratulatory. Cultural improvement rests on European commercial technology – the 'beneficent activities'. For example, Stanley had made 'zealous efforts' to 'induce capitalists' to construct railways, 'knowing [that] they were the best instruments [for the] social elevation of the dark peoples' (*DC*, xix): here is a colonizer who is 'immune to self-doubt'. Conrad, who was also an employee in Leopold's Congo trading company, witnessed the corrosive effects of such 'progress' and represents it in *Heart of Darkness*: native workers are '[b]rought from all the recesses of the coast ... lost in uncongenial surroundings ... they sickened, became inefficient, and were allowed to [die]'.[32] Stanley is silent on this 'performative' dimension of the natives' 'elevation'. His argument in the Preface is not, in Kiberd's terms, 'developed' beyond the commercial: the share price of the Congo Railway – 'today it is fully employed in traffic, and the 500-franc shares are worth 1700 francs' (*DC*, xix).

The Preface expresses a wish that Britain become involved in the colonizing work in Africa, and admonishes its Government for its failure to exploit the continent's resources. However, the narrative shifts from a discussion of 'British' policy to 'England's affairs' (*DC*, xiv–xv). By the time of writing the Preface, Stanley was the MP for North Lambeth: he had attained a place in the English metropolis and had a social status to preserve. In an election campaign in 1892[33] he had promoted the 'spread [of] the British Empire', but it was 'we Englishmen' who had 'the greatest destiny [of] any race' (*A*, 466).[34]

Stanley's Welsh origins had now truly 'receded from view'. Writing to his wife in 1891, he confirms his desire to draw the Welsh towards the central discourse of progress that is espoused in *Through the Dark Continent* and its later Preface. Considering his wife's suggestion that he accept an invitation to preside at the forthcoming National Eisteddfod, he confides:

> [t]he Eisteddfod [is] for the purpose of exciting interest in the Welsh nationality and language [but I] recommend Welshmen to turn their attention to a closer study of the English language, literature, and characteristics, for it is only by that training that they can hope to compete with their English brothers for glory, honour, and prosperity ... [for what] *is* Cambria, alone? ... what hope for her, separate and distinct from her big sister Britannia, or rather Anglia? (*A*, 454–455)

The desire for a 'civilized' white rule that Stanley attributes to African natives is now recommended to the Welsh, but in the form of an English hegemony. His assertion that Welsh 'natives' must be trained to be like the English confirms a wish to 'obliterate' the idea of himself as a marginalized 'Other'.

Earlier in the Autobiography, Stanley refers to African pigmies as 'a degenerate stock of ordinary humanity'; he stresses the 'Otherness' of 'the little people' and declares in more general ideological terms that 'tribes and nations are subject to the same influences as families. If confined strictly to itself, even a nation must, in time, deteriorate' (*A*, 383–384). 'Ordinary human' status is thus achievable only by moving towards pedagogical notions of 'Sameness', and ultimately, for Stanley, that journey concludes with Anglicization. In these terms, he represents his identity as shaped and 'finished', and the way in which he defines himself through narrative offers a model against which the texts of other writers from marginalized origins may be analysed in respect of public positioning. I now turn to an examination of how Stanley's writings shed light on the narrative in *The Nigger of the 'Narcissus'*, bearing in mind that the novella was published as Conrad began to forge a literary career in England.

Joseph Conrad

Conrad was born Józef Teodor Konrad Korzeniowski on 3 December 1857 into a Polish land-owning family 'at Berdichev in Podolia, a part of the Polish Commonwealth that had been appropriated into the Russian Ukraine in 1793'.[35] His father's activism against Russian imperialism resulted in a series of exiles and dislocations during Conrad's childhood. Later, as the seventeen-year-old Stanley had emigrated, Conrad, at the same age, left his family to become a merchant seaman, first with a French shipping company and later on British vessels. Other comparisons can be drawn between the two men. As I note above, both became employees of King Leopold II's regime in the Congo. Stanley had described Africa as a 'blank' waiting to be civilized, and Conrad had been enticed by 'the unsolved mystery of that continent'; as a boy, looking at 'the blank space' on a map of Africa, he had determined to 'go *there*'.[36] Their views of colonialism in Africa were dissimilar, but in their formative years each had been inspired by what was essentially imperial adventure. Stanley admired the work ethic of the men who served on the trading ships in Liverpool docks; Conrad extolled the values of duty conveyed by the British Merchant Marine Service. As Conrad says, the ships and men of the Service were 'the ultimate shapers of my character [and] convictions.'[37]

In *The Nigger of the 'Narcissus'*, the eponymous merchant ship sails from Bombay to London;[38] during the journey, a storm tests the crew. Critics have focused on the novella's initial cultural positioning;[39] written in the fin-de-siècle mood of uncertainty, it recalls Conrad's marine service at the apex of British imperial power. Tim Middleton notes that it was 'carefully' aimed at the 'English literary market';[40] Conrad's artistic objectives were 'to get [at] the *essence* of life'[41] and to 'enshrine [his sea-faring] chums in a *decent edifice*'.[42] These declarations suggest a substantial pedagogical construction. As Allan H. Simmons observes, Conrad's association with the British Merchant Service's character-forming traditions of duty 'strikes [a] national chord'.[43] However, Simmons also notes an identification with a more particular nationalism: in Conrad's sea fiction there is 'an assertion of identity with various traditions of Englishness'.[44] It is not appropriate to suggest that this represents a cultural shift exactly comparable to that of Stanley's. The latter's desire to erase his Welshness, effectively to become English, presents a complication to the more general idea of Britishness, as that term carries meaning for natives of the UK.[45] Such internal differences of nationality would not necessarily have been apparent to the Polish Conrad. However, the narrative form of *The Nigger of the 'Narcissus'*, although more complex than that of *Through the Dark Continent*, may be read as ultimately privileging fixed notions of Englishness over a disruptive 'Other'.

The Nigger of the 'Narcissus' begins with the bringing together of the crew – the ship's community. Baker, the English chief mate, orders, 'bring a good lamp here. I want to muster our crowd' (*NN*, 5). The men have reported to the ship in Bombay harbour amidst the disorientating 'babble of Eastern language' of Asiatic traders; ironically, the crewmen's own 'babble,' their 'voices humm[ing]' (ibid.), perpetuates a 'recursive' incoherence until the character of Old Singleton becomes visible. He is a keystone in Conrad's 'edifice'. An omniscient narrator distinguishes him as

> the oldest able seaman in the ship, sat apart on the deck

> right under the lamps, stripped to the waist, tattooed like a cannibal chief all over his powerful chest ... Between the blue and red patterns his white skin gleamed like satin; his bare back was propped against the ... bowsprit ... he resembled a learned and savage patriarch, the incarnation of barbarian wisdom serene in the blasphemous turmoil of the world. (ibid.)

Singleton, like Baker, is metaphorically associated with light. His bare back bodily fuses with the ship, and the semiotic red, white and blue skin colorations, suggesting the Union Jack, centre him in a 'gleaming' idea of Englishness. Such a polished image in Stanley's texts would confirm a completeness to counter the 'babble' of the 'Other', in the same way that he sets the industry of the Liverpool seamen against the 'vacuity' of the Welsh; here, although Singleton is 'learned', he is simultaneously 'savage', a primitive 'Other'. In contrast to Stanley's shaping binary 'precepts', this passage is *heteroglossic*; in Bakhtinian terms, Conrad's '*double-voiced*'[46] form brings oppositions together within one sentence and within one character.

Bruce Henricksen has focused positively on the novella's multiple 'narrative voices'.[47] In the eulogy to Singleton, another narrator's voice is glimpsed within the omniscient perspective:

> Singleton ... who in the last forty-five years had lived (as we had calculated ...) no more than forty months ashore ... sat unmoved in the clash of voices ... lost in an absorption *profound* enough to resemble a trance. He breathed *regularly*. (*NN*, 8; my emphasis)

The use of 'we' introduces a communal narrator who will re-emerge later. His choric view suggests that Singleton, an 'Other', maintains a civilized *calm, thoughtfulness and order*. The omniscient narrator then introduces 'another new hand', Donkin, by describing his squalor, 'as if he had been cuffed, kicked, rolled in the mud', and characterizing his type: '[t]hey all knew him ... the man that cannot steer

... [t]he man who can't do most things and won't do the rest' (*NN*, 10–11).[48] Although his degradation is juxtaposed with Singleton's integrity, Donkin's request to the crewmen for clothing appeals to their sense of 'Same': responding to the crew's lukewarm welcome, he snarls, '[a]re you men or a lot of 'artless canny-bals?' (*NN*, 11). To be a 'man' like Donkin one must be of his society, not Singleton's 'tribe'. Thus, at this early point in the narrative, it is questionable what constitutes Baker's definition of '*our* crowd', his community.

Of the crewmen who are introduced, only Donkin need declare his nationality: 'I ham a Henglishman, I ham' (*NN*, 12). The corrupted dialect in which the narrator reports this speech, and the scene in which the crewmen throw him clothes, represent a performative mix of 'Same' and 'Other' in one: 'the white skin of his limbs showed his *human kinship* through the *black fantasy* of his rags'; some 'trousers, heavy with tar stains, struck him on the shoulder' (ibid.; my emphasis). Although the trousers are donated generously, their stains mark Donkin, and match his own 'blackness'. The narrator has identified Donkin's humanity, but now suggests his animalism: 'he pawed around [and] looked about for more'; Singleton, who does not donate clothes, is 'unheeding' of the crew's 'sentimental pity' (ibid.). Thus, the 'human' Donkin mimics an animal, and the previously centred Singleton distances himself: the idea of duality earlier established linguistically is repeated in characterization. Unlike *Through the Dark Continent*, which is governed by an emphasis on difference, Conrad's narrator permits the hierarchical sites of 'Same' and 'Other' – those of insider and outsider – constantly to rotate.[49]

Authority is asserted by the boatswain's order for the men to muster. The omniscient narrative then moves in a positive direction by foregrounding the cohesive conduct required to move the *Narcissus* out of its transitional location in the harbour, in order to fulfil its commercial purpose. As the men respond, the contrast between Donkin's dog-like 'yelp[ing]' and Singleton's 'tall and fatherly' (*NN*, 13–14) appearance clarifies who, for this specific purpose, the narrator considers to be 'Other'.

The command structure is evident on the *Narcissus*, but what the narrator espouses most is a shaping discourse: namely, the willingness to serve and to do one's duty, as valued by Stanley and, in Conrad's narrative, through English seamen such as Singleton. Donkin's negative response to that position – '[i]f that's the way of this ship, we'll 'ave to change hall that ...' (*NN*, 13) – represents the performative behaviour of his group. The two positions exemplify what Henricksen describes as 'the historical shift' between social formations: '[g]emeinschaft (community) [and] [g]esellschaft (society).'[50] The former is hierarchical and membership is '*obligatory* and presumed to be "natural" – as shaping, indeed, as Stanley's white Anglicized position; the latter is 'horizontal and membership ... is optional and in a sense "cultural"'.[51] 'Old' Singleton unselfishly fulfils his duty to the community: he has faith in a pedagogical form of social structure. Donkin, the modern 'Henglishman', vocally dissents from that 'norm'. However, as Henricksen points out, 'the ideal ... "gemeinschaft" may never have existed'; rather, it is a 'constructed ideological position from which to critique the present'.[52]

Although the novella is heteroglossic in its various narrative voices, the position that Singleton represents is intended to establish an ideological opposition to that of Donkin. The entrance of the Negro of the title, James Wait, presents more difficulty. Willam W. Bonney notes Wait's 'strange influence',[53] on the 'muster' scene, even before he arrives:

> the blackness of the water was streaked with trails of light ... *similar* to filaments that float rooted to the shore. Rows of other lights stood away in straight lines *as if* drawn up on parade ... sombre hills arched high their black spines, on which [the] point of a star *resembled* a spark. (*NN*, 14; emphasis of the narrator's use of simile as in Bonney)

According to Bonney, this passage prefigures the liminal qualities 'visible in Wait's face':[54]

> [h]is head was away up in the shadows ... The whites of his eyes and teeth gleamed distinctly, but the face was indistinguishable ... The nigger was calm, cool, towering, superb. [His face was] pathetic and brutal: the tragic, the mysterious, the repulsive face of a nigger's soul. (*NN*, 16–17)

Bonney suggests that 'Wait and the night evade the narrator's ability to understand them directly. Consequently, he [alters] his perceptual mode through simile [all founded on] the confusing interpenetration of lights and reflections.'[55] This analysis supports the idea of 'gleaming' definition and 'mysterious' difference: 'Same' and 'Other' are contingent within one identity, as is the case in Singleton. The narrator repeats the racial homogenization seen in Stanley's texts, but his mingling of contemplative qualities, 'calm, cool', with clichéd physical attributes, 'towering, superb', adds a complexity to the community; as Wait says, 'I belong to the ship' (*NN*, 16).[56] In Stanley's writing, it is clear who 'holds' the light and who is condemned to the dark. Wait brings both metaphors to the ship and, in a sense, he 'completes' the crew.[57] However, the narrator also rehearses a racial trope: 'civilized' culture has a sinister 'Other' which, when engaged, will reveal something defining about itself. As Miriam Marcus observes, the novella 'participates in [such] polarised stereotyping as an example of cultural production',[58] and this has implications for the English community it represents, and the associated shaping discourse of duty.

The narrative strategy of the muster scene negotiates several degrees of indeterminacy and culminates in the clearly-defined form of Singleton's regulation and industry: '[a] breeze was coming ... Singleton stepped forward': he commands the ship – 'You ... hold!' (*NN*, 23). Firmly controlled, the *Narcissus* can then depart. With the sails set, 'the ship became a high and lonely pyramid, gliding, all shining and white' (*NN*, 24). Heading home, it achieves a glossy, idealized identity, 'like a small planet' (*NN*, 25), a complete entity, dutifully, as Stanley might have put it, 'guided by the courage of high endeavour' (*NN*, 26).

At the point at which the ship is put to work and the men undertake their duties, the communal narrator begins to play a pedagogical role, the purpose of which is illuminated by reference to Conrad's famous Preface to the novella. Conrad suggests that 'art' must 'attempt to find in its forms [and] in the facts of life, what of each is ... essential'.[59] The omniscient and communal narrators' eulogizing of Singleton are such essentializations; he personifies the enduring 'solidarity ... which binds together all humanity'[60] – the novella's touchstone. Having organised the community, the narrative tests it against the 'Otherness' of Wait, closely associated with the approaching storm.

Wait declares that he is ill and retires to his cabin. He may 'belong to the ship', but, in this liminal position, he is a sinister drain on the crew's resources: 'a black mist emanated from him; a subtle and dismal influence', and the community views him 'like a sick tyrant overawing ... abject but untrustworthy slaves' (*NN*, 29–30). Wait's enslaving 'influence', as his voice suggests, is 'hollow and loud' (*NN*, 30), and this notion is connected to one of Conrad's enduring themes:[61] what is at the centre of a social formation is empty. Marcus notes that the crew's 'ambivalent reaction to [Wait's] illness is constantly linked to his colour'.[62] In Singleton and Donkin, the characteristics of 'Same' and 'Other' rotate, but those characteristics are, nevertheless, visibly defined. Wait, contrastingly, causes uncertainty: he represents a performative dimension that disrupts the shaping discourse of community. Where Stanley resolves uncertainty, for instance by appropriating African 'Others' to the dominant discourse with which he wishes to be associated, *The Nigger of the 'Narcissus'* allows antagonistic values to interact: '[r]acial prejudice is rarely uttered without a qualifier'.[63] So, as Wait deteriorates, a sick-bay is fitted out: the crew are 'delighted to have him removed from the forecastle', yet they still 'attend[] him' (*NN*, 39). The question of Wait's cultural status is in the recurring process of debate.

The storm functions as a crisis point in a dialogic process:

> A big, foaming sea ... made for the ship ... it looked as mischievous and discomposing as a madman with an axe ... the watch below scrambled aft on all fours ... then, groaning, they rolled in a confused mass. (*NN*, 46–47)

The psychopathic personification of the storm visualizes a 'fact of life': within communities cyclical forces operate to 'discompose' civilized order. Stanley's narratives foreground imperial centrality; here, the storm furthers the centrifugal motion instigated by Donkin and Wait. The *Narcissus* lurches over to one side and the crewmen watch as their 'home' disintegrates. Denis Murphy suggests why geometric terminology is appropriate for the historical and cultural narratives:

> [t]he force of the wind and waves ... and the added weight of the water which has entered the ship both conspire to keep her over – but not to turn her over completely. The ship [is at] a point of precarious equilibrium [because of an altered] center of gravity.[64]

Although Murphy does not discuss the play on the name 'Wait' and 'weight', the idea of a destabilizing force 'entering' the ship suggests that the event was foreshadowed by Wait's arrival. The narrative now offers a resolution, a 'lesson', which restores centripetal motion. The ship is '[h]eld down at an angle ... off the perpendicular',[65] ordinarily figured by the ship's masts. Those masts are dragging the ship downward and the crew, urged on by Donkin's yells, 'Cut! Cut!' (*NN*, 49), want the captain, Allistoun, to secure their safety by cutting the masts, thus righting the ship. However, in terms of the community, an English imperial trading one at that, it would then become 'a free-floating derelict'.[66] Allistoun imposes his 'natural'[67] right to reject the idea; Singleton 'st[icks] to the wheel', and Donkin is silenced by an anonymous 'blow over the mouth' (*NN*, 49). In Bhabha's terms, the community is in an interstice, hovering 'back and forth'[68] in performative fashion between order and uncertainty. In such a moment is identity fashioned.

Communal strength is evidenced in efforts to rescue Wait from his cabin, where he has been trapped in the debris caused by the ship lurching over. The crewmen's moral *obligation* demonstrates, in a pedagogical manner, solidarity; but, in practice, they work in an irrational way to aid someone who is potentially damaging. During the rescue scene, there is 'an influx', as Jakob Lothe observes, 'of *we*, *us* and *our*'[69] signifiers that 'iterate' communal values. The use of active verbs, 'we flew ... we tore ... we tugged', supports these signifiers by portraying the men coherently 'in a body'; Wait, contrastingly, is stereotypically passive and malevolent, 'like a bladder full of gas' (*NN*, 57–58).[70] He is dragged, head first, through a tiny hole in the debris. Albert J. Guerard reads this symbolically: the crewmen assist 'the rebirth of evil'.[71] This psychological approach identifies a compulsion to 'descend beneath full consciousness to something "lower"',[72] but equally significant is that during the rescue the men believe 'that the ship had made up her mind to turn over at last. But she didn't' (*NN*, 57).

It could be said that the storm functions in the same way as the Bumbireh Island incident in *Through the Dark Continent*: both create transitional moments in which identity is shaped. The *Narcissus* unites with the 'body', the community, of men. Their conduct at Wait's 'rebirth' – '[we] passed him [tenderly] from hand to hand' – suggests a selfless caring; to echo Stanley, they are 'precepts' who shape a particular identity: this is 'the *kind* of men ... *we* [were]' (*NN*, 58–59). However, in Stanley's conflict at

Bumbireh Island there is a clear-cut and oppositional resolution; in Conrad's story, such an outcome is lacking.

The debate that goes on around Wait suggests that his 'rebirth' represents the assimilation of his primitive 'Other' into the community, despite his 'evil'. William Deresiewicz suggests that the 'moral beauty' of the rescue implies a 'community that cuts across ... cultural difference [and foregrounds] "an essential and generic social bond"'.[73] However, in the aftermath, an ideological enslavement to social order is re-established.[74] The captain is still 'holding the ship up'; Donkin still agitates; Singleton still '[hangs] on by the wheel' (*NN*, 59–67) until Allistoun gives the order to '[w]ear ship ... Lay on your backs and haul!' (*NN*, 68). This manoeuvre rights the ship and vindicates Allistoun's decision not to cut the masts. It demonstrates 'essential' qualities, but, contrary to Deresiewicz's argument, stresses compliance with an obligatory hierarchy, the significance of which is signalled by the *Narcissus* 'fleeing for *her life* [through] clear sunshine' (*NN*, 71). Her journey to England resumes as it began, with the monolithic and monologic Singleton 'alone by the helm'; his role is to do his duty, and thus re-assert the shaping discourse of communal stability: '[h]e steered with care'. (ibid.)

As the *Narcissus* makes for home, favourable winds desert her. During this becalmed period Wait dies and is buried at sea 'under the folds of the Union Jack' (*NN*, 125). The act of covering Wait's body with the flag implies his integration into a civilized national identity, symbolized by the breeze which then springs up to propel the ship. The 'we' narrator offers an alternative perspective: 'his death, like the death of an old belief, shook the foundations of our society. A common bond was gone; the ... bond of a sentimental lie' (*NN*, 123). After his death, the crewmen re-other Wait: he 'didn't back us up, as a shipmate should' (ibid.). Their behaviour at this point illustrates Marcus's view that the text is 'reluctant to face itself with Wait's colour' and that the iteration of 'multiple pronouns' to suggest communal values actually reveals cultural difference and displacement: Wait is the 'catalyst around which [the crewmen] uneasily and unwillingly converge and contradict themselves'.[75] Their 'reluctance' suggests that the 'old belief' of gemeinschaft has always been a 'sentimental lie'; for the omniscient narrator's monologic aims, Wait's death is strategically damaging: '[d]oubt survived [him]' (*NN*, 123). This centrifugal motion must be regulated: the oscillating narrative must be re-centred by the ship's return to London.

Robert Eric Livingston sees the novella's theme as one of 'imminent fragmentation and restored control'.[76] In this sense, its strategy echoes that of Stanley's narratives, in which the threat of 'Otherness' is suppressed by a repetitive imperialist discourse. Thus, once in the reaches of the Thames, the *Narcissus* is transfigured as the unifying 'mother of fleets and nations!' (*NN*, 128). The visionary rhetoric of this idea 'sets in motion a totalizing allegory', which, by its generic nature, is ultimately 'constraining':[77] as the ship docks, 'strange men [take] possession of her' (*NN*, 130). The voyage ends.

As the crewmen are paid off, the community dies. 'One by one' they arrive at the pay-table, where the pay-clerk's impatient, echoing voice reduces their honourable vocation to the lowest common denominator: '[m]oney right? Sign the release. There – there' (*NN*, 133). The 'hollowness' of Wait's voice has followed them home. Singleton is mocked for his inability to write and departs. Donkin 'appear[s] ... at home'; for him, the pay-office symbolizes a competitive gesellschaft: he and the clerk 'discuss ... the account, dropping h's against one another as if for a wager'; this confirms that the linguistic corruption by which Donkin first identifies his nationality also signifies a cultural corruption – 'I'm goin' ter 'ave a job hashore' (*NN*, 134). Donkin invites the rest of the crewmen to join his 'prosperous' (as Stanley might have put it) faction for a drink; they decline and thus consign themselves to the past.

In the context of the crew's attachment to an English ideal, Seamus Heaney's essay 'Englands of the Mind' (1980) offers a view which is relevant to the novella's closing and, perhaps, definitive perspective. Although Heaney analyses writers of the 1950s generation,[78] he identifies a principle that may be applied to *The Nigger of the 'Narcissus'*: Conrad displays a desire for 'a continuity of communal ways, and a confirmation of an identity which is threatened'.[79] As the crewmen stand near the Tower of London, a potent symbol of regulation and national identity, they hesitate, in a 'hazy light' (*NN*, 134). A new narrator emerges: 'I stopped to take my last look at [them]' (*NN*, 135). This appears to be the 'we' narrator, now offering his personal view. The crewmen 'sway' before the Royal Mint, and head for 'the Black Horse, where men ... dispense [illusions] to the paid off crews of southern-going ships' (ibid.). Faced with these modern symbols of national wealth and commerce, and the falseness of, presumably, the imperial adventure, the crewmen are defined as 'creatures of another kind' (ibid.). Their ancient 'wisdom' has weathered the sea-storm, but is now outweighed by the 'blasphemous turmoil'; it is an anachronism in the 'merciless [and] cruel ... roar of the town' (*NN*, 134).

In response to the modernity, the 'I' narrator fashions his 'England of the Mind' – as 'shining' and idealized as the *Narcissus* in full sail:

> [t]he dark knot of seamen drifted in the sunshine ... the stones of the Tower gleam[ed] ... as if remembering ... the fighting prototypes of these men [and their] victories ... And to the right of the dark group the stained front of the Mint, cleansed by the flood of light, stood out for a moment, dazzling and white, like a marble palace in a fairy tale. (*NN*, 136)[80]

He conceives of 'gleaming' 'narratives of originary and initial subjectivities';[81] the darkening processes symbolized by the pay negotiations are purified. The potent civilizing spirit of early, victorious English imperialists is recalled, the meaning of which may be taken to endorse 'a conservative grand narrative'.[82] As Stanley's idealizing colonialist assertions lead us in a specific direction, so Conrad manipulates perspective in a similar manner. However, the 'dazzling ... marble palace' which Conrad's narrator imagines warns of 'premature self-closure',[83] since few would rely on something constructed in the 'hazy light' of a 'fairy tale'.

Stanley and Conrad use their narratives in the pursuit of cultural approval. However, Tim Middleton suggests that the idealizing nationalist traits in *The Nigger of the 'Narcissus'* obscure a double purpose: its narrative 'perhaps tells us more about Conrad's desire to receive critical approbation than it does about his politics'.[84] The 'truth' of the crew's assimilative attitude to Wait is that it offers no more meaning than to iterate the community's own worth and to insist on 'obligatory' membership. Their pity for Wait represents a self-satisfying 'sentimental' belief in community, exercised 'against their will',[85] because of his colour. Thus, they are enslaved to a supposedly 'civilized' version of English 'Sameness', which is compromised in the context of the pay-off in London.

The strategy of Conrad's novella, then, is not pedagogically shaping, but rather, through its 'mimicry' of a 'love of the [S]ame',[86] performatively testing: this is hinted at *before* the 'pay-off' – in fact, immediately the *Narcissus* enters the Thames. The ship has become a symbol of English 'community', but on her return home the omniscient narrator describes her as 'freighted with dross and with jewels' (*NN*, p. 128). At the point at which he establishes a national allegory, he repeats the kind of double-voiced discourse deployed earlier in respect of ideology and character. Ideas of duty, race and belonging, *and* cultural diversity exist on board the English trading ship. However, in the nation to which that ship returns is perceived only self-serving attitudes. It is possible to take from *The Nigger of the 'Narcissus'* a narrative that celebrates a 'continuist' form of Englishness, *and* one that expresses the feelings of recursive displacement in that identity. This doubleness undermines the 'careful' public positioning of the novella.

Conclusion

In each of their texts, Stanley and Conrad support their need to establish a place in the English metropolis. Stanley's 'factual' writings iterate a 'civilized' identity for ideological and political ends through pedagogical discourses that espouse success and progress towards a 'finished' Anglicization. The performative aspect of his marginal Welsh identity is suppressed, but in the iterative nature of his narratives is emphasized his own 'Otherness'. In *Through the Dark Continent*, he integrates accounts of violent oppression of African 'Others', and an appropriation of their purportedly co-operative voices, within the imperial ideal of the 'betterment of mankind'. As Tim Jeal has noted, imperialists' narratives did not usually account for all of their colonizing methods in this manner. Thus, Stanley's comprehensive approach may be seen as an over-compensation for feelings that he is not quite part of the dominant civilizing discourse – the feelings of the Welsh-British 'outcast'.

One might suppose that Conrad's formation of an 'edifice' for his former English shipmates is similarly iterative and obscuring of his own Polish origins. His representation of Englishness in *The Nigger of the 'Narcissus'* may provide social meaning, but, on closer reading, this notion is subverted by the text's multiple narratives and double-voiced strategies. The novella demonstrates the idea that Stanley's 'precepts' seek to efface: namely, that cultural production is a developing and multi-dimensional process: antagonistic values are forced to negotiate with each other in a repetitive interaction between the pedagogical and the performative. The identities that emerge from the process, whether Welsh, Polish, or English, are frequently not quite what they purport to be. Such was the case for Stanley on his death in 1904: his wish to be buried at Westminster Abbey was refused by the dean, 'due to his mixed reputation'.[87]

NOTES

1 The American Testimonial Banquet took place in the same year that *In Darkest Africa*, Stanley's account of his expedition to rescue Emin Pasha, was published. Emin Pasha was the governor of Sudan; he had appealed for help following the Mahdist uprising which had engulfed General Gordon in 1885. Stanley was chosen to lead the rescue mission by William Mackinnon, chairman of the British India Steam Navigation Company. The programme for the banquet is available at http://www.archive.org/details/americantestimon00londiala (accessed 13 June 2007).

2 Allan H. Simmons, *Joseph Conrad* (Basingstoke: Palgrave Macmillan, 2006), p. 1.

3 Homi K. Bhabha, *The Location of Culture* ([1994] Abingdon: Routledge Classics, 2004), p. 208.

4 Ibid., p. 209. David Huddart comments that in the 'narration' of national identity 'there is a pedagogical dimension that foregrounds total sociological facts'; see *Homi K. Bhabha* (Abingdon: Routledge, 2006), p. 121. The *OED* defines a pedagogue as a 'schoolmaster, a teacher; esp. a strict, dogmatic, or pedantic one'; and '[s]omething that serves to teach; a source of instruction or guidance ([c]hiefly with reference to St Paul's use [of the term in] Galatians 3:24'. Galatians 3:24 reads: '[w]herefore the law was our schoolmaster to bring us unto Christ, that we might be justified by faith'. Imperialism, for instance, was fashioned as a discourse in which one could have faith: in such a discourse, national stereotypes convey fixed notions of identity. Huddart, of course, notes Bhabha's identification of the more elusive 'performative' dimension which complicates the 'pedagogical'; each influences the other.

5 Henry M. Stanley, *The Autobiography of Sir Henry Morton*

Stanley: The Making of a 19th-Century Explorer (Santa Barbara: The Narrative Press, 2001), pp. 19–20. All further references are to this edition and are given in the text, abbreviated as *A*.

6 Tim Jeal, *Stanley: The Impossible Life of Africa's Greatest Explorer* (London: Faber and Faber, 2007), p. 24; Richard Hall in *Stanley: An Adventurer Explored* (London: Collins, 1974) suggests that Stanley's escape has 'too many echoes of ... Dickens's *Nicholas Nickleby*, where the heroic young Nicholas rebels against the sadism of Squeers' and flees from his school; see p. 108.

7 Felix Driver, 'Stanley, Sir Henry Morton (1841–1904)', *Oxford Dictionary of National Biography*, Oxford University Press, online edition, http://www.oxforddnb.com/view/article/36247 (accessed 11 October 2007).

8 Stanley's other ventures included the expedition to relieve Emin Pasha; see note 1 above.

9 The *Autobiography* comprises an 'Introduction' and nine chapters written by Stanley; the remaining seventeen chapters were edited and compiled by his wife, Dorothy Stanley, from Stanley's journals, notes and letters: she links these documents together to form a narrative, interspersed with editorial comment. She also included an 'Editor's Preface'. Stanley had married Dorothy Tennant of Cadoxton, Glamorgan on 12 July 1890 in Westminster Abbey.

10 These words are taken from Stanley's letter to his wife, dated 30 November 1893.

11 Emyr Wyn Jones, *Sir Henry M. Stanley: The Enigma* (Denbigh: Gee, 1989), pp. 33–34. There are many factors that support Jones's position: for example, in 1727 a free grammar-school had been founded in the locality by the subscription of landowners. The area is also noted for the beauty of its landscape. Stanley's representation tends to reflect his own displacement.

12 E. J. Hobsbawm, *The Age of Empire*: 1875–1914 (London: Weidenfeld and Nicolson, 1987), p. 9.

13 In the Liverpool dockyards Stanley found his future direction, taking up the offer of a job as a cabin-boy on an American packet boat bound for New Orleans. Lucy M. Jones and Ivor Wynne Jones, *H. M. Stanley and Wales* (Hawarden: Flintshire County Record Office, 1972), p. 17: booklet produced in conjunction with an exhibition about Stanley,

held at the St Asaph Cathedral Museum, 25–30 September 1972. Stanley's mother had married Robert Jones, the father of two of her children.

15 These remarks are the Editor's intervention. At this point (Chapter 10), Dorothy Stanley's use of Stanley's journals, notes and letters begins, interspersed with her editorial commentary.

16 Dorothy Stanley notes that there 'is nothing to show just how or why [Stanley] became a newspaper correspondent', yet this career led directly to what made him famous. The task of finding Livingstone in central Africa was as a result of Stanley's employment with the New York Herald.

17 Publicity material for Henry M. Stanley, *Through the Dark Continent or, The Sources of the Nile Around the Great Lakes of Equatorial Africa and Down the Livingstone River to the Atlantic Ocean, Volume One* (New York: Dover Publications, 1988). All further references to *Volume One* are to this edition and are given in the text, abbreviated as *DC*. References to *Volume Two* are given in footnotes.

18 In 1878 Conrad was twenty-one years of age and four years into his career as a seaman. It was also the year in which he joined his first British ship, the *Skimmer of the Sea*.

19 Andrea White, *Joseph Conrad and the Adventure Tradition: Constructing and deconstructing the imperial subject* ([1993] Cambridge: Cambridge University Press, 2008), p. 100. White also notes that adventure fiction was a further influence on Conrad, but that in 1890, the year that Conrad travelled to the Congo, '*Through the Dark Continent* ... was enjoying a revival'; see p. 109.

20 The American Testimonial Banquet honoured Stanley's achievements in precisely these three realms. When the expedition is deep into the interior, Stanley addresses his officers: '[n]ow look at this, the latest chart which Europeans have drawn of this region. It is a blank, perfectly white'; Stanley confesses to be 'charm[ed]' by the 'enormous void' – the 'singular fascination' for him is to see it 'filled ... with the most wonderful pictures of towns, villages, rivers, countries, and tribes', see *Through the Dark Continent, Volume Two*, p. 152. In other words, Stanley wishes to impose order and coherence on the unknown.

21 The publicity material for the 1988 edition boasts of '[p]refaces. Appendixes. Total of 149 black and white

illustrations. Tables. Foldout map. Total of 960pp.'
22 Letters of 14 April 1875.
23 Jeal, *Stanley*, pp. 221–222; Stanley's expedition was at Bumbireh in May and August 1875.
24 Stanley's notion of justice is explicitly Old Testament – 'an eye for an eye' – a symptom, perhaps, of his Welsh workhouse education.
25 Jeal points out that Stanley gave the impression that the second visit to Bumbireh took place soon after the first attack. This added to the idea of summary 'justice', although the actual three-month interval between visits supports the accusation of premeditation.
26 Jeal, *Stanley*, p. 224. Jeal refers to the comments of Charles 'Chinese' Gordon and notes that '[i]n China, Gordon's [Army] had committed a string of atrocities, and in the Sudan he and his subordinates had killed numerous members of the Bari tribe without ever saying a word'. Jeal observes that Stanley in contrast, not only reported, but also 'exaggerated' the number of natives killed; 'in his diary the figure given was thirty three'. Jeal sees exaggeration as a consistent trait in Stanley, attributable to a 'psychological need to prove that no one ever got the better of him, see pp. 222–224.
27 Stanley, *Through the Dark Continent*, *Volume Two*, pp. 312–316 (the officer was Frank Pocock).
28 Bhabha, *The Location of Culture*, p. 38 (original emphasis). Bhabha identifies the tendency for political movements to 'iterate' their principles so as to 'articulate antagonistic and oppositional elements'.
29 Ibid., p. 195.
30 Declan Kiberd, *Inventing Ireland: The Literature of the Modern Nation* ([1995] London: Vintage, 1996), p. 119; (original emphasis). The 'gleaming' imperial identity would thus be seen as the product of iterative strategies – a repetitive 'polishing'.
31 Stanley, *Through the Dark Continent, Volume Two*, p. 355. This 'quotation' is contained within a letter that Stanley sent to Messrs A. da Motta Veiga and J. W. Harrison of Boma on the Congo River, merchants who dispatched supplies to Stanley's ailing party. The letter, amongst others, is included within his narrative and acts as an authenticating device.
32 Joseph Conrad, *Heart of Darkness: A Norton Critical Edition*, ed. Paul B. Armstrong ([1902] London: W. W. Norton &

Company Ltd, 2006), p. 17.

33 Stanley stood as the Liberal-Unionist candidate in North Lambeth in the election of 1892, but was not elected.

34 This election address of 21 June 1892 is careful to associate the prosperity of England with what can taken to be an English Empire. It is ironic that as Stanley was striving to place himself within a predominantly English Parliament, another Welsh Liberal, David Lloyd George (1863–1945), was rising to political prominence. A matter of ten years or so after Stanley's death, Lloyd George, as President of the Board of Trade (1906), Chancellor of the Exchequer (1908) and Prime Minister (1916), would give English politics a distinctly Welsh face.

35 Simmons, *Joseph Conrad*, p. 2.

36 Joseph Conrad, *A Personal Record* ([1912] Oxford: Oxford University Press, 1998), p. 13 (original emphasis).

37 Joseph Conrad, *The Mirror of the Sea*, Author's Note ([1909] London: J. M. Dent & Sons Ltd, 1950), p. x.

38 Conrad had sailed on the actual *Narcissus* from Bombay to Dunkirk in 1884. The novella's action 'in general ... follows the facts of the historical voyage'; see Ian Watt, *Conrad in the Nineteenth Century* ([1979] London: Chatto & Windus, 1980), pp. 91–93. Unlike Stanley, Conrad does not 'explain' and describe in detail: we are never told the nature of the ship's cargo, for example. Although we take the *Narcissus* to be English, it is not until page 127 of 136 that this fact is reasonably explicit – as the ship speeds 'to its nest' in London. However, a complex industrialized colonial history is hinted at: 'she was born in the thundering peal of hammers ... on the banks of the Clyde. The ... sombre steam gives birth to things of beauty that float away into the sunshine.' Joseph Conrad, *The Nigger of the 'Narcissus' and Other Stories*, ed. J. H. Stape and Allan H. Simmons (London: Penguin Classics, 2007), p. 41. All further references are to this edition and are given in the text, abbreviated as *NN*.

39 The novella was first published in serial form in the *New Review* between August and December 1897.

40 Tim Middleton, *Joseph Conrad* (Abingdon: Routledge, 2006), pp. 31–32; Middleton notes that the *New Review* was 'an influential pro-imperialist journal [read by] a particular literary circle with an appetite for tales of men and empire'.

41 Conrad to Helen Watson, 27 January 1897, in *The Collected*

Letters of Joseph Conrad, Volume 1, 1861–1897, ed. Frederick R. Karl and Laurence Davies (Cambridge: Cambridge University Press, 1983), p. 334 (my emphasis).

42 Conrad to Edward Garnett, 25 October 1896, in ibid., p. 309 (my emphasis).

43 Simmons, *Joseph Conrad*, p. 11.

44 Ibid., p. 53.

45 Norman Davies points out that the editors of the *Oxford English Dictionary*, through the dictionary's definition of 'England', consider 'both 'English' and 'British', like 'nation' and 'state', to be synonyms and that all four terms are coterminous with the 'southern part of Great Britain'; see Norman Davies, *The Isles: A History* (London: Macmillan, 1999), pp. xxx–xxxi. It is reasonable to conclude that the *Oxford English Dictionary* might be used as an instrument of Empire.

46 M. M. Bakhtin, *The Dialogic Imagination: Four Essays*, ed. Michael Holquist, trans. Caryl Emerson and Michael Holquist ([1981] Austin: University of Texas Press, 2004), p. 324. Bakhtin describes 'double-voiced discourses' as incorporating 'two voices, two meanings and two expressions [which] are dialogically interrelated'. Such discourses 'signify a relativizing of linguistic consciousness in the perception of language borders – borders created by history and society, and even the most fundamental border (i.e., those between languages as such)'; see ibid., pp. 323–324.

47 Bruce Henricksen, *Nomadic Voices: Conrad and the Subject of Narrative* (University of Illinois Press: Urbana and Chicago, 1992), pp. 27–29. Jakob Lothe has given a full account of the novella's different narrative modes; see Lothe, 'Variations of Narrative in The Nigger of the "Narcissus", *Conradiana*, Volume 16, No. 3 (1984), 215–224.

48 Singleton is later shown to be the crewman who, in the main, steers the ship.

49 The idea of Donkin being marked by tar stains is an echo of Conrad's description of himself as 'concoction': a Polish nobleman 'encased in British tar' when he became a member of the Merchant Service; see Conrad to Karol Zagórski, 22 May 1890, in *Collected Letters, Volume 1*, ed. Karl and Davies, p. 52. This biographical detail may indicate Conrad's affinity with the 'Other'; in the novella, the Englishman Donkin is also a 'concoction' – part crewman, part animal –– as is the negro Wait. Both are outside the

novella's 'myth' of Englishness.

50 Henricksen, *Nomadic Voices*, p. 29.

51 Ibid., pp. 29–30.

52 Ibid., p. 30.

53 William W. Bonney, *Thorns & Arabesques: Contexts for Conrad's Fiction* (Baltimore & London: The Johns Hopkins University Press, 1980), p. 164.

54 Ibid.

55 Ibid.

56 In Kiberd's terms of images of 'completeness', both Singleton's skin and Wait's teeth are said to 'gleam'.

57 Paradoxically, James Wait is the only crewman who has a 'complete' set of first and second names. The fact that the title of the novella homogenizes him as a 'Nigger', yet also suggests his centrality to its theme, adds to his ambiguity.

58 Miriam Marcus, 'Writing, Race, and Illness In The Nigger of the "Narcissus", *The Conradian*, Volume 23, No. 1 (Spring 1998), 37–50 (p. 42).

59 Joseph Conrad, Preface to The Nigger of the 'Narcissus', in Joseph Conrad, *The Nigger of the 'Narcissus': A Norton Critical Edition*, ed. Robert Kimborough ([1897] New York: W. W. Norton & Company, 1979), pp. 145–167 (p. 145).

60 Ibid., pp. 145–146.

61 As Geoffrey Galt Harpham notes, Conrad 'endlessly constructs forms of containment ... Europeans within jungles [as in the example of Kurtz in Heart of Darkness]', but 'he never places anything substantial at the very center'; see Harpham, *One of Us: The Mastery of Joseph Conrad* (Chicago: The University of Chicago Press, 1996), p. 59.

62 Marcus, 'Writing, Race, and Illness', p. 43.

63 Ibid., p. 44.

64 Denis Murphy, 'Seamanship in Chapter Three of The Nigger of the "Narcissus",' in Joseph Conrad, *The Nigger of the 'Narcissus': A Norton Critical Edition*, pp. 138–139.

65 Ibid., p. 138.

66 Ibid.

67 'Natural', in the sense of gemeinschaft.

68 Bhabha, *The Location of Culture*, p. 2.

69 Jakob Lothe, 'Variations of Narrative in The Nigger of the "Narcissus",' *Conradiana*, Volume XVI, Number 3, 1984, p. 217.

70 In connection with this kind of stereotyping, Marcus refers

to Jeremy Hawthorn's *Joseph Conrad: Narrative Technique and Ideological Commitment* (London: Arnold, 1992); Hawthorn discusses contradictory views in Victorian constructions of marginalized groups: 'the negro is seen to be ... lazy yet capable of working "like a nigger"'; see p. 124.

71 Albert J. Guerard, *Conrad the Novelist* (Cambridge, Massachusetts: Harvard University Press, 1958), p, 112.

72 Ibid., p. 113.

73 William Deresiewicz, 'Conrad's impasse: The Nigger of the "Narcissus" and the invention of Marlow,' *Conradiana*, Volume 38, No. 3 (Fall 2006), 205–223 (pp. 209–210). Deresiewicz quotes from Victor Turner, *The Ritual Process: Structure and Anti-Structure* (New York: Aldine Publishing, 1969).

74 Conrad admired the idea of hierarchical order in the English system; he had seen a similar system destroyed in his Polish homeland by Russian imperialism.

75 Marcus, 'Writing, Race, and Illness,' p. 41.

76 Robert Eric Livingston, 'Seeing Through Reading: Class, Race and Literary Authority in Joseph Conrad's The Nigger of the "Narcissus".' *Novel: A Forum on Fiction*, Volume 26, No. 2 (Winter 1993), 133–150 (p. 137).

77 Ibid., pp. 138–139.

78 Seamus Heaney, 'Englands of the Mind,' in Seamus Heaney, *Preoccupations: Selected Prose 1968–1978* (London: Faber and Faber, 1984), pp. 150–169. Heaney's essay concerns the tendency of Ted Hughes, Geoffrey Hill and Philip Larkin to imply in their poetry 'continuity with another England, there and then' and relate it to the 'here and now'; see p. 150.

79 Ibid., p. 151.

80 The word 'gleam' is carried through the text, from Singleton to Wait, to the Tower.

81 Bhabha, *The Location of Culture*, p. 2.

82 Henricksen, *Nomadic Voices*, p. 26.

83 Kiberd, *Inventing Ireland*, p. 119.

84 Tim Middleton, 'From Menace to Mimicry: Conrad and Late-Victorian Masculinity,' in *Imperial Desire: Dissident Sexualities and Colonial Literature*, ed. Philip Holden and Richard J. Ruppel (Minneapolis, MN: University of Minnesota Press, 2003), pp. 135–151 (p. 145). Middleton's essay concerns issues of male identity; here, I am applying its general principle of a double purpose of

mimicry and menace.

85 Ibid., p. 147. As Marcus says, the crew 'unwillingly' converge around Wait.

86 Ibid., p. 136. Middleton points out that 'self-absorption is ... central to narcissism and Conrad's novel[la] showed how narcissism disrupted a culture's apparently clear-cut social hierarchies'; see Middleton, *Joseph Conrad*, p. 34.

87 Driver, 'Stanley, Sir Henry Morton (1841–1904).'

Winding silkworms' cocoons without a reel:

Betsy Cadwaladyr, Jane Williams (Ysgafell) and the Writing of *The Autobiography of Elizabeth Davis*

Gwyneth Tyson Roberts
Independent Scholar

Betsy Cadwaladyr is currently enjoying a very successful life after death; a hundred and fifty years after she died she is far better, and far more widely, known than during her lifetime. She has acquired a high profile in many schools and colleges in Wales: teaching material about her is available on the web both for primary schools (an outline drawing of her in her nurse's uniform can be filled in with the online paintbox) and at secondary level, while her *Autobiography* appears on the reading-lists of courses in colleges and universities. She is also well-known outside the world of education; for example, she has been the subject of a radio programme (in May 2009 on BBC Radio Wales, in the curiously named series *The Past Masters*), and at the 2009 National Eisteddfod in Bala she was both the subject of a talk and included in an exhibition of the area's best-known characters.[1] She is becoming increasingly well known outside Wales also: Googling her name produces a variety of entries giving accounts of her *Autobiography* and explaining how to get a copy, in Norwegian, Dutch, Portuguese, Danish, Finnish, Japanese and Russian. It may be too early to describe interest in her as a world-wide phenomenon, but global apotheosis is surely only a matter of time.[2]

All this interest in her derives from the republication of her *Autobiography* by Honno Press in a paperback edition in 1987, in their Honno Classics series; this was the first reprinting of the text since the original publication in 1857, and to date the Honno paperback is well on the way to selling twice as many copies as the first edition (750 copies were printed in 1857 and not all of them were sold,[3] whereas at the end of the financial year in April 2009, sales figures of the paperback had reached 1300).[4]

The contents of her autobiography (i.e. the first-person account of her life, here referred to in lower case to distinguish it from the *Autobiography,* the book of which it forms the main part) offer some of the reasons for the book's continuing appeal (and, indeed, could provide material for several more volumes). Interesting, unexpected and often dramatic events follow fast on each other, and one reason for the book's readability is that it is impossible to guess what the narrator will do next; a brief summary of the book's incidents can only indicate a little of the often tumultuous succession of events.

She was born at Pen Rhiw farm outside Bala, one of the youngest of the sixteen children of Judith Humphreys, a farmer's daughter, and Dafydd Cadwaladyr, also a farmer but better known as a preacher with the Calvinistic Methodists. A restless curiosity led her first to Liverpool, then to London and later to a life of travelling the world as maid to the wives of captains of merchant-ships; while working in Liverpool she adopted Davis (based on her father's first name, after the Welsh patronymic system) as her surname instead of Cadwaladyr because 'the English people could not pronounce that surname'.[5] Her reason for running away from Bala to Liverpool was 'I must see something more of the world' (1987: 15) and she did, visiting India, Australia, South America, China and the islands of the Pacific. She subsequently alternated these voyages with periods as a domestic servant, and later as a nurse, in Britain but her curiosity about the world and its peoples remained, and she volunteered as a nurse for the British Army in the Crimea 'to see what was going on, and to take care of the wounded' (1987: 153–4; her order of priorities is significant). In the General Hospital at Balaclava she worked as a nurse for six weeks but was then put in charge of the 'extra-diets' kitchen, which provided food for patients too weak or ill to stomach standard

British Army rations, and worked there for the remainder of her time in the Crimea (1987: 172). Her *Autobiography* was written to provide for her old age by drawing attention to her service to her country, and ends with two names (with addresses) to which 'benevolent readers who may wish to contribute to the comfort of her later years' (1987: 202) can send money (Post Office directories for the period show that one was a lodging-house keeper in Chelsea, the other a 'furnishing undertaker' in Pimlico).

The autobiography, however, is more than the narration of a succession of varied and dramatic anecdotes; a major reason for its popularity lies in the impression it gives of an individual and often highly idiosyncratic personality narrating them, with her own unanalysed and unselfconscious interests and priorities which take no account of what her readers might want to hear about: she says nothing of the reactions of her father and siblings to her flight from the family home, for example, but gives a detailed account of the life and death of Captain Foreman's grey parrot (1987: 135–6); she describes in detail the elopement of a nun from a convent near Venice (1987: 30–3), but says of a tour to Spain merely: "I remember Vigo, Saragossa, Salamanca, Ciudad Rodrigo, Seville and Granada' (1987: 27).

This idiosyncratic approach to what she found interesting and memorable creates a strong impression of a distinctive personality, often opinionated to the point of eccentricity, and this is strengthened by the forthright expression of her views on the people she encounters, often based on their appearance: Lady O'Rourke, dressed to pay a formal call on Spanish royalty, 'looked like a sack of wool tied in the middle' (1987: 26), and while Bishop Heber of Calcutta had 'a fine, heavenly-looking countenance', his wife 'had not the look of a godly woman' (both 1987: 79; she is noticeably sharper in her descriptions of women than of men).

This sense of the narrator's strong and self-confident personality is strengthened by her unselfconscious account of incidents which show her as rash, gullible and unaware, or heedless, of the effect she had on others: when staying with her employers at a duke's castle in Scotland she paraded the ducal wig on a stick in front of his family and guests in spite of the attempts of his son and valet to grab it from her, and apparently took her employer's remark to his hosts – 'My servant is a real child of nature!' – as a compliment rather than a lame excuse for her tactless and presumptuous behaviour (1987: 25); she was conned into giving an intermediary £50 to help a friend and when the conman refused to return it and threatened to kick her downstairs, admitted 'I had not even asked for a note-of-hand or acknowledgement, so I lost my £50 without remedy' (1987: 137), where a more self-conscious autobiographer might have suppressed this evidence of their gullibility; in a violent storm at sea, when a sailor called 'from aloft' for a rope to be released whose name meant nothing to her, she ran round the deck releasing every rope she could get hold of, with the result that 'Down came rushing heavily all the sails at once, bringing many sailors with them like lead upon the deck' (1987: 60; the number of injured sailors is not recorded).

At one point only in the autobiography does she attempt to analyse her actions and reflect on her own character. After the tumultuous and traumatic weeks in which her first fiancé was drowned two days before their wedding and her hopes of making a new life in India with her employers' family were frustrated by her father, she records:

> I saw them all [her employers' family and her fellow-servants who were to accompany them to India] on board, and I almost broke my heart. My father was vexed, and thought that I loved Sir George and my lady [her employers] better than I loved him.

Remembering these life-changing events forty years later seems to have caused her to reflect on the person she had been, and the chapter ends with an analysis of the way the events had changed her:

> I was from infancy so spirited, that my father and my pious friends used often to fear I should get into mischief. He was always more anxious for me than for all his other children, who had quieter dispositions, and therefore gave me more frequent cautions and advice. I became much more thoughtful and steady after Harris [her fiancé] died and the _____ family [her employers] went away. These were great griefs; but, in the midst of my gayest pranks, I had long had the root of right-doing within me.[6]

The last sentence suggests an awareness that she had previously shown herself to be disobedient, resistant to paternal authority and reckless of the consequences of her actions and that she needed to reassure readers (who might be unwilling to 'contribute to the comfort of her later years' if they had doubts about her moral character) that she yet possessed a strong moral compass: that she might sometimes be foolhardy, but would not let her adventurous spirit lead her seriously astray. It is, however, a brief and unusual moment of reflection and self-analysis, and the next chapter hurtles her into her second engagement, her violent rejection of her new fiancé, her flight to London, and the adventures of her new life there; the moment of reflection is over.

Autobiography, which was not identified as a separate genre until the early nineteenth century, has been defined as 'a retrospective, chronological narrative, grounded in truth, whose central theme is the development of the author's personality',[7] and studies of nineteenth-century autobiographies emphasise that a crucial component is the account of the development of the author's personality and the changes effected by his or her experiences;[8] by this definition, Cadwaladyr's *Autobiography* is not an autobiography at all but a book of reminiscences.

Throughout her account of her life the narrator demonstrates the same, very individual, forthright approach to her experiences; her disapproval is made very clear (the effects of her upbringing as a Calvinistic Methodist are apparent in her account of a Good Friday service in the Chapel Royal at Rio de Janeiro, when the Empress of Brazil 'threw herself down on the ground, and made a noise like a dog and crawled along', to be followed by 'an old friar' who 'got a thing like the head of an eight-day clock and played bo peep on it on all sides at the altar': 1987: 107), as is her lack of interest ('I saw in the Mauritius two Welshmen from Pembrokeshire. The name of one of them was Philips. I forget the name of the other': 1987: 83), and her moments of *hiraeth* as a farmer's daughter ('I felt very glad to see hay-fields and Welsh wheat-fields [in Tahiti]. I know there are plenty of wheat-fields in England; but I always thought of my own country, when I met with wheat-fields beyond the seas': 1987: 99).

Throughout the autobiography the sense of a narrator with a distinctive personality talking directly to her readers is reinforced by the frequently conversational style of its prose, which would have been especially remarkable in contrast to the greater literary formality of other volumes of reminiscences of this period. This conversational style is apparent in her references to the timing of events: frequently, after a general suggestion of time passing, the following paragraph begins abruptly with 'on Tuesday', 'on Monday evening', 'on the Saturday morning', etc. (1987, *passim*), which is characteristic of informal oral story-telling but meaningless when, as here, it is not related to any specific dates or other days of the week. Descriptions of food and drink demonstrate an especially conversational style, in which she seems to be addressing her readers directly: after describing a kangaroo hunt in Australia, she says of its tail 'I wish we had it here to make soup; there is none better anywhere' (1987: 74); and later comments that Thames water, treated correctly in barrels on board ship, will keep 'perfectly pure, cold and bright for ever. There is no other water in the world will do this, that I know of' (1987: 123). This conversational style is particularly noticeable and effective when she describes her first sight of wounded soldiers in the military hospital at Balaclava:

> Next day the superintendent and I went to visit the wards and the sights I saw, I shall never forget as long as I live ... When I got to No.5 ward, poor fellows! ... From many of the patients I removed [maggots, in their untended wounds] in handfuls ... There was, I suppose, from three to four hundred patients under their care [three surgeons, one of whom was only there 'occasionally'] ... Not a man there had a bed. (1987: 169–70)

Here the register is particularly conversational, demonstrated in the emphasis given by 'Not a man' at the beginning of a sentence, the use of the homely 'in handfuls', the interjection 'I suppose' as if she was calculating the number of men as she spoke, and especially by the inversion of standard sentence structure in 'the sights I saw, I shall never forget' (rather than 'I shall never forget the sights I saw') which fronts the most important element of the utterance to emphasise its significance, and in the syntactically incomplete 'When I saw No.5 ward, poor fellows!', which conveys powerfully the strength of her reactions of horror and pity at the sufferings of the wounded soldiers, and a sense that her linguistic resources were almost incapable of expressing the depth of her shock and compassion.

This strong sense of a distinctive, confident and often naïvely unself-aware personality talking directly to her readers could lead to the assumption that the rôle of Jane Williams (Ysgafell), described on the title-page of the *Autobiography* as its editor, was merely to take down detailed notes from Cadwaladyr's spoken account, correct grammar as necessary and arrange the resulting text into paragraphs. As Williams's Preface[9] reveals, though, her contribution was considerably more complex than that, and the process of the book's composition is correspondingly more interesting.

The Preface, as well as providing information on how the book was written, is sufficiently variable in tone, and sufficiently different from the preface that might have been expected, to be important in its own right. Readers of the first edition in 1857 might reasonably have expected an unequivocal tribute to Cadwaladyr's adventurous spirit, personal courage and patriotic dedication to the welfare of wounded British soldiers, worded so as to create maximum admiration for her and therefore maximum sympathy and maximum financial contributions; while the Preface begins by praising 'her indomitable energy ... industrious activity and buoyant cheerfulness of spirit', and later commends her 'thorough integrity' and 'dauntless resolution' (Preface: 4–5, 28), by the final paragraphs she is presented as an anthropological case-study of the result of growing up in a highland community ('the mountain region which produced her, and the state of society which surrounded her in early life, moulded and impressed upon the native metal the form and stamp which it has never lost': Pref.: 51–5), which establishes an emotional distance between writer and subject, and therefore between subject and readers, which would have made such sympathy far more difficult to achieve; the Preface's reference to her 'absence of sentiment and air of unsympathising indifference' (Pref.: 52) can only have increased this distance, even in a context which asks that her attitude should not be misunderstood. Further, most of the Preface, instead of the conventional 'it-was-a-privilege-and-delight-to-work-with-her' which might have been considered appropriate (however little it reflected the reality of the working relationship between writer and subject), complains about the writer's difficulties in putting the text together (some of which were created by the book's subject) and the time and effort it took her. While there is no corroborative evidence for the extent of Williams's contribution to the autobiography, the fact that her account of her work on it is detailed, practical and seriously disaffected (rather than, say, loftily self-aggrandising) would seem to strengthen the probability that it is more or less accurate.

In contrast to the (mock-)humble declaration in the

preface to many books – 'any errors are of course mine' – Williams's Preface makes it clear that blame for 'discrepancies and mistakes' (Pref.: 11) lay with Cadwaladyr, who could not be relied on for accuracy of facts, the ordering of events, chronology, geography or orthography – a list sufficiently comprehensive to undermine any expectations that the autobiography which follows will be generally trustworthy (except perhaps by accident), since in many cases Williams had to depend on 'the light of analogy' (Pref.: 14) – a type of illumination which tends to make historians extremely uneasy. The most Williams apparently felt she could commit herself to was the assertion 'that for all thorough students of human nature, the narrative as a whole, bears internal evidence of the light of its truth' (Pref.: 13–14). The significant words here are 'as a whole' (as opposed to 'in detail') and 'internal (evidence)' (as opposed to 'external'), since she was unable to promise veracity either in detail or in relation to externally verifiable facts. The image she uses to illustrate her task is vivid:

> To seize the first floating end of each subject that chanced to present itself, to draw it out, to disentangle it, to piece it, to set the warp straight and firmly in the loom, and to cast the woof aright, so as to produce the true and original pattern of such tapestry, has required sedulous application. The winding of silkworms' cocoons without a reel, is scarcely a task of more difficult manipulation. (Preface: 32–6)

The material she had to work with is here presented as vague and inchoate: each subject is 'floating' and she had to grasp 'the first end' of it 'that chanced to present itself', an especially difficult task since all the tenuous threads were wrapped around each other like a silkworm's cocoon. The task involved taking a firm hold of the thread, drawing it out, carefully separating it from the tangled mass in which it was presented to her, piecing it (i.e. joining it to other threads by spinning), attaching the 'vertical' threads (the warp) to the loom and then weaving the threads horizontally through them (the woof) to create a woven tapestry. The extended metaphor sets up a fundamental contrast between the motley jumble of the threads of information she had been given by Cadwaladyr and the rigour and precision with which she had woven the finished narrative ('to set the warp *straight and firmly* in the loom, and to cast the woof *aright'*: my italics); it presents an image of the creation of order and regularity out of near-chaos. The metaphor illustrates her assertion that the process had been very complicated and delicate (it was like 'winding ... silkworms' cocoons without a reel') and had needed 'much care and labour' and 'sedulous application' from her. She had endeavoured 'to produce the true and original pattern of such tapestry', but her careful listing of six separate processes implies that the tangled mass of threads she had received was in such disarray that it was impossible to be sure that the carefully re-woven tapestry she had produced was an accurate copy of the original design, and emphasises that her task (not only 'cast[ing] the woof' but 'set[ting] the warp' in the loom) required her not to repair or restore a damaged fabric but to recreate the tapestry *ab initio* as seemed best to her. The 'truth' was irrecoverable.

Having issued a series of caveats on the autobiography's content, the Preface then does the same for its style. It might give readers the impression of a distinctive and unselfconscious personality addressing her readers in a direct and conversational style but, declared Williams, 'It was impossible in all parts to give the exact language spoken', adding rather defensively that 'a free translation often renders the original with more truth than a literal one' (Pref.: 19–20), and that she had aimed at giving the reader 'the genuine sense' of Cadwaladyr's account rather than 'literal precision' (Pref.: 22). She emphasised that 'wherever the very words of the heroine were apt and striking, they were retained' (Pref.: 23), but the person who judged whether they were 'apt and striking' was, of course, Williams. To paraphrase: much of the autobiography is Williams's pastiche of Cadwaladyr's speaking style and, although it contains some sentences which Cadwaladyr actually said, it is impossible for readers to know which these are.

This inevitably changes fundamentally the relationship between the autobiography and its readers: Cadwaladyr as ventriloquised by Williams is a very different prospect from Cadwaladyr direct. The result is that the character of Cadwaladyr as presented to the reader – self-confident, decisive, naïvely unaware that her account of events often shows her as rash, foolish or gullible – has to be seen as the entirely self-conscious literary construct of a second person, rather than the unmediated revelation of the narrator's personality.

Although the text of the autobiography itself does not make obvious to readers the major rôle played by Williams in determining its content and style, her presence is overt and pervasive in the rest of the book; the autobiography is framed by the Preface and Introduction which precede it and three Appendices which follow it (respectively: supporting documentation on Cadwaladyr and other nurses in military hospitals, an account of the recruitment of the nurses and details of conditions in the hospitals they worked in and supplies for patients, and 'Remarks on the System of Administration in the War Hospitals of the Crimean Army'). In addition, each chapter of the autobiography is headed by an epigraph and provided with footnotes.

The epigraphs are taken from a range of literary sources – Pope, Bacon, Shakespeare, Cowper, Milton and Crabbe, and other lesser-known poets – as well as a translation of a Welsh proverb and a quotation from the Book of Proverbs, and demonstrate an impressive breadth of reading. They also make a piquant contrast to the contents of the chapters they precede: the autobiography shows Cadwaladyr being and doing, while some of the epigraphs present elaborate literary constructs which reflect the same material (e.g. quotations from Montgomery's *West Indies* and *Voyage Round the World*). The contrast between the self-conscious literary artifice of the poetry and the direct, often colloquial, language of the chapters which follow them serves as a constant reminder that the autobiography is just as much a literary construct as the poetry, though in a different genre and register.

Williams says in her Preface that 'Foot-notes have been added in order to identify persons, to verify facts, to correct exaggerations, and to show the probability of some statements' (Pref.: 24–5). Certainly many of her footnotes merely 'identify persons' and 'verify facts' (e.g. the autobiography mentions a dinner given by Admiral Sotheron: the footnote explains his rôle in the defence of the Bay of Naples under Nelson (1857: I, 23); the autobiography refers to the soap-wood tree: a footnote corrects its English name to the 'soap-berry tree' and provides its botanical name and description (1987: 46, 57)). Other footnotes, however, question and in some cases contradict information stated as fact in the autobiography. In the hospital at Balaclava Cadwaladyr refused to accept the authority of three youthful-looking surgeons who told her they were 15, 17 and 19 years old; Williams's footnote suggested they had 'understated their age on purpose to tease' Cadwaladyr (1987: 186, 190); Cadwaladyr states that on a tour of western Scotland she and her employers stayed at 'Argyle Castle' (which does not exist); a footnote supplies 'Inverary' (1857: I, 86–7). Some footnotes reveal considerable exasperation with the biography's subject:

> The heroine's uncertainty concerning the names of the places which she visited in this expedition, and her want of sufficient geographical knowledge to distinguish between straits, canals, and rivers, have hitherto baffled the writer's efforts to identify the scenes of the adventures related in the present chapter. (1987: 96)

Other footnotes suggest a clash between Williams's attempts at factual accuracy and Cadwaladyr's certainty that she had seen what she had seen: an account in the autobiography of Cadwaladyr's encounter with a unicorn is dismissed in a magisterial footnote: 'The animal was probably a rhinoceros' (1987: 122), and when Cadwaladyr describes a 'strange monster' seen in the West Indies, which had a head like a shark, holes for ears, six wings, twelve feet, was green with a belly the colour of oyster-shells, its front part feathery and its hind quarters 'shelly', Williams gives up all serious attempts at rational discussion and quotes a sardonic verse by Cowper:

> 'Can this be true?' an arch observer cries,
> 'Yes', (rather moved) 'I saw it with these eyes.'
> 'Sir, I believe you, on that ground alone;
> I could not, had I seen it with my own.' (1987: 57)

As in the autobiography, so in the footnotes: what is omitted is often as revealing as what is stated. One of the most important supporting characters in the story of Cadwaladyr's life, her longest-lasting and most persistent suitor, appears for the first time in Vol. I, Chapter 9, and is introduced by a brief biographical sketch, presumably based on Cadwaladyr's memory of what he told her about himself, which begins:

> At Calcutta, a Portuguese merchant took the ship for three years and a half. His name was Andrea Antonio Benjamin Barbosa, and he was principal of the firm of Barbosa, Martin and Burke, general merchants of Macao, Sydney, Lima, Rio de Janeiro and Calcutta.
>
> His father was brother to King John the Eighth of Portugal ... (1987: 82)

Williams's usual practice would require a footnote here on King John the Eighth of Portugal: no such footnote is provided, because no such king existed. In fact, the last

'King John' (João) of Portugal was the sixth of that name, reigning from 1816 to 1826. That the ordinal is expressed in words, rather than by the Roman numeral, indicates that this cannot be the mistake of a compositor unaccountably left uncorrected by Williams; 'the Eighth' is clearly intended here.

The fact that Williams's background reading demonstrated the non-existence of João VIII is confirmed by a footnote to Vol. II, Chapter 2. During a visit to Rio de Janeiro Cadwaladyr became a favourite of the eldest daughter of the Emperor and Empress of Brazil, and the text adds that the 'little princess' later became 'queen of Portugal and mother of the present king' (1987: 127). Williams's footnote to this gives names and dates for leading members of the contemporary royal family of Brazil and Portugal in order to locate Cadwaladyr's 'little princess' in the family tree, and includes the information that the Emperor of Brazil at the time was the eldest son of 'John VI, King of Portugal' (1987: 130); either Barbosa misinformed Cadwaladyr, or she misremembered. The fact that Williams did not include a footnote pointing this out is interesting: perhaps she felt it was acceptable to dispute the names of Scottish castles and the existence of grotesque monsters, but not to challenge Cadwaladyr's memories of information given to her about himself by one of the most important men in her life. Whatever the reason, this reinforces powerfully the impression given by the way in which other of Williams's footnotes relate to Cadwaladyr's account, that Cadwaladyr had control of what went into the text of the autobiography and Williams had control of what went into the footnotes. The friction between the two women caused by their different approaches to the factual basis of Cadwaladyr's reminiscences must be entirely a matter of conjecture.

'John the Eighth of Portugal' is an example of a factual error in the autobiography of which Williams was aware; although most of the facts of Cadwaladyr's life were and are uncheckable, the autobiography contains one factual inaccuracy which Cadwaladyr must have known to be untrue and which Williams, it seems, did not: Cadwaladyr's age.

The reference books say she was born in 1789, and the reference books are right: the Parish Register for Llanycil (which included Bala) records the baptism on 26 May 1789 of 'Elizabeth, daughter of David Cadwaladr and Judith his wife'. The interviews on which the autobiography was based were held in 1856 (Pref.: 2), so at that time Cadwaladyr was either 66 or 67, depending on whether the interviews were held before or after her birthday in May. In the opening paragraph of the autobiography, after expressing uncertainty about her precise age, she states 'I think I am now about sixty-one' – i.e. five or six years younger than her true age.

It is possible that she believed what she said; it is also possible that she was lying. Many people lie about their ages for a variety of reasons, but in Cadwaladyr's case there is a piece of information in the public domain which shows that she had a very strong reason for lying: in the Nurses' Register (the list of nurses enrolled to work in the hospitals of the Crimean Army) the entry about her, from information she gave at her interview in November 1854, states her age to be 54.[10] At the very least, and even if she really had no idea of her true age, she must have known that she could not have been both 54 in 1854 and 61 in 1856; she has to have been deliberately lying in relation to at least one of them (and possibly, of course, both). Certainly, giving her birth-year as 1800 must have simplified the necessary mental arithmetic.

Although it is impossible to be sure why she lied to the Nurses' Register, one very powerful motive suggests itself: if her true age had been known, she would never have been accepted as a nurse with the Crimean Army. Florence Nightingale's instructions were very clear: no woman was to be employed as a nurse who might prove to be in any way unsuitable or inadequate, and being too old would have made her ineligible. Cadwaladyr was confident that she could do the work and cope with the living conditions (and events proved her right) and was determined to go; but her real age would have prevented her from even being considered. Of those whose age is recorded in the Nurses' Register, only eight were over 50, and the oldest was 56; by saying she was 54, Cadwaladyr was dangerously close to the (unofficial) threshold. When the second group of nurses (which included Cadwaladyr) arrived at Scutari, one of them was rejected immediately on grounds of age ('sent home for being too old for work') and returned to Britain.[11] The incident must have confirmed powerfully to Cadwaladyr that she had made the right decision in concealing her true age at her interview; although the autobiography records the dismissal of several other nurses for a variety of reasons during her time at Scutari and Balaclava, there is complete silence about this incident.

She would have known it was very likely that friends and associates of Nightingale would read the book to see if she said anything unfavourable about Nightingale and her organisation (they did: Selina Bracebridge, one of Nightingale's closest friends who acted as her personal assistant and worked with Cadwaladyr at Scutari, described the *Autobiography* in a letter to Florence Nightingale's sister Parthenope as 'that odious, lying book'[12]), and, if she gave her true age, would be alerted by the wide discrepancy between it and the age she had given the Nurses' Register, and might use her lie as a weapon to attack the veracity of other aspects of the *Autobiography*, especially her criticisms of Nightingale and her organisation. Equally, if she maintained in the autobiography the age she had given the Nurses' Register, its difference from her true age might attract the attention of old friends who had known her in her youth and might remember her age clearly enough to know that she was not in her mid-fifties. Saying that she was 'about sixty-one' neatly split the difference between her true age and the one she had given the Nurses' Register.

More important than the detail of this is the question of why an age is mentioned at all in the autobiography, given that this was a subject at the least fraught with difficulty and at worst presenting the danger of being publicly exposed as a liar; it would have been far simpler to let readers draw their own conclusions from the fact that she was a young adult at the time of the General Election of 1812 (1987: 21), for example. A possible explanation is that Williams was aware that making Cadwaladyr's age explicit would show the energy and dedication she had shown in the service of her country as even more impressive and therefore even more deserving of readers' charity. It would have been very difficult for Cadwaladyr to produce a good reason not to give her age, and the hesitation and uncertainty with which the autobiography introduces the subject may reflect Cadwaladyr's reactions when Williams pressed her for the information.

A similar explanation may lie behind another curious detail: that the autobiography says that Cadwaladyr was 'a little more than five years of age' (1987: 6) at the time of her mother's death, while the Llanycil Parish Register records the burial on 10 February 1800 when Cadwaladyr was ten. Certainly adult memories can be fallible about the timing of events in childhood, but the autobiography shows that her mother's death was one the most most traumatic, and arguably one of the most formative, events of Cadwaladyr's life, and therefore more likely to be remembered in detail. If Cadwaladyr had been sixty-one at the time of the interviews for the book, she would indeed have been five years old when her mother died; it is possible that she gave the year of her mother's death and that Williams, realising that making her subject's young age explicit at the time of her mother's death would add greatly to the pathos of the story, decided to save readers the trouble of doing the arithmetic. Certainly, once Cadwaladyr had told Williams her age, it would have been impossible for her to have contradicted herself later. As it is, the inaccuracy calls into question the timing of important subsequent events: the autobiography states that she ran away from her family home to the Lloyds' house in Bala 'when I was about nine years of age' (1987: 13), but since this happened some time after her mother's death it is clearly inaccurate and is perhaps better understood as 'about four years after my mother died', which may have been what she told Williams; her flight from the Lloyds' house to Liverpool, said in the autobiography to have taken place 'about five years later' (1987: 15), would then have happened in her late teens rather than when she was fourteen.

The autobiography, then, has its inaccuracies and omissions; if the Preface has inaccuracies they are not now apparent, but it certainly has its omissions, and investigating them can be very productive. Williams says she first met Cadwaladyr in 1851 and that they met again in 1856 (Pref.: 1–2), apparently when the interviews for the book took place: she says nothing about where and through whom they met or at whose suggestion the book was written. On the evidence of the autobiography, Cadwaladyr was not someone whose immediate solution to the prospect of financial hardship would have been to write a book, and Williams's account of her work on the book in the Preface is so wearily disaffected that if she had been the book's originator she might well have given up on the project. It is therefore possible that the book's prime mover was a third person.

A remarkable feature of the *Autobiography* is the lack of any reference to Lady Llanover (at that time, Lady Hall of Llanover), since both Williams and Cadwaladyr knew her and might have been expected to mention her. Williams had been a friend and protegée of Lady Llanover for some years and owed her a debt of gratitude for enabling publication of the two books which had made her literary name – *Artegall*, her response to the 1847 Report on Education in Wales (Brad y Llyfrau Gleision/The Treachery of the Blue Books) in 1848 and *Literary Remains of the Rev. Thomas*

Price, Carnhuanawc in 1854–55 – while Hall had provided a reference for Cadwaladyr when she enrolled as a nurse with the Crimean Army (which stated she was 'well known and respected by Lady Hall of Llanover'[13]), but in spite of Cadwaladyr's tendency to name-drop the public figures she had met – the Emperor of China, the Infanta of Brazil, Lord Raglan – Hall, as far as the *Autobiography* is concerned, remains curiously absent.

It is, however, possible that Hall makes an anonymous appearance in the autobiography. Cadwaladyr gives the full names of some of the people she had encountered (mainly, it seems, those whom she knew to be dead at the time of the interviews) but omits the surnames of many others, especially previous employers. One of these, 'Lady ____', is described as a Welshwoman who had houses in London and south Wales, and when Cadwaladyr presented herself at the London house for a job interview 'to take charge of a house in South Wales', she received a friendly reception: 'On hearing that I was Dafydd Cadwaladyr's daughter, Lady ____ sent for me, spoke to me, and engaged me.' She worked at the house in south Wales from August to November 1851, and from March to August 1852 worked in Lady ____'s London house as a head-housemaid:

> Lord Raglan's house stood near, and often, when I was cleaning the door of a morning, I used to see Lord Raglan going out on horseback for his morning ride. He never passed me without giving me a pleasant look and a civil word, such as 'Cold morning' or 'Fine morning', and once I heard him say to his groom, 'That woman's always up!' I stayed in ____ Street until August 1852. (1987: 152–3)

In 1855, when Cadwaladyr was in charge of the extra-diets kitchen in the General Hospital at Balaclava, Lord Raglan, Commander in Chief of the Crimean Army, came to inspect her kitchen:

> When he came in, the first words he said, before he spoke

> to any one else, were addressed to me: 'I know you. Did not you live in Stanhope Street?'
>
> 'Yes, my Lord.'
>
> 'Then you know me?'
>
> 'Yes, my lord.'
>
> 'The best woman I ever saw for getting up in the morning.' (1987: 171)

The 1851 Census Returns and contemporary Post Office directories for London show that Raglan lived at no. 5 Great Stanhope Street, and that Sir Benjamin and Lady Hall lived at no. 9; as far as I can establish, Hall was the only woman living in or near Great Stanhope Street during this period who shared the other attributes of 'Lady ____'. If Cadwaladyr did indeed work for her in 1851 and 1852 it would explain not only Hall's reference recorded in the Nurses' Register but also where and how she and Williams could have met (although Williams was living in Talgarth at this period, she made frequent visits to Llanover Court and the Halls' London home).[14] It would also give an additional dimension to the 'respect' expressed in Hall's reference for her and give a private – and piquant – resonance to the description in the Preface of Cadwaladyr's commanding appearance and personality, which had 'a uniform effect upon her employers, in levelling the usual barriers which divide the classes' (Pref.: 47–8).

Cadwaladyr, returned from the Crimea in broken health and with nothing to live on but back pay which would not have kept her for very long (£40-8-0; 1987: 199), would have been likely to contact anyone who might help her, especially previous employers. Hall's reference shows that she had supported Cadwaladyr's spell as a nurse and cook with the Crimean Army, and a book which drew attention to the service to her country of a remarkable Welshwoman, while raising money to support her in her poverty-stricken old age, could well have seemed like an excellent idea to her. And she had at hand someone to write it: a published author who owed her a debt of gratitude for being made a member of the Llanover circle and for the publication of two previous books. Whether or not Hall was the prime mover of the *Autobiography*, she certainly knew and approved of it in advance, since she contributed to it: the autobiography recounts that in Calcutta, Cadwaladyr met Bishop Heber, who recited her father's elegy on Thomas Charles of Bala; two stanzas are included, followed by an (English) 'Translation by G.G.' (1857: I, 230), a reference to Hall's bardic name (Gwenynen Gwent), often used by her and others, including Williams, to refer to her.[15]

Why Hall would have wanted to have her name kept out of the book is an entirely separate question, and any attempt to answer it must be entirely speculative. The reason may lie in a combination of personal, social and political factors: as an MP, Benjamin Hall would have come into frequent social as well as political contact with Sidney Herbert, the Minister at War who had recruited Nightingale to take charge of the nurses for the Crimean Army, and Herbert and his wife Elizabeth were old and close friends of Florence Nightingale. The autobiography's account of Cadwaladyr's immediate and visceral dislike of Nightingale has attracted much attention, but this was so irrational and eccentric that it could be easily dismissed. More difficult to ignore, however, were Cadwaladyr's criticisms of the maladministration and inefficiency with which the Free Gifts for the troops were distributed – or, indeed, not distributed: Cadwaladyr tells of some which were so badly stored that they rotted completely away in a stable in Scutari (1987:163) and of others, on sale in shops in Woolwich and Deptford, advertised as 'Direct from the Crimea' (1987: 201). Nightingale was in charge of the distribution of the Free Gifts, and therefore bore the ultimate responsibility for these failures; animosity to Cadwaladyr's criticisms may explain the refusal of Elizabeth Herbert, who had been closely involved with the recruitment of nurses for the Crimean Army,[16] to extend to Cadwaladyr the 'patronage and protection' requested in a letter from the superintendent of nurses at Balaclava (1987: 210). In the circumstances, Hall may well have thought it expedient to have her contribution to Cadwaladyr's reminiscences kept strictly anonymous.

As the previous paragraphs' 'might', 'would have been likely' and 'could well have seemed' indicate, the degree of Hall's involvement with the *Autobiography* must be a matter of conjecture. It is, however, not only consistent with the evidence that has survived, but also offers a plausible explanation for Williams's defensive repetition of how much time and effort the book had taken her.

Cadwaladyr left the Crimea in November 1855;[17] the treaty which ended the Crimean War was signed in March 1856, and British soldiers began leaving the Crimea four months later. If Williams's rôle had been merely to transcribe Cadwaladyr's words and compose the Preface, Introduction and Appendices, it could have been possible to publish the book in late summer or early autumn 1856, when the war and its management were still live issues. By the time of publication in July 1857, however, although there was still interest in some aspects of the Crimean War (the Royal Commission into the Health of the Army began its work in May 1857, with Sidney Herbert in the chair[18]) other first-hand accounts of experiences during the war had already been published, and the autobiography contained little that was new or unexpected. The Indian Mutiny had broken out nearly two months before its publication, and the focus of British public interest was changing.

At this period, before the royalty system was established, writers were paid a sum on publication for the copyright to their books (sometimes for a specified number of years, sometimes for their lifetime). Unfortunately the financial records of Hurst and Blackett, which would give the sum paid – presumably to Cadwaladyr – have not survived, but the *Autobiography* would certainly have been worth less in July 1857 than in the autumn of 1856.[19] In this context, the defensive tone of the Preface and Williams's emphasis on the time and effort the book took her are understandable; she wished to defend herself against the charge (from Hall?) that her extensive work on the book had unnecessarily delayed its publication and had therefore adversely affected its main object, that of raising money for Cadwaladyr. Her situation was certainly unenviable: she had spent at least many months, and perhaps a year, in detailed and intensive work, she had used her best efforts and her literary and analytical skills, she had done all this for nothing, and in return she seemed likely to receive only criticism from someone whose friendship she valued and whose good opinion she wanted to keep – certainly, someone she did not wish to offend.

At this distance in time, and in the absence of accounts by Cadwaladyr and Hall on the parts they played in the making of the *Autobiography*, many details of its context and composition are irrecoverable; some points, however, seem clear. One is that every part of its title – *The Autobiography of Elizabeth Davis, a Balaclava Nurse*, edited by Jane Williams (Ysgafell) – is either inaccurate or misleading: it is not, in the usual definition of the word, an autobiography; Elizabeth Davis was not the correct name of its subject; she was a cook in the General Hospital at Balaclava for far longer than she was a nurse – approximately nine months as against six weeks (and she is described as 'Cook' in the Nurses' Register[20]); and to call the part Williams played in the book's creation as 'editing' so under-describes her contribution as to be seriously misleading. A second is that its narrative is at times seriously unreliable: the autobiography contains some 'facts' which Cadwaladyr (but probably not Williams) knew to be untrue (her age), and others which Williams knew to be untrue but which Cadwaladyr was apparently convinced were accurate ('King John the Eighth of Portugal').

In the words of the Preface, Cadwaladyr was 'as

different from the ordinary type as are the events of her story' (Pref.: 42–43); she was clearly a remarkable woman who had lived a unique life. But even such a brief consideration as this of her autobiography in the light of Williams's Preface and the context in which the book was written suggests very strongly that it is not the reliable narration of the 'true facts' of her life recounted in her own words which it purports to be, but rather the carefully devised and skilfully ventriloquised literary construct of a second person, with the possibility of a third person in the shadows pulling the strings.

The book for which Cadwaladyr is celebrated should therefore be seen not as the unselfconscious and unsophisticated account of her life-story by a first-person narrator speaking directly to her readers, but as the result of a complex, intricate and sometimes fraught negotiation between two – perhaps three – women who were very different from each other in personality, priorities and interests, education and social class; the light, bright, engaging surface of the narrative rests on a multi-layered process of composition which was both complicated and difficult, and which took place in a context which produced its own problems. Cadwaladyr's autobiography, full of dramatic and unexpected events, grabs the reader's attention and holds it from beginning to end: an awareness of the complexity of the process by which it was created, and its context, can only increase the interest which it holds for its readers today.

NOtes

1 Talk on 3 August by Buddug Medi; exhibition on the stand of the Snowdonia National Park Authority.

2 The increasing interest in her can also lead to confusion: the National Archives website includes a short biography and the photograph of her from the frontispiece of the *Autobiography* to accompany a letter it holds from an Elizabeth Davis, applying for a place in Florence Nightingale's party of nurses

in 1854. Neither the age, address, marital status nor work experience of the letter's author fits Betsy Cadwaladyr, and the date of the letter means that there would not have been enough time for the letter-writer to be interviewed and processed before the second party of nurses left for Scutari, especially given the length of time required for letters and people to travel between London and Southampton (where the letter-writer lived) and back again. The inevitable conclusion, therefore, is that the letter was written by a different Elizabeth Davis and has been wrongly attributed.

3 Information from Jean Rose, Archivist of the Random House Group, which took over Hutchinson, which in turn had taken over Hurst and Blackett, publishers of the *Autobiography*.

4 Information from Helena Earnshaw of Honno, to whom I am also very grateful for alerting me to the exhibition at the 2009 National Eisteddfod.

5 Jane Williams (Ysgafell) (ed.) *The Autobiography of Elizabeth Davis a Balaclava Nurse* (Dinas Powys: Honno, 1987): 18. All further references to this edition are given parenthetically in the text as (1987: x).

6 Jane Williams (Ysgafell) (ed.) *The Autobiography of Elizabeth Davis a Balaclava Nurse* (London: Hurst and Blackett, 1857): I, 119. All further references to this edition are given parenthetically in the text as (1857: x).

7 Adam Smyth, *TLS*, 18/09/09: 24.

8 See, for example, Regenia Gagnier *Subjectivities: A History of Self-Representation in Britain 1832–1920* (OUP, 1991), A.O.J. Cockshut, *The Art of the Autobiography in 19th and 20th Century England* (Yale University Press, 1984) and David Vincent, *Bread, Knowledge and Freedom: a Study of Nineteenth-Century Working-class Autobiography* (Methuen, 1981).

9 This Preface was not reprinted in the Honno reissue; it is reproduced for the first time since the original 1857 edition in the current volume immediately after this essay.

10 LD FNM 0073: 11 (held in Florence Nightingale Museum, St Thomas's Hospital, London).

11 LD FNM 0073: 11.

12 Mark Bostridge, *Florence Nightingale: the Woman and Her*

Legend (Viking, 2008): 269.

13 LD FNM 0073: 10.

14 See NLW MSS 26/9, *passim*.

15 For example, see Tonn MSS 3.109A, letter 45, undated, 1848 (Hall and Archdeacon Williams of Cardigan), and NLW MSS 26/9, Nov. 12 and Dec. 2, 1851 (Williams to Elizabeth Marsh).

16 Bostridge: 208, 236.

17 LD FNM 0073: 11.

18 Bostridge: 318.

19 In 1852 the publisher Richard Bentley told the novelist Margaret Oliphant that it would be necessary to sell 700 copies of her forthcoming novel to justify his offer of £200 (Royal A. Gettmann, *A Victorian Publisher,* CUP, 1960: 131). Her first novel had been a critical success and had gone into three editions, so that her publisher would have needed to spend less money on advertising her next, eagerly awaited book than would the publishers of the autobiography of a nobody (from the point of view of the reading public). Cadwaladyr's two-volume autobiography sold for 21s., the same price as Oliphant's two-volume novel, and the print-runs of the two books are likely to have been comparable; it is very improbable that she would have got more than Oliphant's £200, and far more likely that she would have received less.

20 LD FNM 0073: 10.

The Autobiography of Elizabeth Davis, a Balaclava Nurse

Preface

[by Jane Williams, Ysgafell]

The writer first became acquainted with the heroine and narrator of these adventures in the year 1851. In the year 1856 they met again, under circumstances which led the writer to appreciate more fully the extraordinary character and history of Elizabeth Davis. Though worn by time, and oppressed by illness, her indomitable energy still shone in her eyes, and bore her fine form erect; still manifested itself in industrious activity, and in buoyant cheerfulness of spirit.

She possessed no written records of her life, no memoranda, no letters, no tangible and visible helps to memory. In a desultory and digressive manner, she gave, to the best of her recollection, an account of the principal facts of her own remarkable history. She knew that lapse of time and intermediate events had cast their shadows over some scenes; she was aware that here and there a link in the chain was bent or broken; but she trusted in her vivid impressions of the past, and in her own sincerity of purpose.

Discrepancies and mistakes may be detected in the details, errors in chronology, errors in geography, and errors in the orthography of names and in the designation of persons; but the writer believes that for all thorough students of human nature the narrative, as a whole, bears internal evidence of the light of its truth. With the guidance of its heroine, and the light of analogy, the incidents have been arranged in consecutive order.

It has been the writer's object justly to apprehend the meaning of the narrator, and faithfully to express it.

It is well known that a free translation often renders the sense of an original with more truth than a literal one.

It was impossible in all parts to give the exact language

spoken. The writer has therefore aimed at conveying a true reflex of her exact meaning, preferring the genuine sense to literal precision.

Wherever the very words of the heroine were apt and striking, they were retained.

Foot-notes have been added in order to identify persons, to verify facts, to correct exaggerations, and to show the probability of some extraordinary statements.

The important matter contained in the Appendix tends both to place the public service of Mrs Davis in a just light, and to prove the worth and weight of her opinion upon a great public question.

The narrative of a pure-minded woman, of thorough integrity and of dauntless resolution, and one to whom the Bible formed the chart of life, cannot be altogether useless to society, although like every other record of real experience, it affords matter for warning as well as for example.

A cursory reader may suppose that the writer had merely to listen and to record, but the task of preparing the narrative has really involved much care and labour. To seize the first floating end of each subject that chanced to present itself, to draw it out, to disentangle it, to piece it, to set the warp straight and firmly in the loom, and to cast the woof aright, so as to produce the true and original pattern of such tapestry, has required sedulous application. The winding of silkworms' cocoons without a reel, is scarcely a task of more difficult manipulation.

The reader who supposes the text of the narrative to have cost the writer little trouble, may probably expect that all its most remarkable passages should be illustrated or explained by notes. Extensive inquiries have been instituted for this purpose, and some valuable results have been obtained, but the circulation of a whole edition can alone be expected to bring in the contributions of diffused and personal information necessary to the full execution of this desirable object.

It may be necessary here to call attention to the peculiar

character of the heroine – a character as different from the ordinary type as are the events of her story.

The extraordinary combination in her of the spirit of enterprize, self-dependence, and mental alacrity, with great bodily strength and activity, a commanding figure, noble aspect and perfect self-possession of manner, never failed to exercise a powerful influence upon her associates; and its uniform effect upon her employers, in levelling the usual barriers which divide the classes, is shown throughout this work. To those who are unacquainted with her, the fact may seem incredible. To those who have experienced the power of her blended dignity and deference, no further evidence is necessary.

In her autobiography, the absence of sentiment and air of unsympathising indifference, must not be taken for the want of kindness and humanity.

Her nature was undoubtedly peculiar, imaginative, impulsive and adventurous; but the mountain region which produced her, and the state of society which surrounded her in early life, moulded and impressed upon the native metal the form and stamp which it has never lost.

Visions of Wales:

The Welsh Outlook, 1914–1933

Alyce von Rothkirch
Swansea University

The Welsh Outlook was a monthly periodical which was published in Wales between 1914 and 1933. It stands out amongst similar publications because it aimed to discuss current and political affairs from a Welsh point of view while avoiding 'parish pump' attitudes. It is tempting to view the ephemeral output of newspapers and periodicals mainly as 'a source of historical information, rather than as a subject of historical enquiry.'[1] But instead of taking the *Outlook* as a source of information, I would like to analyse the contents of the periodical itself and attempt to assess, firstly, whether it lived up to the expectations expressed by its first editor Thomas Jones. Secondly, I would like to show how the *Outlook* exemplified the peculiarities of the Welsh public sphere at the beginning of the twentieth century. Thirdly, I would like to speculate why, after twenty years of existence, the *Outlook* finally failed in 1933. My analysis is based mainly on sources such as Ballin (2004, 2008), Jenkins (1985–86) and Williams (1979), as well as on my own analysis of a systematic sample of 60 issues published between 1914 and 1933.[2]

E.L. Ellis provides a good description of the motivations for establishing *The Welsh Outlook*:

> [Thomas Jones] and his friends had come to the conclusion ... that the weekly and monthly press in Wales was too partisan in attitude, too parochial in outlook, and too much concerned with theological and literary subjects to provide effective comment on the great social and political changes that had occurred or were impending. People were bewildered by rapid change and conflicting or uncertain moral standards. There ought to be a proper

> debate in Wales, and enlightened opinion should take the initiative.[3]

The *Outlook* was to fill a gap in the serious periodical press in Wales by engaging with social and political topics. The title was programmatic: expressive of distinctively Welsh views, the magazine was to look beyond Wales at UK and world affairs. The quotation also neatly encapsulates the remarkable certainty of Thomas Jones and his friends that they were the people whose 'enlightened opinion' was to guide their readers.

To assess the *Outlook*'s impact, a few words about the specificities of the Welsh public sphere are appropriate here. Historically, the public sphere as described by Jürgen Habermas developed alongside the political sphere. The public sphere is populated by journalists, opinion formers, think tanks, cultural organisations – in short, by everyone who wants to influence public opinion and has the means to do so. Today, the public sphere exerts a great influence over the political sphere. In fact, the spheres often overlap as politicians moonlight as journalists and as actors in the public sphere become politicians.[4] In England at the beginning of the twentieth century, metropolitan intellectuals and other denizens of the public sphere just began to be able to exert influence over the political sphere.[5] In Wales, however, a different state of affairs prevailed due to the physical separation of the political sphere in Westminster, where Welsh MPs represented their constituencies, and the public sphere located in Wales, for example, in the numerous newspapers and magazines published in Welsh and in English, and in the Welsh 'diaspora' in London, Liverpool and other places. Even as more Wales-specific legislation appeared and as administrative units such as the Central Welsh Board of Education began to be located in Wales, serious public discussion tended to concentrate on cultural, linguistic and religious topics – perhaps because it was in these spheres that this 'nation without state'[6] commanded the independence it lacked politically. Public intellectual commentary in periodicals tended to focus on topics that arose out of, to appropriate the Gramscian term, 'organic culture': publications like *Seren Gomer*, a nineteenth-century Baptist newspaper, could speak directly to the Welsh Baptist community. By contrast, political commentary could not be certain to reach the political sphere in the same way: a well-chosen word in the ear of a civil servant in a select London club could be far more certain to be heeded than a cry of outrage in a Welsh newspaper column. *The Welsh Outlook* was meant to bridge this gap by providing serious political commentary, by looking beyond the Welsh borders and by influencing Welsh politics in Westminster.

The Welsh Outlook appeared when Wales' national self-confidence and unity of vision had reached its zenith. Some of this feeling of self-confidence achieved a tangible presence in the granting of the charter to the University of Wales in 1893, the founding of the National Library in Aberystwyth in 1909 and the establishment of the National Museum of Wales, whose charter was granted in 1907. Social, cultural, religious and linguistic change was undoubtedly in the air, but commentators did not doubt that this change could be incorporated into the greater vision. This vision, which was enthusiastically championed by the members of the Liberal establishment that formed the core of the contributors of *The Welsh Outlook*, was based on a belief in Wales as a 'classless' society, of a people who shared a language, nonconformist religion, Liberal or Lib–Lab political convictions and a pride in an 'organic' culture. Voices like that of W. Llewellyn Williams, who proudly declared that Wales had a 'higher standard of popular culture ... than any other country in Europe', epitomised this sense of optimism even as this image began to be challenged.[7] Ellis calls this a 'populist form of ethnic nationalism'.[8] By 1914 such nationalism had successfully permeated Welsh public and political spheres:

> When Lloyd George assumed a cabinet position in the Liberal government of 1906–1914, he did so secure in the knowledge that the forces of Welsh nonconformist nationalism now virtually controlled the political, cultural, social and economic life of Wales. Welsh political nationalism had worked splendidly and, by all appearances, was advancing from a position of strength at the turn of the century.[9]

The Welsh Outlook was an expression of this sense of national self-confidence and optimism. It gave voice to a particular political, religious and linguistic viewpoint and unhesitatingly applied it to the whole nation.

The unity of vision displayed by *The Welsh Outlook* was centrally influenced by the noted lecturer, adult educator and civil servant Thomas Jones, usually referred to as T.J. 'A periodical is produced by a guiding editorial intelligence, seeking to project an identity'[10] and the *Outlook*'s editorial line, despite frequent changes of editor, remained closely aligned with that of its first editor. T.J. had no experience as a journalist but was keen to reach a wide audience.[11] In 1910 he had met David Davies, the coalowner and philanthropist, and had become a close friend and confidant of the Davies sisters, Margaret and Gwendoline. Hoping for financial backing, T.J. wrote in 1913 a business proposal for a weekly magazine provisionally called 'The Red Dragon', which was 'to assist in the work of Social Reform'.[12] However, these plans did not come to fruition, presumably because David Davies was not prepared to shoulder the financial burden. Then T.J. and a group of friends in Barry and Cardiff came up with a less ambitious project, which David Davies agreed to back: a professionally–produced monthly magazine tackling the social issues of the day. The original editorial board was made up of the Establishment figures of Edwardian Wales. The Rev. Richard Jones, a Calvinist Methodist minister in Llandinam who had originally introduced T.J. to David Davies, took on the responsibility for religion and philosophy. Edgar Jones, the Headmaster of Barry Intermediate School and a close friend of T.J., took on the editorial responsibility for education; a number of contributors to the *Outlook*, like Annie Ffoulkes and the poet R. Williams Parry, also worked at Barry Intermediate School. R. Silyn Roberts, a well-known poet and former Calvinistic Methodist minister who became first secretary of the Appointments Board of the University of Wales, was responsible for literature, poetry and drama. T.J. himself took on responsibility for social and industrial questions and co-operation. W.J. Burdon Evans, David Davies' business secretary, was Davies' nominee on the Board. He looked after health, local government, music, arts and architecture. George M. Lloyd Davies, a pacifist who worked for the Fellowship of Reconciliation in 1914 and entered Parliament in 1923 as a Christian Pacifist MP for the University of Wales and subsequently joined the Labour Party, took on housing. Frank Murrell, a master printer from Barry, was appointed Honorary Secretary and General Manager.[13] All members of the editorial board gave their time on a voluntary basis and only T.J.'s assistant, Frank Wright, drew a small salary. This group of people was highly educated, liberal if not Liberal in outlook and motivated by a high-minded sense of social obligation. However, none of the members of the editorial board were professional journalists or publishers and 'the lack of a serious professional approach was to have a deleterious effect on the magazine in the long term'.[14]

What were the aims of *The Welsh Outlook*? In his second volume of memoirs, *Welsh Broth*, T.J. writes that in 1914 Wales was going through 'a period of comparative national prosperity'. He continues: 'We wanted to translate this wealth into a higher quality of social life in Wales. ... Our first notion had been to found a weekly paper in which to expound and criticize the changes afoot.'[15] The *Outlook* was to raise the quality of social commentary and to broaden the minds of their readership, or, as T.J. put it programmatically in his 'Foreword' to the first edition, '[t]he imagination of our people must be possessed with the vision of a better Wales'.[16] This sentiment is echoed in the *Outlook*'s motto from Proverbs 29:18: 'Where there is no vision, the people perish' and its subtitle 'A Monthly Journal of National Social Progress'. T.J. described the nation the magazine was addressing as 'a seething cauldron of unrest and conflict'. *The Welsh Outlook* was thus poised to respond meaningfully to the social and cultural changes of the period.

E.L. Ellis suggests that a parallel can be drawn between T.J.'s work for the *Outlook* and his involvement with the Workers' Educational Association.[18] T.J., Silyn Roberts and others helped set up and run the WEA in South Wales. At that time it was an organisation providing relatively orthodox, liberal adult education, which was designed to 'graft the values of a liberal university education' on to working-class leaders, who were then meant to be able to detect and reject 'spurious knowledge and bogus remedies' for the social and economic issues with which they were grappling.[19] This kind of adult education can be construed as manipulative, namely as an attempt to take the brightest and best out of the working-class movement, enculturate them in the values of Liberal Wales and thus render them unfit for the class struggle – and this was how many Labour activists, particularly those associated with the rival Plebs League and National Labour College, saw the activities of the WEA. However, it can also be seen as a genuine wish to extend the opportunities of the educated middle class to those in the working class, who had the capacity to benefit, and to engage in a social dialogue that would prevent social conflict. *The Welsh Outlook* shared the latter position and was, in T.J.'s words, to provide 'intelligent guidance' to its readership.[20]

A brief word must be said about the influence exerted by David Davies as the financier and, from 1918, owner of the magazine. The journalistic landscape of early twentieth-century Britain was dominated by newspaper barons like Lord Northcliffe and Lord Beaverbrook. Nick Davies points out that, in contrast to today's newspaper magnates such as Rupert Murdoch, who are primarily interested in sales, these owners took a close and controlling interest in the editorial line their newspapers were taking.[21] After 1917, David Davies began to take an active interest in newspaper publishing and acquired the National Press Agency in 1918, as well as a few journals and newspapers. Even though Davies' media interests cannot be compared with those of Northcliffe and Beaverbrook, he clearly took a similar attitude when it came to controlling what was published in 'his' *Outlook*. There is evidence of censorship, for example, of articles by George H. Lloyd Davies, whose pacifist line displeased Davies.[22] Trevor Williams shows how an ill-tempered David Davies threatened closure of the magazine if an article by Edgar L. Chappell for the January 1917 issue entitled 'The Unrest in the Coalfield', which presented a socialist argument, were printed. He succeeded and the article did not appear.[23] T.J. habitually sent proofs of articles to Davies for approval before they were published and, from 1918, Davies himself contributed numerous articles. His favourite projects received a great deal of editorial attention, for instance, Home Rule, the Welsh League of Nations Union and the King Edward VII National Memorial Association (an organisation dedicated to the fight against tuberculosis). Only the Welsh School of Social Service received an equal amount of attention, presumably because two *Outlook* regulars, the Rev. Gwilym Davies and Daniel Lleufer Thomas, were connected with it as founder and chairman respectively. However, more articles originate from speeches given at the Welsh School of Social Services than take the School as their subject. Editors evidently came to regard the School as a convenient quarry from which to obtain ready-made articles for publication. By contrast, the importance of David Davies-inspired topics can be gleaned from the fact that, out of five special supplements to the

Outlook published between 1915 and 1919, two deal with the League of Nations, one with the National Memorial Association, one with Home Rule, one with the reorganisation of the University of Wales and only one with literature, a topic in which Davies appears to have had no special interest. This is not necessarily an indication of undue pressure: owner and editorial board may have simply agreed on the importance of the causes Davies supported. However, Davies' influence may have made editors fearful of offending him and therefore less likely to commission articles that were controversial.

What, then, were the main subject areas with which the articles in the *Outlook* dealt? My analysis is based on a systematic sample of 60 issues published between 1914 and 1933. From the description of the motivation of founding the periodical and the constitution of the editorial board, it could be concluded that the majority of its space was given to social issues. However, the majority of articles in fact address cultural and literary topics (118). Social topics are dealt with in 81 of the articles. Many articles are of a historical nature or discuss Welsh and other personalities past and present (49). Other topics include education (47), religion (46), nature/agriculture/scientific subjects (26), socialism and labour issues (12), home rule, nationalism and the Welsh Party (20) and war and reconstruction (4). Overall, the *Outlook* strikes a balance between social and literary/cultural topics. However, it cannot be seen as an incisive current affairs magazine. This must partly be due to the fact that articles published in a monthly periodical cannot engage with current affairs as effectively as a weekly. It must also be borne in mind that editors only had access to a limited pool of non-professional contributors, whose work was semi-voluntary. Given such circumstances, the articles probably reveal more about the interests of their authors than about Welsh politics and the social issues of the day. This interpretation is supported by the fact that a high number – about 45% –

of the articles take a historical perspective. There are historical articles on the arts and literature (34), on Welsh personalities of the past (18), on Welsh history, history of religion and extracts of biographies/autobiographies (12), obituaries (9) and so on. Seen in the context of Welsh periodical publishing of the time, this reliance on articles dealing with historical matters, rather than with current affairs, is not surprising. Earlier periodicals, especially those in the miscellany tradition (see Ballin, 2008) include at least as many historical articles. Authors often contributed to more than one periodical and may have fallen into familiar grooves of essay writing. Many of these articles attempt to bring historical Welsh achievement back into the collective consciousness, such as the series on 'Welsh Pioneers', which includes an article on the sixteenth-century mathematician, Robert Recorde, who is remembered for inventing the equals sign, and Henry Richard, the 'Apostle of Peace'. In this way, the current public sphere was meant to be imbued with a sense of the national past and achievement. However, the majority of the historical articles are of antiquarian interest and shed little light on the situation of Wales in the early twentieth century. Apart from the lack of authors who could discuss current news at the required level and with sufficient journalistic flair – a problem all small periodicals and little magazines relying mainly on part-time staff and non-professional contributors face and which must be familiar to present-day editors of publications like *Planet* – there was also a dearth of current news other than local news.[24] The split between political and public spheres becomes especially problematic here as the political sphere was far removed and most authors had no access to it. It is interesting to note that the ratio of current versus historical articles changed over time. In the first five years, the ratio was 75 current articles versus 30 historical ones. This shifts to 76:28 (1919–1923) and then to 62:30 (1924–1928) and finally to 59:36 (1929–1933). This means that during the last years of the *Outlook*'s existence, the balance began to tip over in favour of historical articles. The magazine with aspirations of reporting current affairs had turned into a conventional review.

Looking briefly at articles that address contemporary issues, the balance of subject matter in the sample is the following: the most popular topics were education (46), religion/the Church/theology (39), arts/literature (25), political/administrative issues/housing (22), home rule and nationalism (20), travel writing (16), social issues (14), Welsh culture/Eisteddfod (13), agriculture and the natural environment (13), socialism and the labour movement (10), international affairs (9), women (7) and public health (6). Thus, the articles on contemporary issues do reflect the *Outlook*'s editorial mission quite closely. The weighting of topics reveals a great deal about the reforming zeal of Liberal Wales and about the personal interests of T.J. and subsequent editors. It is perhaps striking that international affairs are not given as much prominence as might have been expected from the rather defensive-sounding editorial note of the January 1915 issue in which T.J. writes that 'we need not apologize for the attention given to other countries in our pages' (3). The majority of commentary on international affairs appears to be contained within the editorial 'Notes of the Month', which were presumably written just before going to press and are the nearest to current political commentary the *Outlook* gets.

A closer look at four subject areas, namely religion, socialism/labour relations/industrial development, home rule/nationalism and education, gives a flavour of the contents of the articles printed in the 60 issues under consideration. The *Outlook* was a secular magazine and, therefore, did not allocate a great deal of space to religious topics. Nevertheless, a familiarity with and an interest in religious topics were assumed by the editors as the relatively high number of articles on religious topics – 46 – shows. True to the *Outlook*'s mission of being a magazine for 'national social progress', the majority of articles discuss the social role and the relevance of religion and Church/chapel for Wales (12). This can be considered progressive in the sense that Church and chapel usually concerned themselves with the spiritual progress of individuals but had very little to say about society. Herbert Morgan, a Baptist minister at the time, conducted a survey of religious and labour leaders entitled 'The Church and Labour: a Symposium'. The results of this survey were published in the February, March, April and May issues in 1918. Morgan's own views lean towards embracing the Church's social role and collaborating with the labour movement. His vision is one of compromise rather than conflict and therefore fits in well within the general tone of the *Outlook*:

> A truly spiritual Church will want to express its spirituality within the economic and social order, and on the other hand a genuine passion for reform in the Labour groups will be directed by a spiritual interest of a broad human kind.[25]

He concludes with a strong affirmation of the social role of the Church:

> It is entirely wrong for Church people to represent Christianity as being concerned merely with the individual. The Church is a society within which the individual is gathered, and it should be a pattern of a more perfect society where each prefers the other in honour instead of grabbing at prizes and honours for the individual as is too often the case in what is called the world. Until the Church takes its own *social* character seriously it has nothing truly impressive to say to the world.[26]

Morgan's impassioned plea for the social role of the Church/chapel was not readily accepted, which may be why he and other left-leaning ministers like R. Silyn Roberts left the ministry. Publishing articles like this placed the *Outlook* at the forefront of non-denominational religious discussion in Wales.

Other popular topics include historical articles (7), articles with broadly theological and philosophical themes (7), articles on religious education in schools (6) and interdenominational issues (5). The same issue that contains Herbert Morgan's final part of his 'Symposium' also includes an article by Ellis Jones, 'A Neglected Book: A Serious Call', which refers 'to the Bible, a book once widely read throughout the Principality, but now, alas! sadly neglected'[27] and contains a detailed discussion of Bible instruction in Sunday Schools, primary and secondary schools as well as teacher training. A few articles address the establishment of a Department of Theology at the University College of North Wales at Bangor (4), a controversial issue as the theological colleges were not overly keen on the university intruding on their territory. Only two articles from 1918 and 1919 deal with the disestablishment of what became the Church in Wales in 1920 and there are a few articles on other issues. As previously mentioned, it is noticeable that the number of socially engaged articles decreases after 1923 while the number of historical articles increases, presumably because of the *Outlook*'s difficulties in retaining authors who could provide such material. The discussion (especially of theological and interdenominational issues) was carried on in the letters to the editor and testifies to the high levels of interest of at least a few engaged readers, who, like J. Arthur Price, were often contributors as well. The *Outlook*'s ongoing engagement with religious topics at a relatively high level of discussion is also documented by the large number of reviews of books on theology, religious issues, religious literature (such as collected sermons) and religious periodicals. While it can be assumed that this interest in religious matters met those of the implied readership in 1914, it probably made the magazine look slightly out of touch by the 1930s. By comparison, the journal *The Welsh*

Review, which was published from 1939, includes almost no discussion of religious themes or book reviews of religious literature.

Given the *Outlook*'s aim to discuss the important social and political movements of the day, one would expect that a great deal of room would be given to the discussion of socialism, the labour movement and related topics. The first few years of publication show an attempt to come to grips with the labour movement and the socialist, communist or syndicalist theories underpinning it, but this interest quickly cools – unsurprisingly, perhaps, considering David Davies' powerful hidden editorial pen. Compared to 46 articles on religion, the total sum of 11 articles on the labour movement and related topics seems meagre. Only one article attempts to elucidate socialist and syndicalist thought, three are about the labour movement and the war and two deal with labour relations more generally. Four articles, which are mainly published around 1927, deal with industry and one is an historical article. The tone of the articles is generally detached, 'objective', and the authors seem keen to inform their readership about the labour movement and its ideas. The tone is usually sympathetic, although some authors warn of the dangers of radicalism. The motivation of these articles is educational: the implied readership is construed as in need of information about this new social movement. The working class and its leaders are the subjects for discussion and not interlocutors or even a projected readership. Only very rarely were selected leaders of the labour movement allowed to put the case themselves. An example is the discussion of the article 'Labour and Welsh Autonomy' by 'G.', which was initiated by Edgar L. Chappell. He sent proofs of the article to selected labour leaders and invited them to write short responses, which appeared in a slightly edited form in the following issues (April and May 1916). Those labour leaders, however, were establishment figures themselves (councillors, MPs, administrators) and do not represent the majority, let alone the radical wing, of the labour movement. No Noah Ablett or A.J. Cook was invited to contribute – but then again they might have refused to write for this magazine of the Liberal establishment. An all too rare exception is an article on 'Unrest in the Coalfield' written by Frank Hodges in the November 1917 issue. Neither are articles on industry written by industrialists to be found – authors here are mostly academics. Most often, the *Outlook*'s contributors write for people much like themselves: educated, interested in social progress, keen to understand the other side and possibly secretly convinced of the superiority of their own convictions.

David Davies was, for a time, enthusiastic about home rule and the *Outlook* reflects this, for example by producing a supplement for the March 1919 issue, which contains the Government of Wales Bill proposed by E.T. John and co-written by David Davies in 1914 in full. The topic was only intensively discussed between 1918 and 1924, however, probably coinciding with David Davies' involvement in politics. The magazine's interest mainly emerges in the 'Notes of the Month'. Here the frustration of the editors Edgar L. Chappell (1918), Thomas Hughes Jones (1919) and T. Huws Davies (1920–1925) with a distant Welsh Party – a grouping made up of Liberal and Lib–Lab MPs – and their somewhat lacklustre promotion of the cause of home rule shines through in biting editorial remarks. A few articles deal with the desirability of home rule in a general way (4) and others deal with the administrative, legal, economic and other implications of home rule (4). As the interest in home rule diminishes, articles about nationalism, including an early discussion of fascism (8), and the newly formed Plaid Genedlaethol Cymru (2) begin to appear. The majority of articles on home rule and nationalism remain at a general level of discussion, thus contributing to the impression of vagueness and dullness of which Trevor Williams accuses the journal.[28] The various possibilities of home rule, from a partial devolution of powers to complete independence, might have been discussed but are not. It seems that contributors were more interested in ideological discussions about what home rule and later Plaid Genedlaethol Cymru would mean for Wales than getting down to political practicalities. Considering that in other subject areas, such as education, town planning or housing, the *Outlook* was quite prepared to print highly technical articles that often look like barely altered academic papers, this lack of concrete political discussion may be a reflection of the distance between political and public sphere even for an editor like T. Huws Davies who lived in London. Unless authors were also players on the political stage or professional political journalists – an unlikely scenario given the pool of regular contributors – discussion would always be hampered by a lack of detailed knowledge.

T.J.'s interest in education ensured that this topic had a high profile in the *Outlook*. Out of 46 articles in the sample, the majority deal with administrative and legislative issues (9), schools (7) and the University of Wales (6), thus demonstrating the impact of Wales-specific legislation in the sphere of education. There are historical articles (5), articles on curricular/pedagogical issues (4), articles on education and the adolescent (4) and articles on commercial/vocational education (3). Articles on school education very often deal with the administrative practicalities of a Welsh education system and argue for the professionalisation of teaching, an issue often linked to teacher training and remuneration. Curricular issues are discussed in fine detail, for example, in 'A History Course for Secondary Schools in Wales', in which J.E. Lloyd develops a detailed curriculum for history teaching (January 1928). Other topics are more ideological in nature and address the role of education in society, such as E. Towyn Jones' article 'The School and Community Service' (May 1928), in which the author summarises the role of education in the following terms: 'It is the duty and the privilege of all educational institutions to provide the facilities necessary for the free development of ideals of social service, and to foster those qualities which are indispensable to good citizenship.'[29] Only two articles in my sample deal with adult education, which seems astonishing given the role in the development of secular adult education in Wales usually ascribed to the *Outlook*.[30] The role of adult education is conceived of in similarly moral terms as school education but with a more obvious class bias. Ronald Burrows' 'Evolution or Revolution' (January 1914) perfectly encapsulates the *Outlook*'s line on the role of adult education. Burrows was Professor of Greek and Principal of the University of Wales College of South Wales and Monmouthshire at Cardiff. He also founded the University Settlement in Splott, which provided educational and recreational facilities for working-class students. Burrows speaks eloquently of the hope for reconciliation between the classes. Adult education is meant to furnish working-class students with the understanding necessary to seek out solutions (evolution) rather than give into 'the inevitableness of a class war' (revolution). Burrows was a social progressive but thought within established social frameworks, which were to be gradually 'remoulded', thus expressing the political views of the Liberal establishment just before the First World War. The *Outlook* was to stick to this interpretation of social relations throughout its existence.

The remaining articles on education are about the philosophy of education, bilingual education, the study of history, education and society, and teaching Welsh in schools. There is a slight whiff of moral panic detectable in the articles on the adolescent, which may be connected to the increasingly desperate unemployment situation especially in the industrial areas of Wales. Contrary to today's policy-makers' unshakeable optimism about the direct link between education and 'employability', the *Outlook* persists in seeing education in terms of personal and moral improvement. It is not regarded as a way out of unemployment but can mitigate the detrimental influence of ‘idleness’. As with religion, articles on current issues decrease and historical articles of little significance for contemporary society increase in the second decade of the *Outlook*’s existence: four out of the five historical articles on education were written after 1927. Current issues were not abandoned: we find an article on ‘Educational Problems of the South Wales Coalfield’ side by side with the reminiscence ‘School in the Early Eighties’ in the January issue of 1932, for instance. However, in this subject area, too, the magazine became increasingly detached from the social reality of 1930s Wales.

To assess the impact of the *Outlook* on the Welsh public sphere, it pays to have a closer look at who contributed to the magazine. Contrary to the practice of earlier periodicals, most articles published in the *Outlook* were signed. Often authors’ names, academic degrees and professional or honorific titles were displayed in full. Nevertheless, editorials and some articles were anonymised. The fact that a considerable number of contributors appear in works of reference like *Welsh Biography Online* or the *Welsh Academy Encyclopaedia of Wales* shows that T.J. and subsequent editors were successful in attracting the ‘great and the good’ of early twentieth-century Wales. Authors were often loyal to the *Outlook* and contributed more than one piece: in the 60 issues under consideration, no fewer than 38 authors published two articles, ten published three, six published four and twelve authors published five or more articles. Often these articles appeared in consecutive numbers, such as the seven essays written by the dramatist John Oswald Francis (January 1919–September 1924). Other contributors, such as David Davies, published throughout the lifespan of the magazine. The engagement of regular authors can be gleaned from the range of their contributions: they often wrote articles, creative pieces, reviews and letters to the editor. The poet, writer, translator and scholar Thomas Gwynn Jones, the first incumbent of the chair of Welsh Literature at the University of Wales College, Aberystwyth, sponsored by Gwendoline and Margaret Davies, contributed five articles (January 1914–December 1933), poetry in English (January 1918 and September 1920), poetry in Welsh (January 1928 and May 1928) and reviews (May 1915 and May 1924). Other particularly loyal contributors were the Rev. Gwilym Davies and the London-based barrister J. Arthur Price. The former published 25 articles between 1918 and 1933, usually in the form of the 'social diary' for the month. He also wrote articles on international peace and co-operation and four of his letters to the editor were printed between January 1920 and May 1926. J. Arthur Price, who mainly wrote on religion and Welsh self-government, contributed six articles (May 1917–January 1931), two reviews (September 1922 and December 1931) and four letters to the editor (May 1925–December 1933). Reprints of speeches, such as those by Sir Harry Reichel, the Principal of the University College of North Wales at Bangor (May 1917–May 1930), were also popular. Overall an impression emerges that a relatively small group of people with a shared political outlook made active use of the public forum established by *The Welsh Outlook* to discuss their favourite topics and each other's contributions. The *Outlook* did not create a new group of active public intellectuals, but it became a convenient and congenial vehicle for those who were already actively involved in Welsh affairs. When the *Outlook* ceased to exist in 1933, contributors simply wrote for other available journals. *The Welsh Review*, a journal that appeared for the first time in 1939 and that resembled the *Outlook* quite closely despite the editor Gwyn Jones' protestations that it was 'a new journal for a new day',[31] gave a home to *Outlook* contributors such as Gwilym Davies, who continued to write on international issues, Huw Menai, A.W. Wade-Evans and Iorwerth C. Peate. *The Welsh Anvil*, published from 1949 and edited by Alwyn D. Rees, gave space to W.J. Gruffydd, H.A. Marquand, Ben

Bowen Thomas and Sydney Herbert, and 1940s numbers of *Wales*, which were edited by Keidrych Rhys, included pieces by H. Idris Bell, Huw Menai, R. Williams Parry, Iorwerth C. Peate, Charles Davies and Walter Dowding.

What set the *Outlook* apart from its competitors in 1914 was the fact that its authors were largely drawn from the secular and often from the academic sphere, thus contributing to a shift away from the popular conception that Welsh opinion-formers and 'organic intellectuals' were ministers and schoolteachers. Authors were largely drawn from one of the four colleges that made up the University of Wales, such as Alfred E. Zimmern, first incumbent of the David Davies-sponsored chair of International Politics at the University College of Wales, Aberystwyth, or Sir Arthur Elijah Trueman, Professor of Geology at the University College of Wales, Swansea. Other contributors included the highly influential Henry Jones, Professor of Moral Philosophy at the University of Glasgow and T.J.'s erstwhile academic teacher. Authors from the theological colleges included two Principals of Bala-Bangor College, Thomas Rees and J. Morgan Jones. Other contributors were drawn from the civil service and other professions, e.g. the contributor and editor Edgar L. Chappell, who was an inspector for the Housing Department of the Ministry for Health (1918–1921), then became Secretary of the South Wales Regional Survey Committee for the Ministry of Health (from 1921) and later left to form and manage land development companies in South Wales and London. About 28 authors were ministers – a relatively small number considering that the overall number of contributors in my sample is 264. It appears that *The Welsh Outlook* moved public discourse into a secular public sphere, which, in this case, was dominated by a highly educated, socially cohesive group of professional people, a great number of whom were connected with T.J. in some way. A considerable number of contributors did not live in Wales, thus confirming that the Welsh public sphere included a large Welsh diaspora.

With twenty years of publication, the *Outlook*, despite 'sometimes [being] dull, even in some respects, despite its initial high-toned pretensions, shallow and mundane'[32] was one of the most successful Welsh periodicals in English ever produced. However, in the late 1920s and 1930s it went into a decline from which it was not to recover and it finally ceased publication in 1933. What were the reasons for its demise? Probably the main reason for failure of periodicals is that they, after having carefully cultivated close relationships with their audiences, eventually fall out of step with them.[33] The *Outlook*, which belonged to a 'a tradition of review journals which reached the peak of their popularity in the Victorian age',[34] most probably fell out of favour not so much because it was out of sympathy with an established audience but because it failed to attract a new audience. In the absence of sales and circulation figures except for 1914, 1918, 1919 and 1933, actual impact on the public sphere is difficult to gauge. Sales figures hovered around 3,000 in the first nine months of the *Outlook*'s existence, probably never went much above 4,000, and, by the end, fell to about 700.[35] The initial circulation figures sound impressive but they cannot compare with those of popular magazines such as O.M. Edwards' *Cymru'r Plant*, which had a circulation figure of 12,000 copies every month.[36]

The circulation figures point categorically to a limited readership based on the university towns, the major cities of south Wales, Cardiff and Swansea, and among exiled Welshmen in London, Liverpool, Manchester or abroad. The *Outlook* hardly penetrated into the south Wales valleys and the same is true for the more rural parts of Wales. The *Outlook*'s readership consisted for the most part of the well-educated Welsh middle class and this is borne out by an analysis of the list of subscribers, many of whose names are to be found among the pages of *Who's Who in Wales*. By 1933 it had also lost touch with many of the strands of Welsh radicalism which were now channelled into the labour movement and, in a minor though growing contributory, the Welsh Nationalist Party.[37]

Jenkins probably slightly underestimates readership figures. Each subscribing household would have had more than one reader. Also, a number of public libraries subscribed to the *Outlook*, such as Cardiff Public Library and the Carnegie Free Library in Rhyl. Other libraries include the Brecon Memorial College Library and the library of the Swansea Training College. Some miners' and workingmen's institute libraries subscribed: records exist for Bargoed Workingmen's Institute and for Aberbargoed workingmen's Institute for 1923.[38] It is likely, though, that many institute libraries would have cancelled their subscription by the end of the 1920s due to the desperate unemployment situation in the industrial areas and the subsequent drop in revenue for the institutes.

In some ways the *Outlook* failed to grasp the enormity of the social change taking place under its nose and, therefore, by 1933 had become obsolete. A few examples shall serve to illustrate this. At its inception in 1914, the editors of the *Outlook* made several tacit assumptions about the nation they were commenting on. One concerned the degree to which Welsh culture had a Welsh-language core, even as more and more cultural expression was mediated through the English language. An example of this is the publication of poetry in Welsh in an otherwise wholly English-language magazine. The *Outlook* simply assumed that all its readers were able to read and enjoy poetry in Welsh. However, the changing ratio of Welsh versus English poetry shows something of the changing linguistic realities in Wales. In 1914, 80% of the poetry published in the *Outlook* was in Welsh. From 1916 onwards (with the exception of 1919, 1922 and 1928), more than 50% of the poetry is in English. Numbers with poetry exclusively in English are to be found in 1921, 1924, 1929, 1932 and 1933. It is unlikely that the *Outlook* was able to commission poetry. The choice of poetry published reflects the editors' connections in the literary world, as well as the amount of poetry that arrived unsolicited in the editors' postbag. Assumptions about a culture centrally based on the Welsh language were becoming tenuous.

A second assumption was political. The magazine was imbued with a Liberal spirit in 1914 and it retained its affiliation with Liberal and Lib–Lab politics with a focus on Welsh national issues throughout its existence. The political affiliations of authors are difficult to trace. Overall, it is easier to establish authors' support for civic and cultural institutions of Wales, such as the National Library, the National Museum, the National Eisteddfod, the Society of Cymmrodorion, the Board of Celtic Studies and the University of Wales and its Guild of Graduates. This may be proof of the split between the public sphere, which tended to be concerned with cultural issues, and the political sphere in Wales. It also shows that the *Outlook* had but a limited impact on the political sphere. Out of the few contributors whose political affiliations can be established with any certainty, Liberal Party MPs outweigh Labour Party MPs by a factor of 6:1. Several contributors were friends of Lloyd George at one time or another. The swelling political support for the Labour Party and other, more radical, left-wing organisations in the late 1920s and 1930s seems to have passed the *Outlook* by.

A further clue why the *Outlook* failed to attract a new readership is the age and gender profile of its contributors. One might expect a generational shift to occur within 20 years of publication as 'older' authors are slowly replaced by 'younger' authors. In fact, the majority of contributors whose birth dates can be identified belong to roughly the same generation regardless of when their article or piece of creative writing appears. More than half of all authors identified were born between 1870 and 1890. It appears that newer voices were either not interested in publishing in the *Outlook*, were not commissioned by increasingly out of touch editors or did not have the same impact on the public sphere as 'older' authors, as they do not appear in standard works of reference. Further, the gender balance of authors remains resolutely male-dominated. I can identify only 23 female authors of articles. Female authors were also unlikely to submit more than one piece. Rare exceptions were Lilian Winstanley, a lecturer in English at University College of Wales, Aberystwyth, and author of several novels, such as *The Scholar Vagabond* (1909), and 'M.M.' who contributed a regular 'Welshwoman's Page'. Nevertheless, when female authors were invited to write articles, the editorial practice was not obviously discriminatory, i.e. female authors were not confined to 'female' topics. Topics range from Olive A. Wheeler's article on 'The Education of the Adolescent' (January 1924) to Mrs John Lewis' article on 'A Plea for Hungary' (May 1919). One area in which the number of contributions by female authors rose steadily was creative writing, especially of short stories, although here, too, authors are difficult to trace. An example is Dorothy N. Bonarjee, who might have been the first female Law student who took an LLB at University College London in 1917[39] and who published poetry in English between January 1915 and January 1916. Lilian Winstanley published poetry in English between September 1915 and January 1921. Dilys Cadwaladr published short stories between May 1928 and September 1929 and her work can also be found in *The Welsh Review*.

Finally, the range of subjects never changed in 20 years. An editorial note written by the editor William Watkin Davies (1925–1927) sounds much like the ones written by T.J. some twelve years earlier: 'We endeavour always to remember that ours is a Welsh magazine; and that it exists, primarily for the discussion of matters pertaining to Wales, – politics, education, religion, music, literature and art.'[40] The December 1933 issue made a point of commissioning overview articles. The choice of topics for these articles is therefore important as they summarise what the *Outlook* had been about. They are: 'Literature', 'Education', 'Religion',

'Yesterday and To-day in a Border Village', 'Yesterday and To-day in a Mining Valley', 'Drama', 'Music', 'Health', 'Politics', 'Wales and the World', 'The Story of Porthdinllaen' (II) and 'Shakespeare's Welsh Characters'. What are interesting about this list of topics and titles are the topics that are omitted: the lack of science writing had already been regretted by T.J., but nothing was done to remedy the omission.[40] The widespread unemployment in the industrial areas was deplored in a few articles, but no effort was made to think creatively about economic change. Very few articles deal with industrial development. The *Outlook* paid almost no attention to popular culture, such as sport, radio, cinema and popular theatre.[42] Exceptions were articles like George H. Green's 'The Cinematograph and the School', in which discussing film becomes acceptable because it is pinned to the topic of education, regular 'notes' on 'The Gramophone', which focus on classical music, and dispersed editorial notes on topics like the radio (May 1928) or rugby (May 1930), which cannot be said to amount to any serious discussion. Attempts by editors like Edgar L. Chappell to give the *Outlook* 'bite' did not succeed – whether that was due to David Davies' continued interference or the timidity of the editors is difficult to tell. What cannot have helped was the resolute refusal of Margaret and Gwendoline Davies, who had taken over the *Outlook* after their brother lost interest in 1927, to countenance a popularisation of the magazine.[43] Instead, page after page was filled with long book reviews – a favourite strategy of editors when there were more pages to fill than articles available – and some frankly boring serialisations such as 'The Recollections of a Welsh Doctor', which appeared in 1932 and 1933. Articles on current affairs continued to appear, but it must be assumed that the *Outlook* had less and less impact in the public sphere of commentators and opinion-formers. In a political sphere now dominated by the Labour Party, the *Outlook*, with its increasingly out of date profile, had a negligible impact.[44] The fact that T.J. returned to oversee the final issues of the

Outlook in some way only confirms that its time had passed.

It is perhaps unfair to judge the overall impact of *The Welsh Outlook* by its failings, many of them due to its semi-professional status and dependence on the largely voluntary efforts of editors and contributors. The *Outlook* provides documentary evidence of a fleeting 'in between' period between Liberal Victorian Wales and a twentieth century in which the political split between the Labour Party and Plaid Cymru can be read emblematically for a deeper cultural and social split of the nation. While obviously failing to make itself heard in the political sphere, it can be credited with influencing central shifts in the Welsh public sphere: in the *Outlook*, secular academics largely replaced ministers of religion as opinion-formers, and while its editors were assuming that the Welsh language was to remain at the core of Welsh culture and identity, it supported the permeation of the public sphere by the English language. Importantly, though, English was not to replace Welsh. The *Outlook* noted the increasing divergence of English-language and Welsh-language Wales and the new, divisive, class-based politics. It struggled against these fissures and held on to a vision of a unified Wales for as long as possible. It is an alternative vision of Wales to the one that was to gain prominence later in the century and, for all the eye-watering class-based and other assumptions, it is perhaps to be regretted that its time passed so quickly.

BIBLIOGRAPHY

Horn Melton, James van, *The Rise of the Public in Enlightenment Europe* (Cambridge: Cambridge University Press, 2001).

Krippendorf, K., *Content Analysis: An Introduction to Its Methodology*, Second Ed. (London: Sage, 2004).

Llyfrgell Genedlaethol Cymru/National Library of Wales. *Welsh Biography Online*. http://yba.llgc.org.uk/en/index.html (accessed 2008 and 2009).

Stephens, Meic, ed. *The New Companion to the Literature of Wales* (Cardiff: University of Wales Press, 1998).

NOTES

1 Gruffydd Aled Jones, *Press, Politics and Society: A History of Journalism in Wales* (Cardiff: University of Wales Press, 1993), p. 5.

2 See: Malcolm Ballin, *Irish Periodical Culture*, 1937–1972: *Genre in Ireland, Wales, and Scotland* (Basingstoke: Palgrave Macmillan, 2008) and his 'Welsh Periodicals in English 1880–1965: Literary Form and Cultural Substance', *Welsh Writing in English*, 9, 2004, pp. 1–32; Gwyn Jenkins, 'The Welsh Outlook, 1914–1933', *Cylchgrawn Llyfrgell Genedlaethol Cymru/The National Library of Wales Journal* 24, 1985–1986, pp. 463–496; Trevor Williams, 'Thomas Jones and the "Welsh Outlook"', *Anglo-Welsh Review* 64: 1979, pp. 38–46.

3 E. L. Ellis, T.J.: *A Life of Dr Thomas Jones*, CH (Cardiff: University of Wales Press, 1992), p. 158.

4 See: Jürgen Habermas, 'The Public Sphere', *Rethinking Popular Culture: Contemporary Perspectives in Cultural Studies*, ed.s Chandra Mukerji and Michael Schudson, 1973, transl. 1989 (Berkeley: University of California Press, 1991), pp. 398–404 and his *Strukturwandel der Öffentlichkeit*. [1962] (Frankfurt/M.: Suhrkamp, 1990).

5 Stefan Collini, *Absent Minds: Intellectuals in Britain* (Oxford: Oxford University Press, 2006); see also Thomas William Heyck, 'Myths and Meanings of Intellectuals in Twentieth-Century British National Identity', *The Journal of British Studies*, 37: 2 1998, pp. 192–221.

6 Montserrat Guibernau, *Nations without States: Political Communities in a Global Age* (Cambridge: Polity, 1999).

7 W. Llewellyn Williams, 'The Prospects of the Drama in Wales', *The Transactions of the Honourable Society of Cymmrodorion*, Session 1912–1914 (London: Cymmrodorion, 1914), p. 141.

8 John S. Ellis, *Investiture: Royal Ceremony and the National Identity in Wales*, 1911–1969, (Cardiff: University of Wales Press, 2008), p. 26.

9 John S. Ellis, 2008, p. 33.

10 Ballin, 2008, p. 2.

11 E.L. Ellis, 1992, p. 158.

12 Jenkins, 1985–86, p. 464.

13 See: Jenkins, 1985–86; E.L. Ellis, 1992; John Davies, Nigel Jenkins, Menna Baines and Peredur I. Lynch, ed.s *The Welsh*

Academy Encyclopaedia of Wales (Cardiff: University of Wales Press, 2008).

14 Jenkins, 1985–86, p. 464.

15 Thomas Jones, Welsh Broth (London: W. Griffiths & Co., [1951]) p. 141.

16 Thomas Jones, 'Foreword', *Welsh Outlook* January 1914, p. 2.

17 Thomas Jones, 1951, p. 141.

18 E.L. Ellis, 1992, p. 158.

19 Richard Lewis, *Leaders and Teachers: Adult Education and the Challenge of Labour in South Wales, 1906–1940* (Cardiff: University of Wales Press, 1993), p. xv.

20 Jenkins, 1985–86, p. 466.

21 Nick Davies, *Flat Earth News* (London: Chatto & Windus, 2008), pp. 15–16.

22 Jenkins, 1985–86, p. 470.

23 Trevor Williams, 'Thomas Jones and the "Welsh Outlook"', *Anglo-Welsh Review* 64: 1979, pp. 38–46.

24 Gruffydd Aled Jones, 1993; Jenkins, 1985–86; see also Roland Mathias, *The Lonely Editor: A Glance at Anglo-Welsh Magazines*, University College Cardiff Annual Gwyn Jones Lecture (Cardiff: University College Cardiff Press, 1984).

25 *Welsh Outlook* May, 1918, p. 164.

26 *Welsh Outlook* May, 1918, p. 166; italics in original.

27 *Welsh Outlook* May, 1918, p. 157.

28 Trevor Williams, 'Thomas Jones and the "Welsh Outlook"'.

29 *Welsh Outlook* May, 1928, p. 120.

30 Ballin, 2008, p. 153.

31 Gwyn Jones, 'Editorial', *The Welsh Review*, 1: 1, 3–7, 1939), p. 3.

32 E.L. Ellis, 1992, p. 177.

33 Ballin, 2008, p. 6.

34 Jenkins, 1985–86, p. 463.

35 Jenkins, 1985–86, p. 486; E.L. Ellis, 1992, p. 160.

36 Mari Jones, *Language Obsolescence and Revitalization: Linguistic Change in Two Socio-linguistically Contrasting Welsh Communities* (Oxford: Oxford University Press, 1998), p. 21.

37 Jenkins, 1985–86, p. 485.

38 Hywel Francis, 'Workers' Libraries: The Origins of the South Wales Miners' Library', *History Workshop Journal* 2: 1,

1976, pp. 183–205 [195].

39 Rosemary Auchmuty, 'Early Women Law Students at Cambridge and Oxford', *The Journal of Legal History*, 29: 1, 2008, 63–97, p. 65.

40 *Welsh Outlook* , 'Notes of the Month', January, 1926, p. 4.

41 E.L. Ellis, 1992, p. 177.

42 See Jenkins, 1985–86, p. 484.

43 Jenkins, 1985–86.

44 Jenkins, 1985–86, p. 486.

Spaces of International Comparison in Welsh Periodicals in English: 1882–2008

Malcolm Ballin
Cardiff University

I

'Periodical journalism', says Stefan Collini, 'is the noise of a culture talking to itself.'[1] While Welsh periodicals in English are surely prone to such introversion, they do also sometimes address themselves to the world. From the nineteenth century onwards they work hard at defining, as Daniel Williams suggests, 'a highly respectable Welsh identity that could nevertheless be contrasted to Englishness'.[2] Indeed, England provides the first and most evident space of comparison, so obvious that it may easily be overlooked. In the first issue of Owen M. Edwards's *Wales*, published in May 1894, T. Darlington MA worries about the extent of the English-speaking population of Wales, over 45% according to the census of 1891, compared with 20% in 1801.[3] The second issue in June has an article 'Wales to English Eyes' that records 'the stock libels about Wales' and proposes to show 'from what hole of a pit they are dug'.[4] Edwards goes on to show that the Welsh can reciprocate this prejudice by citing a range of fifteen triads of which one fair example is 'Three things attack the weak – the cat, the sea crow, and the Englishman.'

In the same issue, however, Edwards publishes a poem 'To a Mocking Bird (Heard in the Graveyard at Spring-Hill 1st May, 1834)' written by Thomas Lloyd Jones (whose bardic name was *Gwenffrwd*) – composed in Mobile, Alabama, shortly before his death and burial there. It contains the lines

> Alas! Like glimpses of an exile's dream,
> My soul thou hast beguiled to haunt my native stream.[5]

In thus turning his eyes to the diaspora, Edwards opens up another space of comparison that is frequently occupied by the periodicals. Tinged often, as here, with *hiraeth*, it can operate in both directions, giving both Welsh perceptions of the exilic experience and the contrasting point of view of the Welsh communities overseas.

Other international spaces of comparison that are exploited by the periodicals include: Celticism, language divisions, travel memoirs, missionary work, relations with the Empire and the Commonwealth, involvement with The League of Nations, The United Nations and the European Community. Periodicals at various times demonstrate interest in imperialism, globalisation and climate change. The Subject Indexes for Welsh Periodicals held in the National Library of Wales cover both Welsh- and English-language journals and extend from 1931 to 1980 with a gap between 1955 and 1968.[6] They are not always easy to interpret, especially since the various compilers do not have a consistent method of selecting their headings. However, my recent rough examination suggests that throughout these fifty years there was a relatively small but consistent interest in other countries, providing probably around two per cent of the total number of articles (i.e. about 1,200 listings out of a total of over 68,000). To put this into some context, there are nearly 3,000 articles about religion and more than 4,600 articles about literary topics. The 'international' listings represent sometimes as few as ten articles in a year but rise to 50–60 articles per year during the decade 1970–80. These articles deal with over twenty countries in all and although the percentage of articles is low, the range is wide.[7] This article will therefore need to be highly selective and will proceed by sampling individual issues of these periodicals and giving some examples of the variety of international spaces of comparison that are occupied within them.

Rather than proceeding chronologically, I will group the material under two main headings: first, the periodicals' handling of relations with the English-speaking world;

second, their treatment of countries in Europe and overseas. Under the first heading I will consider especially the articles about America (usually so described; it is rarely characterised as the United States) and Commonwealth countries such as Canada, Australia and South Africa. Under the second heading it will be necessary to consider the concept of the 'Welsh European' as well as to think about experiences linked to such interventions as missionary work and the formation of international organisations.

II

The connection with England is one I will not have space to explore further in this article, although both the antagonistic and the supportive elements of the relationship are frequently implied in many of the articles that ostensibly deal with other countries. The very idea of Wales having an international presence on its own account is itself a kind of national escape from under the British or Imperial umbrella. Ernest Bowen Rowlands introduces the first issue of *The Welsh Review* in November 1891 by stating the aim to create 'a literary organ in which the views [of the Welsh] could be interchanged with those of other nations'.[8] He argues that

> Now in every part of the habitable globe the sons of Wales are to be found treading the paths to success ... In the Antipodes, the Americas and the continent have been carried the characteristics of the Brythonic race. (2)

As an indirect assault on England, in the same issue, he includes an article by the Irishman Thomas H. Grattan Esmond about Samoa (58–63), condemning German aggression, and saying

> I am not an Englishman. As things go I do not care two straws for British Imperialism. Were England's relations with my own country different from what they were I might look upon the Samoan position from a different point of view. (58)

International articles play to both nionist and nationalist constituencies, emphasising Welsh 'contributionism' or proposing Welsh difference. Perhaps this explains why some editors seem to feel uneasy in this field. *Welsh Outlook*'s editorial 'Notes of the Month' for January 1915 remarks that 'it is part of our national duty to understand other nations, and we need therefore not apologise for the attention given to other countries in these pages' (3).[9] The international space in *Welsh Outlook* was, indeed, unusually generous. Owned by Lord Davies of Llandinam – and edited for much of its life by Thomas Jones (who later became Lloyd George's Cabinet Secretary) – the magazine carried two supplements on the League of Nations, and aimed to convince a largely pacifist Wales that the 1914–18 war was a Christian crusade. It allocated much space to travel writing and carried numerous editorial chidings about the dangers of narrowness and parochialism.[10] In December 1914 the 'Notes of the Month' makes a comparison between Belgium and Wales, both nations being fractured between rural, pastoral cultures and urban, industrial areas, and both riven by divisions over language. *Welsh Outlook* paid much attention at this time to Belgian poets and artists, such as Verhaeren, Maeterlinck and Meunier, in well-illustrated articles such as those it carried in October and November 1914 (423–6; 463–5). It imported articles by eminent writers on international affairs, such as Albert Zimmern (January 1921, 303–6) and Erskine of Marr (April 1921, 83). The Reverend Gwilym Davies had a regular column 'Wales and the World', covering for example the post-war Manchurian crisis and the disarmament negotiations. This series continued right up to the final issue of *Welsh Outlook* in November 1933 where Davies recorded Germany being outvoted 52:1 at the Geneva conference on disarmament: 'in the court of public opinion Germany stood alone' (293).

The most frequent coverage of the anglophone world outside England is that of America. The earliest reference I have been able to trace comes from Charles Wilkins's *Red Dragon* in 1883 with its cautionary 'Notes on Southern California' (III, 548–55). The anonymous English correspondent thinks that his observations

> would be of interest to such of your English readers as find that the battle of life in the old country is too hard for them and the competitors for the prizes of wealth too many ... Much harm has been done by misrepresentations, especially by agents in England, who undertake to place gentleman's sons in comfortable quarters with American farmers ... As a rule, English farmers do not do well in America. In England land is dear and labour cheap; In America land is cheap and labour dear ... the further that one goes from England, the more stagnant, I think, do the waters of existence become. But if it is so for men, it is ten times more for women. (548–50)

He lists his regrets for what has been left behind: beauties of nature, sport and social intercourse. He dismisses American praises of California as 'very characteristic American speech: gross exaggeration without absolute untruth' (552).

This sense of Welsh (or indeed, as specified here, 'English') superiority is a regular feature of diasporic writing about America in early Welsh periodicals. In *Red Dragon*, in 1887, W. B. Jones writes two articles from New York, 'What Americans Owe to Welshmen for the Formation of her Government on the principles of Civil and Religious Liberty' (249–60; 305–13). He singles out Roger Williams, who obtained the charter for Providence Rhode Island in 1643 (243), and Dr Richard Price, a friend of Benjamin Franklin, whose *Observations on the Nature of Civil Liberty* ... (1876) sold 60,000 copies (305). The article also records the seventeen Welshmen who signed the Declaration of Independence and the four Presidents Jones claims to be of Welsh descent: Jefferson, Madison, Monroe and Harrison (312). Similar claims surface again in *Wales*, at least twice, in October 1894 in O. M. Edwards's 'Editor's Notes' about

'Welsh Americans' (280–3) and in 'The Welsh in America' in December 1894, which describes an Eisteddfod in Scranton attended by over 3,000 people (349–52). This article, however, also criticises those Welsh émigrés who 'cling too stubbornly to their own customs and language.' The theme of eminent Welshmen in America appears again in January 1896, in W. P. Morgan's article 'The Welsh in the United States' (17–24), citing the story of Madoc as the original discoverer (while readily conceding that the veracity of the legend has been destroyed by Thomas Stephens). He lists a shipload of Welsh Quakers arriving in 1682, founding towns like Morganstown, Swansea and Lloydsville. A Welshman called Jones was the Captain of the *Mayflower*, and no fewer than seven Presidents claimed Wales as the Land of their Fathers (21).

From January to September 1897 *Wales* publishes a series titled 'A Young Welshman Abroad' relating the privations of a steerage passenger, later 'unmercifully quizzed' by 'admitted jokers, as the Yankees are', as he travels by river-boat up the Hudson. He delights in the relatively luxurious nature of the American railroad with its provisions of iced water, books and newspapers. In his last communiqué (September 1897) he articulates his version of the American dream:

> Here in America, far enough away from the evil that follows the gossip of a neighbour, he finds a new life teeming with examples of individual success, and he rises to positions in the social life of the country which at home would be denied him. This may be regarded as an uncharitable view to take of the old country; but to a very great extent it is borne out by experience. On all sides you find a prosperity awaiting the young Welshman never to be looked for at home. (200)

It is not wholly clear whether this anonymous series is autobiography or an imaginative creation. It nevertheless reflects the tone of much diasporic writing: at once warning about hardships and stressing the difficulties of cultural adjustment while still managing to convey an essential optimism about the processes and the outcomes of emigration.

The American exilic press reinforced these themes, mingling nostalgia and some triumphalism. In April 1895 *Wales* has a list of about a dozen papers sent from abroad (mostly from America) including *Y Drych* (*The Mirror*), subtitled *The American Organ of the Welsh People* (187). In the following month, under 'Notes and Queries' (283–4) *Y Drych* is said to be 'very indignant about the introduction of women – Welsh women from Morriston – into the tinplate works recently established at Pittsburgh'. America, says the article, 'is not tin-plate Paradise'. Aled and Bill Jones have given a very full account of *Y Drych*, which was published from January 1851 and was incorporated into *Ninnau* in 2003.[11] Peter Garrett, Nikolas Coupland and Hywel Bishop have produced an account of the photographic images in the journal.[12] Among their other complex and detailed observations and arguments, Jones and Jones draw attention to the 'relative weakness of the Welsh as an ethnic group'[13] within the United States and suggest that *Y Drych*'s bilingual texts may have discouraged earlier researchers. However, the publication was widely distributed throughout America, with a claimed circulation of 12,000 in 1890[14] probably dipping to around 2,000 in recent times (*Reflections*, 117). It 'articulated the changing definitions of the Welsh in America, (ibid., 44). Like some of the contributors to home-based periodicals, early issues sought to advise potential Welsh émigrés (*Identities*, 45) about difficulties and opportunities awaiting them. It passionately supported the North in the Civil War and 'sharply criticised British neutrality' (ibid., 46). It contested the claim of Patagonia (incidentally the site for another Welsh-language magazine, *Y Drafen* [*The Mentor*]) as a proposed location for a Welsh colony (ibid., 49). Garrett, Coupland and Bishop make a useful distinction between the 'Tourist gaze' and the

'Romantic gaze' in their study of the magazine's iconography (545–6), giving examples of these tendencies in both Wales and America. They remark on the scarcity of urban as against rural images, suggesting that the journal represents Wales as 'in some ways antithetical to a busy, prosperous, urban and modern America' (559). An issue in February 1986 continues this tradition with cover photographs of country scenes, such as St Hilary's Tower, Denbigh. Literary topics feature more prominently in later issues. March 1992 has a review of a book about Kate Roberts and a recommendation of the 'Writers of Wales' series. In February 2009 *Ninnau* has an article about the National Botanic Gardens and a review of Barry Morgan's book about R. S. Thomas. In these pages, the tourist and the romantic, the rural and the urban, present contrasting geographic spaces of comparison.

However, indigenous anglophone Welsh periodicals of the twentieth century and beyond appear rather less interested in American topics, though there are some exceptions. Relative American prosperity drew editorial attention after the Second World War. In Keidrych Rhys's *Wales* in June 1946 Rhys J. Davies writes about 'The Mood of the Americans' and draws attention to endemic labour problems in Chicago and Los Angeles. He remarks on the American terror of socialism (55–8). In *Wales* in November 1948, Myfanwy Roberts writes about 'The American Welsh'. She believes that, although by this point in time there has been no significant Welsh immigration for twenty years, the Welsh immigrant families are still 'Welsh to the core'. But she worries that there is a lack of understanding of Wales among most Americans and fears that Welsh identity will disappear within a generation. John Idris Jones gives his 'Impressions of the United States' in 1967 in the *Anglo-Welsh Review* (38, 69–73). He is dismayed by the contrast with the 'class-ridden society' he perceives in the UK following his return, advising readers to go to the Mid-West 'to see the genuine America'. He says that, in the post-war era, despite a continuing high level of parochialism, 'The American working man is better dressed and better spoken than his British counterpart. He is also much better paid.'

More recent Welsh periodicals move away from the diasporic theme and instead debate some of the cultural influences coming from the United States. In the *Anglo-Welsh Review* in 1986 (82, 78–84) M. Wynn Thomas writes about 'Walt Whitman's Welsh Connection', describing the stereotypical picture of Wales relayed to the poet by Ernest Rhys, leading him to the conclusion that 'the Welsh are an inbred, gesticulating people'. In an interview with David Lloyd in *Poetry Wales* (January 1993), Peter Finch accepts that the influences on his radical magazine, *Second Aeon*, were primarily American. The Beat Generation features positively in *Second Aeon*, which prints a poem, 'Wales Visitation', by Allen Ginsburg and pays tribute to Laurence Ferlinghetti and the City Lights bookshop in San Francisco. City Lights is also the topic of a 2003 article in *Planet* by Paul Clements (160, 44–7). However, *Poetry Wales* appears, certainly in its early years, more ambivalent about American models. Duncan Glen compliments the magazine in a letter in 1971 on 'its rejection of a facile and fashionable cosmopolitanism that would have us all mid-Atlantic writers' (Winter 1971, 27–31). Robert Minhinnick's interview with Tony Curtis in *The New Welsh Review* in 1990 touched on Curtis's visits to the US and elicited the response: 'If you've got a little talent and you put it on a jumbo jet it gets a lot bigger' (*NWR* 4, 1990, 52). Minhinnick's own editorial in *Poetry Wales* in January 1999 records a recent tour of the United States and describes New York as 'a literary furnace. In Manhattan alone every night of the week will see ten or more readings and launches.' Minhinnick is generally positive about international influence: 'this magazine urges writers in Wales to pack their bags, whether physically or intellectually, and explore fresh ways of achieving what they want to say'.

Other recent periodicals have been anxious to follow up political developments in the US, often expressing serious concerns about the trends of American foreign policy. *Planet* has carried articles on Presidential elections, like Peter Morgan's 'Walking into the Propeller', a title that describes George Bush's intense devotion to action rather than words or thought. Roger Caldwell's treatment of '9/11 and the aftermath,' ventilates his 'sceptical thoughts' about the Terrorist threat (189, June/July 2008, 51–7). Caldwell identifies an element of *Schadenfreude* in European responses to American policy and believes that fears of further attacks in Europe may have been orchestrated for political effect (56–7). *The New Welsh Review* has a number of specific American numbers, such as its spring 1996 issue, 'Looking Towards America (and Back)'. Tony Conran writes about 'A Special Relationship', observing that 'the valleys are more like America than they were like England' and pointing out how many Anglo-Welsh writers since Dylan Thomas have regarded America as a potential audience. In 'Through Welsh-tinted Glasses' (37–45), the American/Welsh poet, Joseph Clancy, understands why many Europeans have preferred to react against the excesses of American nationalism. He accepts that this 'manifests itself in ... crass and ethically doubtful ways' but he still regards himself as an American poet despite Welsh influences upon him. Charlotte Davies, an American anthropologist, brought up in Kentucky and South Carolina and currently studying Wales as an 'exotic culture', notes that Welsh people are unaware of the extent of regional variations in the United States (46–9). Jon Dressel's 'Looking Both Ways' imagines 'an extended dialogue with Benjamin Benoni Jones, his Welsh grandfather who emigrated to America in the 1890s (56–64). Despite early 'romantic infatuation with Wales', he concludes ironically that by now 'whatever disillusion I had with America has been fully balanced by disillusion with Wales'. Introducing the winter 2005 issue of *The New*

Welsh Review (subtitled 'Wales and the Americas') Francesca Rhydderch says that: 'American foreign policy has had such a bad press since 9/11 that it has become easy to forget, or at least to overlook, Wales's love affair with American continents, North and South' (6–7). The thread of this recurrent ambivalence runs throughout the treatment of American topics in the later periodicals.

The periodicals also appear to be in two minds about the Empire and the British Commonwealth – the other main sources of relations with the English-speaking world. The prospectus for the International Labour Organisation at its ten-year anniversary in 1929 shows that (following the Balfour Declaration of 1926, which created the British Commonwealth of Nations) Australia, Canada, India, New Zealand and South Africa are recognised as members in their own right (as is the Irish Free State). However, the whole of the rest of the Commonwealth – all the African states including South Africa and all the West Indian and Asian dependencies, together, obviously, with Northern Ireland, Wales and Scotland – are still subsumed under the title of 'The British Empire'.[15]

In the late Victorian and Edwardian eras the Imperial theme is heard in Welsh periodicals, usually without criticism or irony. It is often linked to missionary activity and careers seen as civilising activities. The serial story of 'Gabriel Yoreth' by the Rev. E. Cynffig Davies appears in *Wales* in nineteen episodes over two years between June 1894 and June 1896. Gabriel is a virtuous young Welsh miner, who heroically rescues several of his fellows after an explosion and then attempts to act as peacemaker in a subsequent demonstration. Falsely accused of involvement in the death of a policeman, he is sentenced to transportation to Van Diemen's Land. On the voyage he meets a missionary couple en route for South Africa who intercede on his behalf and eventually secure him a pardon. He achieves prosperity, becomes a wise and successful socialist mine owner and his son later returns to Wales, is ordained as a Minister and then decides to go back to Van Diemen's land as a missionary. This lengthy serial supports some continuing themes about emigration. Gabriel experiences 'intense longing for the old home, its scenes and elevated pleasures' (September 1894, 223) together with a strong sense of Welsh mission as a reforming influence in unpromising colonial settings. Gabriel tells his fellow mine-owner, Mr Jackson, that 'missionary zeal and Christian activity of all kinds are inseparably connected with one another and with the higher forms of Christian life' (February 1895, 96).

This missionary urge to combine good deeds and successful careers is repeated in *Young Wales* in June 1896. Linked to *Cymru Fydd* and edited by J. Hugh Edwards, the magazine mediates between Welsh aspirations to home rule and loyalty to the Empire. J. Young Evans's article 'Wales and the Empire' sees his exhortation in this 'Welsh University Celebration Number' to a greater pride in British citizenship as 'a call to magnanimity':

> What will be done by the University of Wales towards making the Welsh National life, while jealously retaining its individual characteristics, more potent in the life of the Empire? ... It is but a clap-trap and vapid patriotism that attempts to isolate and alienate the life and thought of Wales, thus causing Welshmen to fail in their duty to themselves and to the world. (51–2)

A later series of articles titled 'Sons of Wales' in *Wales* (again edited by J. Hugh Edwards, published between 1911 and 1914) suggests that this call has not gone unheeded. Welsh involvement in Empire is celebrated fully:

> There is not a quarter of the Globe where Welshmen are not to be found. All the world over they are occupying positions of distinction and responsibility ... we propose chronicling each month ... the activities and triumphs of our countrymen. (May 1911, 47)

This article goes on to record the appointments of Welshmen as Presidents of the Supreme Courts of Canada and Australia, where yet another Welshman serves as Attorney General – and as Chief Justice in India (48). Welshmen are shown as leading academics in India and in New Zealand (March 1914, 62; May 1914, 112).

Careerist delight in Imperial opportunity (however well-intentioned) is a common enough target for post-colonial critics. An example of the unconscious exoticising 'otherness' that Homi Bhabha identifies at the root of colonial stereotyping[16] appears in the innocent observations of Miss S. B. Williams, Professor of History at the University College of Trivandrum, South India, in *Wales* in July 1895:

> It is the queerest place in the world, full of the wildest contrasts. It is a world of broad red leaves and cocoa nut palms and brown naked figures; and at night hanging brass lights and torches and star-light make the scene like an Arabian Night's entertainment. (334)

But I have to report one far more explicit example. The unthinking, alienating racial and misogynist language of the journalist Perceval Gibbon, 'A Young Welshman in South Africa', hidden away in the midst of his lengthy account of a day in Ixopo, Natal, published (it may now seem incredibly) in the Liberal *Young Wales* in November 1901, reads

> Now a Cape Boy is a nigger you know, and I had not heard him say 'Sir' and out here we hold familiarity with niggers worse than communion with the devil. So I was about to ask him if he knew he was talking to a white man ... (249)

and (a few pages later)

> I am not a lady's man as you will bear me out; nothing gars me hate a woman so as having to talk to her. (252)

It is difficult to imagine a much more blatant example of what Edward Said calls 'the imperial dynamic and its separating, essentialising, dominating and reactive tendencies'.

It is a relief to turn to Alun Lewis's unusually sensitive perceptions of the weakness of Empire in his 'Letter from India' in *The Welsh Review* of June 1945. The sub-continent is

> an amazing spectacular land but something seems to have gone wrong at the root of it. I sense a perpetual undercurrent of mockery and hostility towards us among the people. (92)

My research in the subject indexes suggests that interest in the Commonwealth in the Welsh journals seems to decline quite sharply after 1945, as the processes of independence take place. The indexes from 1950 through to 1980 record as few as half a dozen articles per year devoted to Commonwealth countries. Nevertheless, in May 1948, Keidrych Rhys noted the presence of additional subscribers for his *Wales* in Australia, New Zealand, Canada, Malta, Uganda and Jamaica. However, the 250 subscribers listed by *Dock Leaves* in March 1953 include only three from the Commonwealth. On the other hand, Mike Jenkins's valedictory April 1992 special issue of *Poetry Wales* on 'International Poetry' has articles about Nigeria and Malawi, together with an account of a visit to the Kalahari, and letters from India and Barbados.

Planet is the most likely journal to deal with Commonwealth topics, although my sampling of its contents does not suggest that the periodical actually gives them very high priority. There are, however, articles about the Caribbean in 1971 (Feb/Mar, 48–58) and 1987 (Feb/Mar, 81–6) and about Bangladesh in 2000 (Aug/Sept, 46–53). There are articles about Canada, especially about the possible secession of Quebec. Keith Buchanan's 'Quebec: New World Emerging' appears in 1978 (January, 4–13) and Ned Thomas writes 'The View from Montreal' in 1986 (June/July, 3–7). John Canning's 2003 contribution suggests that the frequent citation of Quebec as an 'exemplar for the autonomy which can be achieved for nations without states' (Aug/Sept 2003, 81) is misleading. It is perhaps surprising that nationalist feeling in Wales does not appear to have energised more active support in the periodicals for the aspirations of British colonial dependencies to self-rule.

III

The anglophone Welsh periodicals' approach to the non-Welsh, non-English world seems to have developed in the first place through the keen interest many contributors displayed in Celtic links and comparisons. Wales has not developed the same depth of mythical relation to the Orient that Joseph Lennon has discovered in Irish writing over the centuries.[18] But Lennon's observation that 'cultural continuity is the rule not the exception' (xxiii) also fits Wales and explains many aspects of the character of its self-definition in international terms. Lennon argues that 'accumulation, continuity and cohesion rather than invention define the progress of most traditions and cultural discourses' (2). He also points out that the fact that many myths of origin and theories of history are eventually shown to be wholly inaccurate does not prevent them in any way from having a substantial impact, as in the example of Ossianic writings (89). Meta Williams claims in Owen M. Edwards's *Wales* in February 1895 that

> Silently and all unconsciously, the Celtic element in the population has moulded the genius of the races with which it has mingled; and without it English literature and French art could not have been. ... When the conquest of South Wales by the Normans was begun, the intellectual reaction of the conquered on the conqueror began also. (49, 51)

In J. Hugh Edwards's *Wales* in May 1914, in an article about 'Pioneers of Welsh Nationalism', J. E. de Hirsch–Davies remarks that few of 'the worthy writers' on the history of the subject 'cared in their love of thoroughness and comprehensiveness to stop short of Adam' (137). The following excerpts from the article emphasise the power of myth in the formation of a Welsh historical persona:

> In trying to estimate and analyse the forces that have been operative from the earliest days in welding together the Celtic people into a homogenous community, we must not minimise and certainly not overlook the enormous influence of the illusions which play, and always have played, so notable a part in the earliest stages of a country's history. ... A nation lives and moves and has its being in great ideas and fruitful fantasies. ... We must not forget that the present Welsh people were once a portion of a widespread Empire in the very heart of Europe and that we once had the pleasure of sacking Rome. ... The primitive Celts, truly, wandered over many a land and sampled many a climate before they finally settled down in the little land which has been their home for at least two thousand years. (137–9)

However, an interest in Celticism also influences more realistic forms of alliance, often associated with language differences, leading to expressions of solidarity with other nations. In *Wales* in July 1896 an article on 'What the Celts are Doing' seeks to strengthen links between the Cymmrodorion, the Highland Association and the Society for the Preservation of the Irish Language (290–2). Welsh concerns about the problems of linguistic division appear in *Young Wales* in September 1901, once more citing the example of Belgium (193–8), and again in *Welsh Outlook* (January 1932) with R. T. Williamson's article 'A Language Lost and then Revived' about the problems of the Czech language in Bohemia (23–5). Gwyn Jones's editorial in the winter 1948 issue of *The Welsh Review* urges support for a petition to provide for the teaching of Breton in schools in Brittany (230). *Planet's* second issue in 1971 features articles on French regionalism, and on the fate of several linguistic minorities in Europe including Bretons, Basques and Catalans. Matthew Jarvis has recently quite rightly pointed out that an article of mine in *Welsh Writing in English* in 2007 understated the international element in early issues of *Poetry Wales* and especially the extent of that magazine's engagement with Breton poetry. Jarvis does accept, however, that these concerns of *Poetry Wales* were then linked mainly to what he describes as 'a linguistic-cultural situation which in some ways parallels Welsh circumstances'. He recognises that, unlike Peter Finch's *Second Aeon*, they 'do not generally seem to embrace cosmopolitanism for its own sake.'[19] *Poetry Wales* was, in this respect, closely aligned with the editorial practice of many other Welsh periodicals in English.

Raymond Williams articulated a vision of Wales as being able to by-pass its historic connections with England, instead linking itself directly to Europe:

> Suddenly England, bourgeois England, wasn't my main point of reference any more. I was a Welsh European, and both levels felt different ... I am in a culture where I can breathe.[20]

The force of this was recognised by Gwynfor Evans in his book *Fighting for Wales*: 'The growing interdependence of nations in Europe is matched by a growing awareness of the value of diverse identities.'[21] John Osmond suggests that the nation state is capable of being overtaken by what he calls 'continental patterns of governance' in the context of a *Europe des Regions*.[22] The case for and against closer Welsh alliance with Europe is debated in various ways in the periodicals from the late nineteenth century onwards.

Cymru Fydd marked the death of Henry Richard in September 1888, saying that

> He was the inspiring influence of the Peace Society. The authoritative objects of this organisation are international and it is no exaggeration to say that they were to Mr. Richard as 'the very life of his life'. (504)

The periodical welcomes Richard's meetings with Victor Hugo at the International Peace Congress held in 1849, and his success in getting a parliamentary motion establishing a system of international arbitration (524). It lists his visits to Brussels, The Hague, Berlin, Dresden, Vienna, Venice, Milan and Turin (529).

However, a year later, in 1889, Ivor Bowen, also writing in *Cymru Fydd,* makes a pointed comparison between 'Welsh Radicalism and German Socialism' (57–63). He is keen to distinguish Welsh Liberals from those who are 'imbued with the vague teachings and fearful uncertainties of the German School, as represented by Lassalle and Karl Marx' (57). These German ideas are 'not much more valuable than the impoverished [German] Princes and Royal hangers-on who are supported by a patient and long-suffering electorate'. Bowen asserts the character of the Welshman as 'a fierce and uncompromising radical [who is] everywhere against class interests, is for the elevation of the individual, in order to obtain the moral integrity of the multitude'. German socialism is declared in emphatic italics to have '*no common ground with Welsh aspirations and sentiment*'.

However, this fierce, politicised insularity is relaxed in other journals. Owen Edwards, in *Wales*, promotes the value of European travel. In June 1896 he applauds the University College of North Wales for its educational European residencies,

> recognising 'the importance of sending our teachers abroad for part of their training. ... Residence abroad gives the intellectual awakening and the wide sympathy which mark off a real teacher from a useless one.' (285)

However, in February 1896, Edwards resisted another European comparison when acknowledging receipt of a 'well written article' by 'JR' on 'Young Italy and Young Wales', but judging it 'glaringly unjust to modern Welsh politicians when comparing them to Mazzini and Cavour and Garibaldi. It is too partisan ... to find room in these pages' (90). The magazine's 'Peeps Abroad' series starts with 'A Visit to the Pyrenees' in January 1897 by Mary Annie Foulkes of Llanberis, who makes comparisons with 'the dear familiar old mountains of Eryri'. The series continues with 'Walks in the Eiffel' (March 1897) and 'In the Land of Floods', a diary of a visit to Norway in April 1897 (91). At this stage European cultural and tourist experiences are welcome but radical European politics appear too challenging.

J. Hugh Edwards deplores Welsh isolationism in *Young Wales* in August 1899. He says that

> A [Welsh] national weakness is that embodied in our spirit of exclusiveness, in that proneness to live our national life in complete isolation. In the maze of European politics 'splendid isolation' may mark the wisest policy, but in the world of nationalism, of national interests and influences, it cannot but be a mistaken one. (177)

He worries that other countries (including, he says, England) have no clear picture of Wales.

By 1914, however, the spaces of comparison have broadened. I have earlier remarked on the extent of the engagement of *Welsh Outlook* in the politics of the 1914–18 war and in the processes of international diplomacy through the 1930s. The first editor, Thomas Jones, stated in his opening editorial piece that he wanted to strike a balance between celebrating Welsh national achievements and involving Wales in wider international contacts:

> ... we wish in these pages to witness to the unity of our national life and to deepen and enrich it. This we would do not by refusing what other nations have to offer but by taking of their best, making it our own and returning it with interest. We believe we can make some contribution, however small, to the common treasury of the nations. (January 1914, 1–2)[23]

There was a sequence of pieces on international topics throughout 1915: in January on 'Famous Frenchmen', in February on 'Politics and Philosophy in England and Germany', in March on 'The War and Small Nations', in June on 'Some Aspects of Russia' and in September on 'Songs of Serbia'. In the inter-war period, *Welsh Outlook* was a constant supporter of the League of Nations, Gwilym Davies reporting in 'Notes of the Month' in January 1921 that its first meeting had been 'a great, though a somewhat qualified success' (301). Albert Zimmern recognised 'a vein of deep pessimism and anxiety' (303) which was, of course to be justified by subsequent events. But Gwilym Davies continued to cover the disarmament negotiations in great detail right up to the magazine's closure in 1933. It is curious, given the extent of the involvement of Welsh volunteers in the Spanish Civil War, that I have not been able to trace any significant material about this subject in the periodicals. This contrasts with the very detailed coverage in James O'Donovan's magazine *Ireland To-Day*, which was probably suppressed because of its opposition to the Fascist revolution in Spain.[24]

Gwilym Davies also wrote for Gwyn Jones's *Welsh Review*. In July 1939 Gwyn Jones's editorial expresses disquietude at the naivité of ministers over the Manchurian crisis, accusing them of granting 'aggressor states ... the exact rights of smash-and-grab we found so profitable in our empire-building days' (305). The use of 'our' in this context suggests that Jones recognises the past involvement of Welsh people in the imperial project. In his editorial on the outbreak of hostilities in September 1939 Jones remarks that 'every individual who has helped in however small a way ... to sabotage the League of Nations carries his share of dreadful responsibility' (65). Gwilym Davies is by now near apocalyptic:

> The democratic governments in the second decade (1929–38) were given chance after chance and at every turn they failed ... Either we are witnessing the twilight

> of Western civilisation or we are actors in a tremendous drama ... Our generation is in travail with the world state. (August 1939, 46–7)

At the same time, Keidrych Rhys, in his magazine *Wales*, was resisting international involvement, concentrating instead on perceived distinctions between Welsh and English culture. He remarks in the end paper to the first issue (Summer 1937) that the magazine will provide a platform for 'creative work by the younger progressive Welsh writers'. In his second editorial (August 1937, 35) Rhys insists that *Wales* 'ought to be a sort of forum where the "Anglo-Welsh" can have their say', remarking that 'we pride ourselves on being intelligent enough not to dogmatize on the military loyalists in Spain and elsewhere. Criticism of No. 1 was seldom tonic. We've been accused of being European' (35). It is not until October 1939, after the commencement of hostilities, that the new editor, Nigel Heseltine (Rhys being by then in the services), declares in an editorial that 'blood and horror have been forced on us lately at peace' and that 'our fight will be against any establishment of Fascist principles in this country' (254). *Wales* has been drawn, despite itself, into engagement with contemporary international conflict.

In the period after the Second World War periodicals often express increased interest in European and world affairs. After Raymond Garlick becomes editor, *Dock Leaves*, which now describes itself as 'The Voice of Pembrokeshire Speaking to Wales', the journal avoids accusations of provincialism by including, for example: translations from Mallarmé and the Swedish of Frans G. Beningsen, a poem on the arrest of Cardinal Mindzenty and editorial comment on floods in the Netherlands, the Mau Mau atrocities and the death of Stalin.[25] Keidrych Rhys's *Wales* in Winter 1946 has articles about the USSR (an enthusiastic encomium from a J.P.), an account of taking medical supplies to post-war Yugoslavia and a diary by Emyr Humpreys of his wartime experiences in Florence. *Dock Leaves'* successor, the *Anglo-Welsh Review* institutes a section called 'Abroad' which, in a single issue in 1959, has features on Dutch writers, on settler life in Israel, on anti-Semitism in the west and about a writer's experience on the 'Second Floor Back in Montparnasse'. There are short stories set in the Spanish Civil War, and biographies that often feature the subject's overseas exposure to foreign cultures, for example citing T. E. Ellis's 'compulsive wish to visit foreign lands'. Much of this may be seen to reflect the exotic appeal of foreign travel to a generation largely starved of the experience during periods of recession and war.

Welsh periodicals in the period after devolution regularly spread their wings beyond Europe. There is little space here to deal with the profusion of their international materials in any depth. However, the three most prominent recent periodicals in Wales, *Poetry Wales*, *The New Welsh Review* and of course *Planet*, all work at asserting their credentials in respect of major issues about the environment, climate change and globalisation. In his recent book, *Welsh Environments in Contemporary Poetry*, Matthew Jarvis underlines the degree to which Robert Minhinnick's poetry celebrates Welsh space in an international context, involved deeply with global politics and environmental concerns.[26] Minhinnick's first editorial in *Poetry Wales* – written in October 1997 in the immediate aftermath of the yes vote in the second devolution referendum – emphasises the cultural value to writers of direct international experience:

> There is no profit and no future in the dour, respectful regional introspection that underlines much art in this country ... writers should get out more. ... then come back and for all our sakes share what has been discovered. (2)

A single issue of *Poetry Wales* in 2001 features contemporary Hungarian poetry, a letter from Serbia, an article by Duncan Bush on Francophilia and an account of Robert Minhinnick's visit to Belgium.

Richard Reeves, the second editor of *The New Welsh Review*, is described in the introduction to his archives in the

National Library as a 'Welsh European' and his successor, Victor Golightly, advocated in his first editorial the concept of 'a critically interlinked world'. A special issue in Summer 2007 takes as its theme 'On the Continent: "Wales and Europe"'. *Planet* (which adopted the sub-title 'The Welsh Internationalist' in 1980) consciously takes a global view, for instance, in David Sullivan's article, 'Wars End', in May 2002, asking whether the spread of democracy can create the conditions for world-wide peace. Or in John Lovering's article '9/11, Neo Liberalism and the New Conformity' in January 2004, discussing globalism and the American Empire. One could multiply many such examples.

IV

It is my conviction that periodical literature is substantially representative of the play of educated opinion in the anglophone public sphere in Wales. If this is so, a few tentative conclusions may promote further debate. However, international interests must be kept in reasonable proportion. As I pointed out at the beginning, only a relatively small – though growing – extent of space in Welsh periodicals in English is devoted to this area. This suggests that interest in international matters may still be quite marginal in Wales. Perhaps a close examination of Welsh-language periodicals would tell a different tale; but the subject indexes include them and their listings do not immediately suggest that they are very different in this respect. It would be, however, an interesting future question for research.

Ambivalent relations with England invade many of the comparisons: these recognise the Welsh contribution to Empire, and the importance of career opportunities for Welshmen in England and the British Commonwealth, but they also involve rivalry, resentment and sometimes hostility. Diasporic contributions and the missionary nature of some overseas relationships appear stronger in the nineteenth century and in the recession-hit 1930s. The prevalence of American topics is significant. There does, however, seem to be a switch in interest after the Second World War from giving primacy to relations with the English-speaking world towards linking Wales more closely with Europe and the wider world. Tourism and travel feature strongly, especially as restrictions on mobility diminish in the aftermath of the Second World War. More recently again, global considerations have featured more prominently (and perhaps coincidentally) in the period after devolution. It does seem that Welsh links to other countries have been most strongly forged by personal contacts, especially through outstanding individuals, such as Henry Richard or Raymond Williams, rather than through formal institutions such as the European Community or the United Nations. Internationalism creates tensions throughout this history between what sometimes appear as three rival projects: establishing a coherent Welsh identity; ensuring that Wales is properly informed about the wider world; and guaranteeing that Wales is well-represented and not misunderstood. The spaces of comparison in these periodicals are seen as offering opportunities for Wales, as sites for validation, but, just occasionally, they appear as threats.

APPENDIX

Summary of subject indexes for Welsh periodicals: 1931–55; 1968–80

Two series of subject indexes are available, covering almost 50 years but with a 13-year gap after 1955. The following notes describe the volumes and my methodology.

1. The first series from 1931–55 is in 7 volumes, edited by Arthur Gwynn and/or Idwal Lewis, published by the Wales and

Monmouthshire Branch of the Library Associations in Cardiff or Swansea: I: 1931; II: 1932–33; III: 1934–5; IV: 1936–7; V: 1938–40; VI: 1941–45; VII: 1946–55. Each volume covers between 40 and 60 journals.

2. The second series from 1968–80 is in 3 volumes: I: 1968–70; II: 1971–76; III: 1977–80. These are published by the National Library of Wales, Aberystwyth, with introductions by David Jenkins and R. Geraint Gruffydd. Volumes I and II each cover 97 titles and Volume III covers 84 titles.

3. For the purpose of comparison I have estimated the number of articles falling under a selection of headings. The choice of headings within these publications is not always consistent and the compilers have also listed alternative references (e.g. 'See under …') for most significant topics.

4. Under 'International' I have assessed the numbers of articles under the following headings: 'International'; Ireland/Eire; USA/America; Great Britain; France; Germany; Greece; Israel; Italy; Canada; India; Africa; Hungary; Czech; Pakistan; Russia/Soviet Union; South Africa; Argentine; China; South America; Patagonia; Spain; Japan; Palestine.

5. The table summarises the outcome of this analysis in respect of 'International' articles, compared with the numbers of entries for literature and religion.

TOTAL LISTINGS PER INDEX/LISTINGS PER YEAR/PERCENTAGE OF TOTAL

	1931 1 yr 1500	1932-3 2 yrs 3300 1500	1934-5 2 yrs 2700 1400	1936-7 2 yrs 2400 1200	1938-40 3 yrs 3000 1000	1941-5 5 yrs 2800 560	1946-55 10 yrs 6000 600		1968-70 3 yrs 13k 4.3k	1971-6 6 yrs 22k 3.8k	1977-80 4 yrs 15k 3.8k
INT	32 2%	79 40 2%	67 34 3%	58 29 2%	57 19 2%	67 13 2%	104 10 2%		147 49 1%	376 62 2%	259 65 2%
LIT	69 5%	125 63 4%	115 57 4%	140 70 6%	148 49 6%	194 39 7%	358 36 6%		740 247 6%	1930 321 9%	796 199 5%
REL	131 9%	151 75 5%	186 93 7%	137 69 6%	196 65 6%	158 30 6%	326 33 5%		395 132 3%	647 107 3%	529 132 4%

This article is based on a paper delivered to the Association for Welsh Writing in English Annual Conference, 'Spaces of Comparison: Welsh Writing in Comparative Contexts' held at Gregynog Hall, 27–29 March 2009. I acknowledge in these notes a number of sources of helpful advice and comment. Any errors are, however, my own.

NOTES

1 Stefan Collini, *Absent Minds: Intellectuals in Britain* (Oxford: Oxford University Press, 2006), p. 434.
2 Daniel G. Williams, *Ethnicity and Cultural Authority, Arnold to Dubois* (Edinburgh: Edinburgh University Press, 2006), p. 17.
3 T. Darlington, *Wales*, 1, 1894, pp. 11–16.
4 'Wales to English Eyes', *Wales*, 2, 1894, pp. 51–2.
5 'Gwenffrwd', 'To A Mocking Bird (Heard in the Graveyard at Spring-Hill 1st May, 1834)', *Wales*, 2, 1894, p. 64.
6 First series (1931–55) edited by Arthur Gwynn and Idwal Davies, 7 volumes. I: 1931; II: 1932–3; III: 1934–5; IV: 1936–7; V: 1938–40; VI: 1941–5; VII: 1946–55, published by the Wales and Monmouthshire Branch of the Libraries Associations in Cardiff and Swansea. Second series (1968–80) edited by David Jenkins and R. Geraint Gruffydd, 3 volumes. I: 1968–70; II: 1971–6; III: 1977–80, published by National Library of Wales. I am grateful to Meic Stephens for drawing my attention to these publications.
7 See the Appendix for a summary of my analysis.
8 Ernest Bowen Rowlands, *The Welsh Review*, 1, November 1891, pp. 1–5 (2). All further page references to the periodicals will be given parenthetically in the article.
9 I wish to thank Alyce von Rothkirch for pointing out the extent of international coverage in *Welsh Outlook*; for further information, see her essay in the present volume.
10 See Tecwyn Lloyd, 'Welsh Opinion and the First World War', *Planet*, Feb–Mar 1972, pp. 25–37.
11 See Aled Jones and Bill Jones, '*Y Drych* and American Welsh Identities, 1851–1951' in *North American Journal of Welsh Studies*, I, 1, Winter 2001, pp. 42–58 and Aled Jones and Bill Jones, *Welsh Reflections: Y Drych and America* 1851–2001, (Llandysul: Gomer, 2001).
12 Peter Garrett, Nikolas Coupland and Hywel Bishop,

'Globalization and the Visualisation of Wales and Welsh America', in *Ethnicities*, V, 4, 2005, pp. 530–564, accessed via Sage Journals Online, March 2009. All further page references will be given parenthetically in the article.

13 Aled Jones and Bill Jones, '*Y Drych* and American Welsh Identities, 1851–1951', op. cit., p. 42. All further page references will be given parenthetically in the article.

14 Aled Jones and Bill Jones, *Welsh Reflections: Y Drych and America 1851–2001*, op. cit., p. 38. All further page references will be given parenthetically in the article.

15 Thanks are due to Stephen Thomas, Director of the Welsh Centre for International Affairs, who has discussed this article with me, made a number of helpful suggestions and who kindly loaned me a copy of this ILO publication.

16 Homi Bhabha, *The Location of Culture* (London: Routledge, 1994), pp. 66–7.

17 Edward Said, *Culture and Imperialism* (London: Vintage, 1994), p. 42.

18 Joseph Lennon, *Irish Orientalism: A Literary and Intellectual History* (Syracuse, New York: Syracuse University Press, 2004). All further page references will be given parenthetically in the article.

19 Matthew Jarvis, 'International Elements in Early *Poetry Wales*: A Response to Malcolm Ballin' in *Almanac*, Yearbook of Welsh Writing in English (Cardigan: Parthian, 2009), pp. 190–201 (196). Jarvis critically examines some aspects of my article, 'Welsh Periodicals in English: *Second Aeon* and *Poetry Wales* 1965–1985' in *Welsh Writing in English: A Yearbook of Critical Essays*, 11, 2006–2007, pp. 147–87. He challenges my conclusion that there is relatively little international material in *Poetry Wales* throughout the periods of Meic Stephens's and Gerald Morgan's editorships during 1965–73. He convincingly argues that I pay too little attention to the extent of engagement the periodical had at that time with translations, Breton poets and regional cultures. He accepts, however (p. 197), that *Poetry Wales* took a different stance from Peter Finch's *Second Aeon* in this respect and that the references he cites were designed mainly to offer 'a perspective on Welsh cultural conditions'. I am happy to set the record right and to attempt to offer a more balanced assessment in this article.

20 Raymond Williams, *Politics and Letters: Interviews with New Left Review* (London: NLB, 1979), pp. 295–6.

21 Gwynfor Evans, *Fighting for Wales* (Talybont: Y Lolfa, 1991), pp. 208–16.

22 John Osmond, *Welsh Europeans* (Bridgend: Seren, 1995), pp. 144–56.

23 See: Trevor L. Williams, 'Thomas Jones and the *Welsh Outlook*' in *Anglo-Welsh Review*, 64, 1979, pp. 38–44, for a wider appreciation of the role of Thomas Jones in relation to this periodical. His interest in international articles is highlighted on p. 44.

24 For a full account of *Ireland To-day* and its involvement with the Spanish Civil War see Frank Shovlin, *The Irish Literary Periodical*: 1923–1958 (Oxford: Oxford University Press, 2003), pp. 80–87.

25 See *Dock Leaves*, Easter 1950, pp.19 and 54; Spring 1953, pp. 1–2.

26 Matthew Jarvis, *Welsh Environments in Contemporary Poetry* (Cardiff: University of Wales Press, 2008), p. 87.

Exact Mystery:

Some Aspects of Vernon Watkins's Poetics

John Powell Ward
formerly Swansea University

Vernon Watkins's *Collected Poems* was published by the Golgonooza Press in 1986. Its re-issue in 2000 and the poet's centenary in 2006 have been followed by a stir of new interest, notably in articles by M. Wynn Thomas and the Archbishop of Canterbury Rowan Williams, together with an Introduction by Watkins's latest editor Richard Ramsbotham to the *New Selected Poems*.[1] Yet it still seems that, even so, many readers are chary of Watkins and do not see a feasible way of reading him, certainly not at this time, perhaps at no time. These and other recent pieces of criticism have concentrated on presenting Watkins as one would normally treat an established figure. They are drawn to him already, and wish mainly to celebrate him by throwing light on broad positions Watkins held and which his poetry evinces. Interestingly delineated, this would newly secure his place on the critical map, whether of Wales or Britain more widely. But, alarmingly, Watkins actually isn't on that map at all. A decade back John Greening concluded that Watkins had 'dropped into almost complete obscurity', a view confirmed quite recently by Ramsbotham, who states that Watkins has 'disappeared almost completely from the commonly perceived map of twentieth-century poetry'.[2]

The reasons given for this neglect are familiar. Watkins was too ethereal-minded to bother to describe the natural world he supposedly loved. There is no narrative; in fact, he often veers away from a story-line exactly when one seems imminent. His weight of classical and mythological reference, sincerely presented without affectation, is still too much for contemporary readers. His congested obscurities leave his meaning, if any, hard to grasp; his insistence on regular formal rhyming grows monotonous, and he seems to have eschewed irony entirely. And his persistent belief in a world beyond time[3] takes him right out of the everyday mortal world, its metallic technology, street-wise noisiness and messy domestic scenery, all that someone – I believe Richard Hoggart – once called 'the reek of the human'. As a result, Watkins saw the past and present as one, and often felt, as he once put it, that 'a poem is not finished until it attains its most ancient form'.[4] The adjective is important; it does not mean 'antique', but is more like a reversal of Pound's 'make it new' into 'make it old', although that is doubtless too simple an opposition in which to have complete confidence. All this shying away from Watkins follows despite the fact that an impressive roll-call of poets has praised him in strong terms of admiration and (so to call it) bardic affection; Dylan Thomas of course, but also T.S. Eliot, Marianne Moore, Kathleen Raine and, surprisingly in light of that poet's own realism, his friend Philip Larkin – to name a few.

The question, then, is how to approach Watkins critically. In the last few decades the common approach to any poetry – when it is not theory-bound from the start – has been to discern what a poem is 'about' and then place *that* in the current social and cultural scene, or alongside the poet's own biography, as detective-like evidence of the personality revealed. Vernon Watkins cannot be treated like that. Seeking only what can gainfully be said, movingly, enrichingly or otherwise, his poems are often about the words they contain. Or, despite an allusive or referential title, they reach for an unnamed thing beyond it. The unnamed thing may be simply unidentified by the poet momentarily – hence the poem at all – or may be metaphysical, and so unnameable in principle. So we are more likely, in describing a Watkins poem, to note its verbal inventory and combinations thereof, see where it is pointing or whence it has come, and describe a final effect, and its value, that we discern in it. There is no parallel-prose rendering to most Watkins poems, as there is to many of Larkin's, even though such renderings of, for example, 'The Whitsun Weddings', would omit most of what mattered in them.

In Watkins's own case, critics often try for a centre in his work by taking one of the clear groups of poems he occasionally wrote, and go from there. These include the 'Music of Colours' group, the Taliesin group, the poems for Dylan Thomas, those addressed to other poets or on poetry itself, and the ballads, notably the two long ones, 'Ballad of the Mari Lwyd' (41) and its sequel 'The Ballad of the Outer Dark' (440).[5] Such treatment then takes the critic into wider considerations of Watkins's main beliefs about the poetic tradition; life and death; and the metaphysical attitude of Watkins. This has clear importance and will come up from time to time no doubt in the present article. But in general I would rather avoid this approach. It seemed preferable, for once, to look at Watkins's verse close-up most of the way, seeking aspects, features, moments of unique voice, and much-favoured single terms, from any poem that seems most to evince them. It might then turn out that some of the above-listed adverse criticisms of Watkins can be seen from different angles, and that more is present than such readings so far have recognised. Of course this may not still convince, but it seems worth trying. Those eminent poets who supported him so strongly were surely not entirely mistaken.

Accurate vivid description

First, then, there is the charge that Watkins lacked accurate, vivid descriptive power. The view of some adverse critics is that he was normally distracted by his own metaphysical beliefs. The solid things of nature – plants, sea-shells, rocks, fish – matter for what they signified in the further and timeless world beyond nature; in Blake's words, 'the eternal World of which this vegetable Universe is but a faint shadow'.[6] That being so, it is argued, Watkins's natural items needed only simple reference, and they therefore fail to grip the reader. As Roland Mathias put it, Watkins's observations of nature don't seem to happen 'on a particular day, a particular occasion', and so are no guide to his 'life, mood or predicament' at the time.[7] But Mathias had no doubt at all as to Watkins's real experience and knowledge of the natural world, and his acute power of observation in its presence. From such factors, this area of criticism of Watkins still raises debate.

There are indeed times, and modes, where Watkins didn't 'grip' – a favoured term for him – his material as tightly as he might have done. Stanzas of no great exactitude occur here and there:

> Truth is simple: out of the mouth of babes
> Flows the living word to correct the proud.
> All great acts are serene and
> Born in the bands of acknowledged glory.
>
> ('Ode', 219)

True no doubt, but hardly realised. Elsewhere, the welter of seemingly endless imperatives and rhetorical questions can disconcert the reader and distract us from the tangible and real things that any poem in question contains:

> 'Not yet! Do not yet touch,
> Break not this branch of silver-birch,
> Nor ask the stealthy river why it laves
> Black roots that feed the leaves'
>
> ('The Turning of the Leaves', 10)

The rhetorical questions, overtly anyway, sometimes feel almost empty. 'O what's the good of a man in a rock?' ('Ballad of the Rough Sea', 187); 'Who am I to load the year with continual misunderstanding?' ('Triads', 392). What and who indeed?

But if we look more closely, we find something intriguingly different, more solid and more approachable, and maybe of profound worth. Watkins's knowledge of and familiarity with the beaches, tides, wooded valleys, streams, birds and trees of the Gower peninsula was such that he could transform them as he wished while retaining their inimitable earthly character too. His imagery is thus seldom the verbal high-definition photograph. That would be information-overload; what he sought was unforgettable invocation.

For example, the wren is the smallest British bird apart from its relative, the goldcrest. So when Watkins says 'ask first the flickering wren' ('The Turning of the Leaves', 10) we may be wondering where the question comes from, and so miss how 'flickering' is exactly right for the way so small a bird does what a larger one would do in 'flapping' or 'fluttering' its wings. 'Flickering' is what a candle's tiny flame does in a big dark church. Elsewhere, it is the sea that gets such exact attention:

> Sharp rocks drive back the breaking waves,
> Confusing sea with air.
> Bundles of spray blown mountain-high
> Have left the shingle bare ...
>
> ('The Heron', 176)

Anyone who has seen waves hit a cliff and shoot upward fully vertically can recognise this at once; but the triply-mixed image – 'bundles' as of hay, the sea's 'spray' itself and 'blown' as by dynamite in a quarry – confirms the 'confusion' of the previous line as more than a two-dimensional picture. It is a rounded experience, opening further possibilities. Watkins's best-remembered sea-image, however, comes in one of his best-recalled poems, 'Music of Colours: White Blossom' (101), where the poet saw the same stretch of coast two days running:

> The spray looked white until this snowfall.
> Now the foam is grey, the wave is dull.
> Call nothing white again, we were deceived ...

– a ‘deception’ in that our earthly vision falls short of a Platonically perfect one. Another sea-image captures a quieter event:

> And I hurl a stick to the wave
> And watch it slowly come ...
> Here, brought by foam, it lies,
> A spent and weary log ...
>
> (‘Ballad of the Equinox’, 189)

Again, anyone who has thrown a stick into a wave thinning out on sand as it arrives on shore will know this experience. And so this can be developed, for the log – humanised now as ‘spent and weary’ – is also contrastingly thickened to log from stick, a growing just as the stick’s journey grows, going out and coming in. All this takes us further forward than a camera-cannot-lie image would allow. Equally, in the Thomsonesque ‘The Tributary Seasons’ (252) we see a small event – actually two – quickly evoked:

> A skater goes
> Skimming across the pond. A stone
> Stays on the ice where it is thrown.

Neither ourselves nor the poet needed to see the stone actually being ‘thrown’, for the experience is familiar, it *looks* thrown when lying there like that on the ice.

But these rich accuracies aren’t confined to the world of nature. James Davies is right that Watkins normally avoided ‘ordinary, work-based, domesticated existence or the urban setting in which he spent so much of his life’.[8] But such things are not absent entirely, and when needed they come with the same characteristic precision. In ‘The Mother and Child’ we find a real – certainly ‘domesticated’ – baby on its mother’s lap: ‘He kicks and strikes for joy ... / he climbs her ... / she drops her arm, and feeling the fruit of his lips, / tends him cunningly’ (37). Elsewhere town imagery appears, including during the World War II bombing of Swansea. In two other poems, brutal air attack is mingled with metaphysical implication: 'Under the wind and whine of bombs, / when the pavings flew up to the stars'; 'from a crippled engine's fall', 'who laid the mechanical trap? / till a bullet snaps the myth' – all poignantly taking place in 'a skipping-rope world of to-morrow's names and games' ('The Spoils of War', 121; 'Unveiling the Statue', 122). These are not fulsome, multi-detailed images. Rather they are quick glimpses of an evil in the sky the more menacing for not offering clearly knowable targets, and so seeming to emanate from a more universal wrong. Back on the ground is 'a lamp nightly lit / Till it burnt a hole in the shade.'

Some critics see all this differently. A common aim in Watkins criticism has been to show how his poetry moves from the world of nature to the ethereal or timeless world beyond it. Roland Mathias has described the position as clearly as anyone.[9] But some critics assert that in this process Watkins leaves nature behind too soon. He starts with it, but briefly, and immediacy and detail thereby suffer. John Barnie has criticised Watkins's *lack* of precision, as he sees it, with natural imagery, while a generation earlier, in a seminal and surely influential whole-page *TLS* review of the *Collected Poems*, Andrew Motion averred that Watkins's poems 'profess a love for life which is [not] substantiated by close looking'. Motion's example is equally important in accurately identifying what happens in a Watkins poem, while – as it seems to me – missing the point of his own observation: 'In "Poet and Goldsmith" [233] a bird (species not identified) is driven away from a promisingly naturalistic pose into a tree where it rapidly ceases to matter as a thing in itself.'[10] On the contrary, it now matters in itself doubly, that is to say, metaphysically as well as just physically. With a critic of different persuasion, 'promisingly' might have been 'excessively' or 'reductively'. What matters is that Watkins has already long made clear his central working principle:

'I marvel at the beauty of landscape, but I never think of it as a theme for poetry until I read metaphysical symbols behind what I see ... a poem that only reflects the natural world is an incomplete poem ... something must be added by the poem itself.'[11] Furthermore, with that somewhat sardonically bracketed 'species not identified' Motion may have taken a risk too many. Birds named in Watkins's poetry include the coot, peacock, swallow, dove, shag, heron, woodpecker, lyre-bird, raven, curlew, kestrel, crane, eagle, vulture, swan, wren, moorhen, kingfisher, razorbill, herring-gull, lark, ptarmigan, plover, grouse, cormorant, pewit, auk, blackbird, swift, hawk and finch. The first fifteen named are in the relevant poem's title, usually its main subject. 'Taliesin in Gower' (184) names nine birds, 'Ode to Swansea' (285) seven. But most are not described fully. Rather, a feature or two is accurately and vividly rendered, and that rendering itself then made allegoric of some transcendental form, or ultimate possibility.

Other critics take a more positive view. Philip Larkin wrote to Watkins in 1967 with considered praise. He said of the *Collected Poems*, 'I admire profoundly the incredible gloss you put on life ... for all their (to me) abstract quality your poems are full of concrete images, beautifully so. I wish I had your talent – I shouldn't use it in your way, but I wish I had it.'[12] From a largely secular town-and-countryscape poet like Larkin, that surely counts highly. Larkin's switch of poetic mentor in the early 1940s from Yeats to Hardy is well known; all the more notable, then, that he still recognised Watkins's different gifts so long afterwards. Rowan Williams has replied to those who hold that Watkins 'somehow empties out the specificity of the landscape or personality', by contending that it is 'impossible ... to think of [Watkins's Gower landscape and its details] as abstract'.[13] Elsewhere, Rowan Williams adds a point which may serve to clinch this natural-metaphysical link; this time, in reverse. Writing of the poem 'Good Friday' (271), Williams sees that dark day as holding 'the moment of total loss without which nothing can be said that has honesty', precisely *because* 'there can be no image-making in the face of God's death'.[14] That extreme moment reaches back into the happier implication of all the others. Watkins can only see through nature into the beyond by evoking what in the natural enables that more sublime contact.

Absence of narrative

The non-narrative aspect of Watkins's poetry has also been noted. But in this case it is more or less uncontentious. In the words of Watkins's widow, the writer Gwen Watkins, who presumably knows: 'narrative played no part in Vernon Watkins's life. He read no novels, thrillers or plays, and often failed to understand them when passages or chapters were read to him. Apart from Kierkegaard he read very little prose of any kind.'[15] Indeed, any disagreement over the issue is usually over whether it is a fortunate quality or a failing.

Clearly, this inward tendency might be to do with the poet's repeated affirmation – once he decided on it as a young man – that his poetry aspired to escape the bonds of time; or, better still, not to have emerged from a time-bound world in its conception at all, if such is possible. But that is to anticipate. What matters more is what follows; namely, that Watkins rarely if ever seems to attempt narrative and fail at it. Instead, topics which would stir the narrative impulse in many poets are treated by Watkins otherwise. At times, in fact, he will suddenly turn away from the narrative opportunity when a poem is already under way. In 'Ophelia' (114), addressed to Laertes's sister in *Hamlet*, 'passion recalls the tumult of your story, / Midnight revives it'; but the story is left untold, the poem evoking rather the 'mouse, bird and insect' who witnessed it and the flora and river-scenery surrounding. In 'The Smoke of Cities Passed' (315) we are told of an 'expected face' the poet had gone to

London to meet; but no one comes, for 'the power to reperceive [*sic*] was mine alone'. The event, then, was mystical or imaginary. The poem 'The Sunbather' (11) begins, 'Inert he lies on the saltgold sand'. Inert he remains.

The very greatest poets, Homer, Dante, Shakespeare, Milton, Wordsworth, have been great narrators. But this doesn't prevent others achieving stature by other means; for example, Horace, Emily Dickinson and Donne. But with those poets, narrative seldom appears as an option; the starting-points are elsewhere. With Watkins the narrative possibility is briefly allowed, only to vanish. One example stands out immediately. Strong narrative might have been expected from the major poem 'Yeats in Dublin' (59), where the poet recaptures his visit to W.B. Yeats in Dublin in 1938 with his own friend Francis Dufau-Labeyrie. Yet the very first lines of the poem find the pair already in Yeats's house: 'A rich lupin-garden, / A long, amber room, / A bronze head, bookshelves ...' The journey itself appears fleetingly and only symbolically: 'After the ten years' journey / ... I look him in the eyes.'[16] For this is a visit to Watkins's oracle, his very source, so whatever is remembered of Yeats is transmuted into Watkins's own patterns of rhythm, symbol and reference as though they had already originated there. The whole is part-reverie, part-discourse, an idealised one around the very heart of Yeats's poetics. Indeed, even the discourse is at times other-worldly, as though the words overtly coming from Yeats are really the two poets chanting in unison. Glimpses of event occur, but they are infrequent and tiny: 'My friend and I were silent ...', 'With visionary footsteps / Slow, he crossed the room ...', and so on. The end is ambivalent, as poetry so often must be, with living and dead, wave and sky, blind and seeing, age and youth, each circling the other; so the quotidian ending from Yeats himself, 'I am sorry you have come so far / For so little ...', seemingly bringing us back to earth, actually makes us realise what a flight we have experienced. The final couplet: 'the blue wave moves beneath me: / above, the white bird flies' is the only hint, ethereally presented as ever, of the journey home. It clinches the whole in the metaphysic Watkins always wants and needs.

The poem 'The Return' (236) has a more dramatic theme, that of the bombing of Swansea in World War II. The opening could be taken to offer a narrative account to come:

> I lay, pulse beating fast,
> While the night-raider passed
> And gave each hovering tick
> The speed of dream ...

But in the very next stanza, again a rhetorical question is the upshot:

> What life-uprooting year
> Sent him, an envoy, here
> To set two states at war?

– followed, seven stanzas later, at the close where the same question is generalised: 'Why let two states at war / Destroy the mind?' Again hints of action have intervened: 'Where wings had made / A single engine stop, two hearts afraid', with later the enemy aircraft's lights shining their 'converging, crossing beams'; but they remain undeveloped, as Watkins surely intended. For that is the problem, namely as to whether Watkins just can't manage what other poets might, or, as I prefer to think, he deliberately evokes touches of the horrid, messy world of war in order to move from them to something universal. If it is the latter, then the rhetorical questions in this case underline how war's havoc can block the eternal verities unless humans, and their spokespersons the poets, spell it out otherwise.

This whole issue is highlighted most clearly in some of Watkins's Christian poems, many of which are based on vivid biblical narratives. 'Good Friday' (271), already mentioned, is about one of the major human stories, yet the poem starts and ends quite elsewhere, for the reason Rowan Williams suggested. But Watkins's most intricate and complex attempt, perhaps not entirely successful but still a truly remarkable poem, was the 'Cantata for the Waking of Lazarus' (185). This most famous of biblical stories[17] appears in the gospel of John – no other gospel tells it – at great and sinuous length; forty-six biblical verses no less. Much of it is a kind of sublime dialogue, of anxiety and reassurance; Jesus speaks first to his doubting disciples and to Lazarus's distraught sisters, Mary and Martha. The poem is somewhat similar in that respect. Surprisingly, in part, it actually does narrate.

Yet this is an evocation; it chants the story, even somehow causes it, by the poem's awesome power of evocation. That effect is partly due to its extraordinary and unique rhyme scheme, which captures the stillness within which the miracle is achieved. But Watkins probably chose this subject for the story too, and then mainly avoids the narration the poem unusually risks, by giving two central stanzas to Jesus's own uplifting/uplifted words, making use of John's comparable, though rather different version. The first of these stanzas is the key one. It starts the first line, and ends the last, with a divine command, 'Lazarus dead, rise up'. Its rhyme scheme is best given in full, with its play on '-ing' rhymes interspersed with others: 'obeying, crown, delaying, renown, glory, light, story, raying, white, swaying, cup, playing, up'. The way the sequence 'glory, light, story' leads us to expect another '-ight' rhyme only to return to the '-ing', is just one of the surprises the scheme affords. The reader's resulting sense, I suggest, is that as there 'sang' a 'fountain' (as the opening line tells us), Lazarus is in effect frozen awake, until each huge stanza stirs the dead corpse into another tiny breath nearer life.

The poem's last fourteen lines are another evocation, this time a paean of praise, and not from Jesus but from the poet: 'Come, O Redeemer, come; come down, and make Earth new. / Love, newly born, come down: for you the fountain playing / Leaps into light, then spills, and fills the basin's brim .... ' That brief refrain 'come down' is strangely beautiful, as though a story is completed but of an ethereal kind. But in between this and Jesus's words has appeared the one piece of pure narration, as though the poet enters that world knowing he has sufficiently eluded time – his common aim – because the subject permits it. First is the short sentence 'That moment, Jesus wept.' That echoes the Bible's shortest verse out of hundreds of thousands, 'Jesus wept' (John 11.35). Then follows a brief but straight piece of accounting typically ordinary and secular:

> ... all the folk drew near ...
> For the young man came forth, and it was he they knew;
> And they drew back amazed; it shook their hearts with fear
> To see the young man walk. Then that white retinue
> Knew that their own last resurrection had come near.

Rarely did Watkins confront narration and yet so fully rise above it.

Some might feel it is too simple to see absence of narrative in Watkins's poetry as straight evidence of his early decision never to write poetry dominated by time. The crisis that brought on that commitment – a nervous breakdown when he was a young man – came when he had already written many poems, nearly all of which equally lacked any strain of narrative. But narrative is time-bound in its nature, and the two elements of narrative and time do square fairly exactly with each other.

The bardic tradition and rhyme

Watkins has also been accused of monotony and repetitiveness. And there is truth in the charges, in that a sameness hangs over the entire oeuvre, for Watkins chose his modes of lexicon and form early, and stuck to them. Nearly all his poems use regular rhyme schemes, and he strongly believed that poetry's value to civilization stemmed from the bardic tradition. This surely arose mainly from the influence of his major mentor, W.B. Yeats, who most valued the work of poets committed to 'certain heroic and religious truths, passed on from age to age, modified by individual genius, but never abandoned'.[18] Watkins was an overtly Christian poet; but even so, no poet is thereby excluded; it was merely that poets need the fullest engagement, however differently, with what religion also engages with. Rather, both these issues – rhyme and the bardic stance – suggest an outwardness of attention, verbally formal rather than colloquial, and humanly communal rather than individual.

But for some decades now poetry's prevailing tone in Britain has commonly been different. It often deals with the individual's small immediate experiences: the shifting voices, odd rooms and clothes and car journeys; domestic, schoolroom and office life; chance events, quiet disappointments, or moments of thankful relief. From Philip Larkin (after his early 'Yeats period') to Carol Ann Duffy, via such poets as Alan Brownjohn, Anthony Thwaite, Carol Rumens, Peter Porter, U.A. Fanthorpe, Andrew Motion, Simon Armitage and countless more, the palpable quotidian detail is there, however varied its ambience and treatment. Of course there are contrasting cases such as Elizabeth Jennings, Ted Hughes and Geoffrey Hill, and indeed in this present decade there has been some return to a more incantatory and symbolic mode. But even in the poets just named – apart from Jennings – the tangible qualities, however distant in their cases from normal experience, are seldom missing. The poets of religion and nature, such as R.S. Thomas and Seamus Heaney, equally give their messages via the earthly existence we do experience. So all this poetry's internal energies and rhythms are to do with the poet's own vulnerable psychology or that of his/her poem's characters. But there are the bigger topics too, of course: international headline news; major sexual experience; or the poet's long sojourns abroad. Such varied concerns can yield as many incidents as a free society's activities give rise to; and each poem is one more breath of millions in a society's lifetime.

An unremittingly rhymed poetry might then seem likely to stifle this plurality, and the bardic vocation of highlighting long-established verities could equally chill out anything much new at the level of meaning. Indeed, we have earlier remarked that, while psychological nuance is not absent from Watkins's poetry, he certainly fell back, in poem after poem, on the rhetorical imperative and the rhetorical question: 'Not yet! Do not yet touch ...'; 'Go to that place where men can look no more ...'; 'O, have you seen the leper healed ...?'; 'What branches rouse above his head? What noise of wind and sea?'; scarcely a poem in the entire oeuvre lacks one or other of them. These two very public modes often seem the metaphysical poet's necessary recourse, if they usually prefer not to voice the endless hesitations, protests, melancholies or bits of fun and joke to which most poets of today's world instinctively turn. But debate about that is not our aim here.[19] The aim here, given Watkins's poetry as it stands and its broadly bardic aspirations, is rather to seek to identify aspects of the poetic richness achieved. Apart from the quite massive lexicon – consider, for example, just 'Sea-Music for My Sister Travelling' (68) alone – there are three areas worth looking at. These are the huge variety of rhyme schemes employed (Watkins rarely used exactly the same form twice); great play with the individual single word, and commonly the monosyllable; and, rather differently, Watkins's varied allusiveness to poets of the past, both distant and more recent. This last may be the true key to his authenticity as member of the bardic tradition.

Rhyme-scheme variety in Watkins goes along with variety of line-length, stanza-length and poem-length too.

There are the long twisting lines – 'Late I return, O violent, colossal, reverberant, eavesdropping sea' ('Taliesin in Gower', 184); 'Then I enter the steep prison-walls of salmon-circled Carmarthen' ('Money for the Market', 104); but there is also the straight pentameter and the six-foot line in the six-line stanza:

> Strange, that in all we make
> A solemn purpose can,
> More than most things, break,
> While some lesser plan
> By accident will wake
> The deepest roots in man.
>
> ('Rebirth', 365)

The short-stanza rhyming could hardly be more varied. The six-line form evinces *ababab* as in the verse just quoted; *abcbdb* as in 'Yeats in Dublin' itself; *ababcc* ('Poets, in Whom Truth Lives', 223) and that reversed to *aabcbc*, as in 'Trust Darkness' (235); *aabccb* ('Unity of the Stream', 374); *abcbac* ('The Scythe', 226) and others. *Ababab* appears in the four-foot line too, as in 'Touch With Your Fingers' (257) and elsewhere. Five-line stanzas give us *ababb* ('Earth and Fire', 339); *ababa* ('For a Christening', 261); and a curious variant in 'The Beaver' (389) where the first two lines are *aa*, followed by alternatives, *bcd*, *bbb* or *bcb*, in different stanzas. Seven-liners have *abacbcc* ('Digging the Past', 381) and *abcacbc* ('Belief and Praise', 376) while eight-liners use the quatrain doubled: *ababcdcd* ('The Spring', 227), as also in the magnificent 'Camelot' (249) with its exact rhythm of the Christmas carol, 'Good King Wenceslas', 'Bread and the Stars' (258) has the same but with the second 'b' going to line eight: *abacdcdb*. Very long stanzas have increasingly unique rhyme schemes, as in the Lazarus poem discussed above, and 'Sardine-Fishers at Daybreak' (111), much admired by Watkins enthusiasts. There the first stanza goes *ababcbcbddeeffgg* but the second is *abbacddceffeeghhg*, with only the third 'e' breaking an otherwise standard 'xyyx' pattern. After shorter stanzas there comes *abbbabccddcceecffa*.

Such heavy and indigestible analysis could go on forever; but what is the significance? In the space available here we can only generalise. What today's more typical poet hears as the question 'What am I trying to say?' the bardic poet senses as 'What is able to be said?'[20] In practice, and with of course varying refinements, Watkins might light on a tried or untried rhyme scheme, mentally tie it to an emerging lexicon he found himself with, and then seek intuitively what could be done with that rhyme-lexicon combination. The metaphysical chance would beckon hard. That sounds a touch formulaic no doubt, but a much-practised poet would move fluently in such waters. Extended examples of this would be ideal here; we can only name a few prototypes: 'Prime Colours' (6), 'Yeats' Tower' (13), 'Bread and the Stars' (258) and 'Unity of the Stream' (374). These and other poems seek to work first from a set of gathering, half-conscious poetic notions, and hold them steady with just one or two firm physical entities – colours, tower, bread, stars, stream – in order to find 'what can be said' (or sung, or chanted) in some nevertheless still more ethereal universe. It all implies, as Yeats suggested, that there are deeper truths available within the culture's bones, and maybe beyond them, which the poet's task is latently to embody by whatever linguistic forms can achieve that end. Such was Watkins's lifetime aim too.

Along with rhyme variation, Watkins has an intriguing way with individual words along a thin but remarkable vein of selection. His use of monosyllabic words, in work marked by immense lexicon and a reputation for the arcane and abstruse, would need a separate study of its own. We can only point to some random examples. For example, the monosyllabic line. The heavily polysyllabic opening of 'Taliesin in Gower' (184) already cited – 'Late I return, O violent, colossal, reverberant, eavesdropping sea' – is strongly contrasted by what follows. There is that stanza's closing line, 'I have been taught the script of the stones', and the opening lines of later stanzas: 'Yet now my task is to weigh the rocks on the level wings of a bird'; 'Now let the great rock turn. I am safe with an ear of corn.' All these seem to bring intermediate lucidities, as indeed do many of the poem's shorter phrases, 'a life locked fast in the cliff', 'but first I must cut the wood'. It is as though, by virtue of the monosyllabic words, Taliesin's mythical actions are rendered defiantly present, easily accepted by the reader, so that the metaphysical setting can work its own deeper meanings via longer terms elsewhere: 'in a hundred dramatic shapes I perish', 'these holy creatures proclaim their regenerate joys', 'every boulder is hung on a breath's miraculous birth'. Numerous other poems are strong on monosyllable, giving Watkins's oft-criticised opacity a reassuring guarantee of underlying clarity.

Watkins also has a way of suddenly injecting a single but sharply profiled mundane term into an otherwise ethereally evoked scene. 'Let him look softly, with some seventh sense' ('The Lady with the Unicorn', 150). Seventh? In 'The Feather' (120) come these lines:

> The perfect into night must fly;
> On this the winds agree.
> How could a blind rock satisfy
> The hungers of the sea?

Perfection in night flying, and the sea's hungers, get a down-to-earth jolt with the winds 'agreeing'; it gives some measure of hope – to doubting readers – that Watkins's feet are nearer the ground than often seems the case. 'Dust drops from campions where the hedge is hottest' ('Music of Colours: Dragonfoil and the Furnace of Colours', 322); with that 'hottest' the sun's symbolism switches briefly to what we feel on our necks in high August. Sometimes the mundane term is dynamic, active. 'Thought into shape I shove', in a poem on poetics ('A Prayer against Time', 21). 'The act itself is prayer, deliberate in its speed' ('The Interval', 277); speed is rarely a feature of the prayerful attitude. 'Dive, then: receive/This water with our prayer': diving in Watkins is usually done by gulls and cormorants, but this poem is about a christening ('For a Christening', 261), and the priest touching the child with the sign of water is granted a curiously athletic power. Yet the same drops of water are 'stunned'; perhaps here time is stilled, even materially, for eternity to enter. And finally here: 'that tall ship / ... / Built out of light, whose faith his hands equip' ('Sonnet: Infant Noah', 33). Faith equipped, as with tools or camping gear; that goes back to St Paul, yet here feels strange and new.

In short, Vernon Watkins's body of work is not so monotonous and repetitive as might appear when we first encounter it. His capacity for variation can be found everywhere. There are, for example, the powerful, and commonly monosyllabic, k-rhymes (a technique incidentally much used by Wordsworth), notably 'Yeats in Dublin' with its ten clear groups of k-rhymes occurring in its seventy-odd stanzas. The poem 'Niobe' (165) begins sombrely, 'If we shall live, it must be from this rock / The stream shall break', but in 'Yeats in Dublin' (59) we suddenly find ' ... Blake / And Burns had a public style; / But others found a fake' – a different register altogether. The monosyllabic k-rhyme seems to come to Watkins very naturally. Then there are the curious contrasts, 'you are my nearmost, you who have travelled the farthest' ('Taliesin and The Spring of Vision', 224); 'Who touches one dead blossom touches every star' ('Music of Colours: The Blossom Scattered', 162). There is also the single-term synecdoche, where key terms are repeatedly used in place of the larger unit they belong to. Leaves, thread, wave, bird, jet and grief stand in respectively for trees, cloth, the sea, water empowered wherever, and all that is tragic more widely. Why so often 'leaves' (not twigs or buds) and 'thread' (not cloth)? It is because each term accrues a symbolic meaning which survives its many contingent occasions.

Finally for this section, the bardic poet not only hallows

the poetic past but alludes to it. In Watkins this applies to poets of the distant and more recent past, as for example classical drama and epic: George Herbert and John Donne; Tennyson and Arnold; W.B. Yeats of course; major Europeans of the past such as the Germans Friedrich Hölderlin and Heinrich Heine; and the Welsh tradition. Watkins was not a speaker or writer of Welsh, but was well versed from childhood in the *Mabinogion*, in translations of the early poets Aneirin and Taliesin, and in the englynion poems about Llywarch Hen, as his own poetry of course indicates.[21] The question is how far such voices remain mere derivation, and how far they are truly absorbed. Vernon Watkins listened to his poetic forbears from instinct and belief alike; and this was no young man's sycophancy, for it never stopped. From 'Yeats' Tower' (13) and 'In Memory of Elizabeth Corbet Yeats' (34) in his earliest collection through to 'The Breaking of the Wave' (483), the very last poem in the *Collected Poems*, it is seldom far away. A late collection, *Affinities* (1962), makes an overt theme of the matter. Again this absorption's variety of mode and method is great, further suggesting its depth in the poet's apprehensions.

Sometimes an ode is written to one poet but its mode is that of another. 'The Exacting Ghost' (237) is an elegy for Dylan Thomas, yet the model is clearly Tennyson's 'In Memoriam AHH'. Here is Tennyson ('In Memoriam', 42, 85):

> I vex my heart with fancies dim:
> He still outstript me in the race;
> It was but unity of place
> That made me dream I rank'd with him ...
>
> Whatever way my days decline,
> I felt and feel, tho' left alone,
> His being working in mine own,
> The footsteps of his life in mine ...

And here Watkins:

> By the new year you set great store.
> The leaves have turned, and some are shed.
> A sacred, moving metaphor
> Is living in my mind, though dead.
>
> I would have counted good years more,
> But all is changed: your life has set.
> I praise that living metaphor
> And when I sleep I see it yet ...

While Tennyson's renowned *abba* rhyme scheme is now *abab*, the tone of bemused grief trying to make sense of itself is remarkably similar. Yet the poem is Watkins's own, for he sharpens Tennyson's fear of forgetting his friend into pain at seeing him the more vividly in dreams at night.

And Tennyson's tone pervades Watkins's entire poem. But in other examples a single word or short phrase reveals who is in mind. Watkins's line 'first each drop, then all the sphere' ('For a Christening', 261) is a clear echo of Donne, despite that the 'sphere' is here a drop of baptismal water; such is echo's occasional indirection. In 'Westminster Bridge' (128), a sonnet very different from Wordsworth's, the word 'garment' recalls Wordsworth's line 'This City now doth, like a garment, wear ...' Watkins's term for clothing is usually 'thread', as noted above; but not here. In 'Apple-Tree' (407) 'their juice, their joy' comes straight from Hopkins's poem 'Spring': 'What is all this juice and all this joy?' Early in 'The Keen Shy Flame' (22) the word 'mummy-cloth', from Yeats's 'Byzantium', was surely brought to mind by both of Yeats's Byzantium poems with their burnished effect and flame-and-fire imagery.

Sometimes one particular feature of an earlier poet's work is adopted. Not surprisingly, Yeats is object of at least a dozen poems, but Watkins's 'A Prayer' (171) and 'The Precision of the Wheel' (275) are both clearly modelled on Yeats's 'A Prayer for my Daughter' in their carefully arranged procedures and their wishes for the children addressed. 'I pray that he may have / Recourse in argument ...'; 'May you be given / Peace ....' Elsewhere, a group of poets, or other body of cognate work, seems to have saturated the poet's consciousness. The long poem 'Sea-Music for My Sister Travelling' (68) seems broadly mindful of such works as *The Tempest*, *Moby Dick* and to an extent Eliot's 'Dry Salvages' from *Four Quartets*. Rather differently, Matthew Arnold's 'The Forsaken Merman' is surely behind 'The Ballad of the Mermaid of Zennor' (296). In Watkins's poems the sea's huge and pitiless power is a single opposition to the usual metaphysical concerns. Then there are the seventeenth-century metaphysical poets, whom Watkins admired deeply all his life. Thomas Traherne and Henry Vaughan figure briefly[22] but Donne and Herbert are a main source. Much might be said of them all, but specially notable is perhaps Watkins's apparent use of Herbert's title form '*The*-plus-noun'. Watkins has 'The Eastern Window' (36), 'The Burial' (132), 'The Sinner' (140), 'The Return' (236), 'The Interval' (277) and many others. Herbert's 'The Pulley' and 'The Collar' are his best known, but others abound: 'The Dawning', 'The Elixir', 'The Flower', 'The Size' and 'The Sinner' too. In such titles the mix of common, abstract or metaphorical nouns may mean that for both poets a poem was a special kind of *object*, mirroring creation itself and then granting that creator homage.

Watkins addresses, alludes to or otherwise makes hoveringly present many more poets, including Shakespeare, Milton, Shelley, Blake, Keats, Wilfred Owen and Edward Thomas. Is it mere derivation or further homage; something too-easily copied or something deeply internalised? Occasionally there is a ventriloquism, but usually Watkins's fundamental concerns prevent this safely enough. Each reader must decide, but I have two comments. One is that the problems posed by Watkins's variety have long been noted by readers.[23] We must simply judge each poem as it comes and know the entire oeuvre enough to make this reliable. The other point is that some poems are so unmistakably Watkins's own. Without defending the choice here we could cite 'Two Decisions' (19), 'Music of Colours: White Blossom' (101), 'The Heron' (176) and 'A Prayer against Time' (21). Surely we are grateful for these.

This section has necessarily entailed a scatter-shot process of many close-up cases; I can only invite the reader to pursue further any of them which seem appealing or promising. Vernon Watkins once wrote, in an oft-quoted couplet from 'The Precision of the Wheel' (275), that

> There is, within our lives,
> An exact mystery

– and it is what his poetry strove to express, despite the forbidding mode which, quite understandably, for many readers blocks the route to their grasping it.

The metaphysical

All these features we have just pointed to are more or less local, and therefore identifiable easily enough. But a poet's stance toward reality in general is less readily focused upon by using just close-up cases. It is more difficult still when – as so often with Watkins – the 'reality' is elusive even to those who acknowledge it, which many in a secular world do not. This aspect of the matter, then, is complex, as may soon appear.

Watkins is usually called a 'metaphysical' poet and he saw himself as such.[24] As previously mentioned, he valued highly the metaphysical poets of the seventeenth century, John Donne, George Herbert, Henry Vaughan and Thomas Traherne – all of whom notably were Welsh, of border country background or provenance, or both. But a leading authority on that group and its contemporaries, Barbara Lewalski, seems to have found the term 'metaphysical' in their context no longer necessary.[25] Thirty years earlier this would have been critically unthinkable. But Lewalski retains the liveliest sense of these poets' grasp of things palpable in the spiritual realm; whether or not metaphysical, they are firmly religious. The Bible stories and Christian festivals; the elements of church and sacramental life in bread and wine, stained glass, robes and music; the portrayal of heaven itself, whether angels, paradisic gardens or the throne of the almighty. In this respect it is poets like George Herbert, and in our era R.S. Thomas, who have attracted greater attention. But those two were priests, inhabiting that tangible world of the church daily. Dictionaries tend to see 'metaphysical' as far less concrete. 'Metaphysical' for them pertains to the visionary or spiritual, or a philosophical stance toward knowing and being. Vernon Watkins held tight to the natural world as I have tried to show, and he wrote much specifically Christian, in fact biblical, poetry; but the latter is not where he characteristically pursues the metaphysical search, although there are some cases as we shall suggest.

It seems rather that his metaphysical-as-elusive theme ties to a belief that our world and universe are secondary to a more fundamental existence elsewhere. It matches William Blake's belief mentioned earlier,[26] but it also underlines Watkins's own declared parallel statement, also cited above, as to what that infers for his own poetic practice: 'I marvel at the beauty of landscape, but I never think of it as a theme for poetry until I read metaphysical symbols behind what I see .... '[27] But there is a further feature. Watkins thought of his poems as themselves originating, perhaps pre-existing, in such a further world. It was his task to identify their delivery. He seldom speaks of anything as overt as 'automatic writing' or 'divine dictation' – granted at times to Yeats and Blake[28] – but it isn't always far off. Early in adult life his poems 'were dictated, or partly dictated, to him – by what or whom, he did not know, and did not try to find out'. There was indeed the poem's own 'need to be written. Like Michelangelo's statues, the poem had always been there: it needed to be chiselled out, and the muse and the poet were both necessary to this'; 'poetry's deepest utterances are given rather than claimed ... a poet cannot choose his subject matter, it is given completely and unpredictably, and [the poet] must do his best to get it right.'[29] Watkins's poems, then, sought the exactness of phrase which would reach toward the mystery they could never fully express; but the poetry's quality lies in that act of reaching-out.

An obvious case, partly because the poem is much admired, is 'Music of Colours: White Blossom' (101). The theme is whiteness itself, a prototype for the elusive metaphysical entity in that white is all colours and none; and pure whiteness, Plato-wise, isn't tied finally to any one locus of its earthly existence. The poem starts with those earth-bound cases, the apple-blossom and the snow which makes yesterday's white waves on the shore now seem a dirty grey. But the inference follows: 'Call nothing white again, we were deceived ...', and the poet can then only repeat the single term, white, white, white – twenty-eight times in the poem's forty-six lines – as items of physical nature or earth-bound myth are tried out one by one to evoke the unattainable. To convey the effect, we too need to cite most of them:

> White blossom, white, white shell; the Nazarene
> Walking in the ear; white touched by souls
> Who know the music by which white is seen,
> Blinding white, from strings and aureoles,
> Until that is not white, seen at the two poles,
> Nor white the Scythian hills, nor Marlowe's queen ...
>
> White must die black, to be born white again
> From the womb of sounds, the inscrutable grain,
> From the crushed, dark fibre, breaking in pain ...
>
> ... Where they alight in air, are white asleep.

They will not break, not break, until you say
White is not white again, nor may may ...

If there is white, or has been white, it must have been
When His eyes looked down and made the leper clean ...

Lovers speak of Venus, and the white doves,
Jubilant, the white girl, myth's whiteness, Jove's,
Of Leda, the swan, whitest of his loves ...

In the churchyard the yew is neither green nor black.
I know nothing of earth or colour until I know I lack
Original white, by which the ravishing bird looks wan.
The mound of dust is nearer, white of mute dust that dies
In the soundfall's great light, the music in the eyes,
Transfiguring whiteness into shadows gone,
Utterly secret. I know you, black swan.

The final short sentence is a masterstroke, citing as it surely does Karl Popper's famous illustration of scientific falsifiability. Popper argued that an assertion like 'all swans are white' remained scientifically true until somebody just once saw a black one.[30] The swan illustration became philosophical currency. In Watkins's poem it thus links logical reflection with wider meanings. 'I know you, black swan' could be defiant, the swan breaking the rules of both nature and virtue (white as pure, black as evil) with the poet resisting that. But equally it might pick up the 'know' (twice) in the stanza's second line. There it is failure to know, 'I know nothing ...', this poem's marvellous whiteness being in a realm beyond human understanding. So the final short sentence would then come to mean 'I see you, black swan, but no more than that.' Either way, the poem shows the metaphysical as good, infinite, beyond us; but at least the reader is taken to its boundaries.

After such an extraordinary poetic tour-de-force, further cases may look likely to promise little. But a very different poem appears only two pages after this one in the *Collected*

Poems; namely 'Returning to Goleufryn' (103). Perhaps Watkins's 'Fern Hill', the poem evokes the house near Carmarthen where his uncle James lived (not 'grandfather', as the poem has it but which the rhythm requires). But the tone is very different from that of 'Music of Colours: White Blossom'. Detail after detail is shiningly offered, 'Gooseberries and currants are gay / With tranquil, unsettled light'; 'Gold butter is shining, the tablecloth speckled with crumbs, / The kettle throbs.' Yet this real house and garden is recalled as perfect, it becomes a transfiguration of itself by virtue of the intervening exultings. 'Sing, little house, clap hands: shut, like a book of the Psalms ...,' 'I shall not unnumber one soul I have stood with and known / To regain your stars struck by horses, your sons of God breaking in song.' How far we are ourselves thus taken forward into the realms the poet seeks, lies with the individual reader; but there is little doubt of Watkins's intention and, I would say, his success in rendering it.

Biblical stories, if surprisingly, sometimes get metaphysical treatment despite that this eschews the palpable, as we have suggested. Two such poems, 'Zacchaeus in the Leaves' (143) and 'The Song of the Good Samaritan' (146), follow each other in the *Collected Poems* and both work on the same principle. In each case a mass of palpable detail is evoked only then to be stripped away, leaving a now etherealised human entity holding the sanctified centre field. In the first poem it is the tree which Zacchaeus climbed in order to see Christ as he passed by underneath. Thick-coiled leaves, branches, light, sap, hollowed-out wood, seeds, nesting-birds and their wings and claws, and the trunk itself are all cited. But the poet builds all this up simply to remove it, clearing space in which Christ becomes transcendently visible: 'Known, unknown, / Where seen, unseen, / Were one alone; / Jesus passing / The Nazarene.' In the Samaritan poem it is even more pronounced. Virtually everything in nature, eternity, the pagan world, symbol, life-forms, stars and gold, all seem to surround the Good Samaritan's great act of love. In the final stanza it is left uncompromisingly, and 'the mocked, unpremeditated bowl of the hand / Makes the world nothing, pouring in oil and wine.' It returns us to the start, where the Samaritan evinces the eternal ones who 'heal the Earth with silent tumult of love'. In 'Good Friday' (271) the details of that day are touched in more softly, for the inference aspired to is only that this day supersede all others in our apprehension:

> Day must die here that day may break.
> Time must forsake
> Time, and this moment be preferred
> To any copy, light or word.

Two other topics remain to touch on here; that of space, and that of poems on poetry itself. As said throughout already, the time and out-of-time theme is consistent across Watkins's work. So it might make us ask about its concomitant, space. If the metaphysical aspires to some eternal world, it must presumably seek to probe the boundaries of our time-space existence inseparably. Yet Watkins's solid renderings of the Gower landscape, its geology, birds and fish, trees leaning over rushing streams, sea coast and real or mythical human activity in that terrain (climbers, sunbathers and others), surely cut out any resolution never to write a poem dominated by space; there is just no suggestion of it. But again, space is the home of the palpable. Space has to be overcome by taking it on its own terms, but with those then transposed from self-sufficient matter into symbol of what is beyond matter. Finally, we should at least mention Watkins's various poems on poetry itself, or art generally: 'A Prayer Against Time' (21), 'Art and the Ravens' (182), 'Demands of the Poet' and 'Demands of the Muse' (both 281), 'Ode to Nijinsky' (289) and others. If, as Victor de Waal has suggested,[31] the arts are 'sacred in character', then there could be a connection (sometimes insightful, sometimes confusing) between the aesthetic and the metaphysical as areas of human endeavour which aspire, in one way or another, beyond the earthly human condition. But the topic is a vast one, and we might best leave it with some of Watkins's own typically lucid adages: 'Art is miraculous ... The raison d'etre of a poet is not to be competent but to perform wonders ... The power to contract is the means of praise most compelling ... A poem is not true because it is beautiful, it is beautiful because it is true.'[32]

*

I hope these examples have given some idea of how Watkins moves from something sensed in this world – a rock, a tree, a pattern of music – to the metaphysical evocations he seeks. But if for some readers they have not, it might at least give rise to a final question, both for this section and for all that has been said earlier. Reading the entire *Collected Poems* as I have this year, it increasingly seemed to me that any reader of it may gradually find, not that they have to make a choice, but that their own dispositions toward life in general may mean the choice has already long been made. I mean of course the choice of whether they already possess or reject the sense of the metaphysical which Watkins's poetry usually requires. I mean, even (though am less sure of this), that there may not be many 'conversions'; it may be very hard for anyone to come to cherish this poetry without that metaphysical orientation. That is certainly not meant to sound pessimistic or discouraging; anyone can try, and much might happen. But it is different with other religious poets such as Herbert, Milton, Eliot or R.S. Thomas. Many secular and sceptical readers find those poets most rewarding, for their approachable speech-voices, sense of daily human existence, homely or communal imagery and so forth. By contrast, Watkins's firm stance, toward his own poetic aims and the provenance of poetry generally, leaves readers needing qualifications before they begin. So if any claim is to be made for Watkins's greatness, then those who quite understandably doubt it may be doing so at a level somewhat beyond poetry itself.

Or so it may seem. Is Watkins a great poet, as some have contended? Even to his supporters, an air of strange unreality occasionally hangs over the whole body of work, and loyalty can be strained. Yes, but he continued to make unassailable signs, strongly and boldly, of lasting nature and beyond, for anyone prepared to live with them, and in a visionless and material world which has all but trampled such things out of existence. This has become rare, and the supposed unreality suddenly feels like something most precious. Actually the devotee can perhaps hope too that Watkins's doubters may take away at least something from his work; his dedication, his near-perfect lyrical ear, his masterly control of a wide vocabulary, and from these, in James Davies's words, his 'constant ability to create lines of great beauty'.[33] The same critic, not always one of Watkins's greatest supporters, also concludes where we began; that 'Watkins, undeservedly, has become a marginal figure within the Anglo-Welsh canon.'[34]

NOTES

1 M. Wynn Thomas, '"Fidelities where beams together run": Vernon Watkins and Henry Vaughan', *Scintilla* 11 (2007), pp. 169–84; Rowan Williams, 'Swansea's Other Poet: Vernon Watkins and the Threshold between Worlds', *Welsh Writing in English*, 8 (2003), pp. 107–20; *Vernon Watkins: New Selected Poems*, ed. with Introduction by Richard Ramsbotham; Foreword by Rowan Williams (Manchester: Carcanet, 2006).

2 *Poetry Wales* 31, 3 (1996), p. 48; Richard Ramsbotham, p. xi. Watkins rarely appears in the journal *Welsh Writing* in English or its successor *Almanac*, in either critical articles or the annual critical bibliography; a scan shows much the same with Wales's other literary magazines. In the last decade three collections of critical essays have appeared from the University of Wales Press: *Dangerous Diversity: The Changing Faces of Wales* (1998) edited by Katie Gramich and Andrew Hiscock; *Seeing Wales Whole: Essays on the Literature of Wales* (1998) edited by Sam Adams; and *Beyond the Difference: Welsh Literature in Comparative*

Contexts (2004) edited by Alyce von Rothkirch and Daniel Williams. Two of these have no Watkins index entry; *Seeing Wales Whole* has no index but a scan of text and footnotes reveals the poet again scarcely mentioned. A decade earlier appeared *Wales: The Imagined Nation: Essays in Cultural and National Identity*, edited by Tony Curtis (Poetry Wales Press, 1986), with just three index references to Watkins. In the text they all prove to be one-phrase comments.

3 Others of the modern era, as different from Watkins as from each other, have taken Watkins's attitude to time. The Russian Orthodox Christian philosopher Nicolas Berdyaev (1874–1948) wrote that 'I have ... above all, never been able to acquiesce in the ephemeral, perishable achievements of time, in all that lives but for an instant, ... I could never be reconciled to the fact that time is in a perpetual flux and that each moment is devoured by, and vanishes into, the preceding one.' The painter Ben Nicholson (1894–1982) once described himself in his abstract period as 'outside place, outside time and outside generation-idea'. Nicolas Berdyaev, *Dream and Reality: an Essay in Autobiography*, trans. by Katharine Lampert (London: Geoffrey Bles, 1950), p. 29; Virginia Button, *Ben Nicholson* (London: Tate Publishing, 2007), p. 33.

4 *London Magazine*, 1, 11 (1962), p. 43.

5 Throughout this article, the number after a poem's title gives the page where the poem referred to in the text appears in Vernon Watkins's *Collected Poems* (Ipswich: Golgonooza Press, 1986).

6 William Blake, *Complete Writings*, ed. by Geoffrey Keynes (Oxford: Oxford University Press, 1966), 'Jerusalem' f.77. But, in support of our argument here, Watkins would have strongly refuted Blake's contention that 'I do not behold the outward Creation ... to me it is hindrance & not Action; it is as the Dirt upon my feet.' William Blake, *Complete Writings*, p. 617; cited in David Jasper, *Coleridge as Poet and Religious Thinker* (London: Macmillan, 1985), p. 14.

7 Roland Mathias, *Vernon Watkins* (Cardiff: University of Wales Press on behalf of the Welsh Arts Council, 1974), p. 68.

8 James A. Davies, 'Dylan Thomas and His Welsh Contemporaries' in *A Guide to Welsh Literature VII: Welsh Writing in English* (2003), p. 147.

9 Roland Mathias, pp. 67–70.

10 John Barnie, review of *New Selected Poems* (op. cit.) in *Poetry*

Wales, 44, 3 (2008); Andrew Motion, review of *Collected Poems* in the *TLS*, 3 July 1987.

11 Cited in Ramsbotham, pp. xix–xx from a private MS.

12 *Selected Letters of Philip Larkin* 1940–1985, ed. by Anthony Thwaite (London: Faber and Faber, 1992), p. 392.

13 Ramsbotham, p. ix.

14 Rowan Williams, 'Foreword' in Ramsbotham, p. 1x; Rowan Williams, pp. 112–13.

15 Personal note from Gwen Watkins to myself. I am most grateful to Gwen Watkins for much information she has given me with her husband's work, as well as her encouragement in writing this article, and her unceasing wider friendship.

16 In fact Francis Dufau-Labeyrie wrote an account of the journey and visit in down-to-earth (but vivid and interesting) prose nearly forty years later. Francis Dufau-Labeyrie, 'Notes in memory of the Dublin Visit', *Poetry Wales*, 12, 4 (Spring 1977) (special issue on Vernon Watkins), pp. 78–83.

17 London football club Queens Park Rangers once had a come-back victory in which their late winning goal was scored by Mike Lazarus. Current football commentators still use the phrase 'back from the dead' in such context.

18 Kathleen Raine, *Defending Ancient Springs* (Ipswich: Golgonooza, 1985), p. 18. In the relevant chapter in her book, 'Vernon Watkins and the Bardic tradition', Raine herself summed up the issue with – apart from the final sentence here quoted, her own judgement – firm neutrality. 'The evocation of the "other" mind [the metaphysical mind] by incantatory rhythms is as old as mankind; and whatever the reason may be, the gift of lyrical and incantatory speech seems at all times to accompany "inspired" utterance and to be the natural gift of those who know how to tap the springs ... Vernon Watkins has this gift to a marked degree.' Raine, p. 23.

19 A debate which in the present context could start by comparing Andrew Motion's *TLS* review of the *Collected Poems* with Kathleen Raine's chapter on Watkins in her book *Defending Ancient Springs*. See notes 10 and 17.

20 A contrast to compare with Watkins's contention that any poem worth writing 'comes out of exaltation, or moves towards it'. *London Magazine*, p. 43.

21 Roland Mathias, pp. 97–9.

22 For example, Henry Vaughan's theme of darkness-as-

benevolent seems present in 'Five Poems of Magdalenian Darkness' (326).

23 At a Gregynog Conference on Welsh Writing in English held in 1994, Antony Conran remarked in a post-lecture discussion that 'the critical problem with Watkins is how to know which are the good poems and which are not ... Is this a (very) good poem or possibly a (very) bad one?' (quoted from present writer's personal note). Watkins himself has written a curiously intriguing piece of critical advice: 'When you find you are writing well, stop writing ... When you are writing badly, go on, and stick to your theme' (*Poetry Wales*, 12, 4, p. 55).

24 See *New Welsh Review* 13, 11 (Autumn 2000), p. 13.

25 Barbara Lewalski, *Protestant Poetics and the Seventeenth Century Religious Lyric* (Princeton: Princeton University Press, 1979).

26 See above, note 6.

27 See above, note 11.

28 The phrase 'automatic writing' is usually associated with William Blake and W.B. Yeats. In 1803 Blake told Thomas Butts that 'I have written this Poem from immediate Dictation ... without Premeditation & even against my Will ... all produc'd without Labour or Study ... I dare not pretend to be other than the Secretary; the Authors are in Eternity.' It was Yeats's wife, Georgie Hyde-Lees, who used this practice. Yeats himself came to reject automatic writing entirely, but some poems, including late ones, probably still stemmed from his wife's work. S. Foster Damon, *A Blake Dictionary* (London: Thames & Hudson, 1973), pp. 275–6; Richard Ellmann, *The Identity of Yeats* (London: Faber and Faber, 1954) pp. 149, 151, 163, 283.

29 Gwen Watkins, 'A Poet in Miniature', *New Welsh Review*, 13, 11, pp. 11-14. The first quotation is Gwen Watkins's commentary, the second is the poet's own words.

30 Karl Popper, *The Logic of Scientific Discovery* (London: Hutchinson, 1959), pp. 93–4.

31 Sermon at the Thomas Traherne Association annual weekend, Weobley, Herefordshire in June 1990 (quoted from present writer's personal note).

32 For the first, Ramsbotham, p. 102; for the rest, Gwen Watkins, *New Welsh Review*.

33 Davies, pp. 147–8; 152.

34 Davies, pp. 147.

Vernon Watkins, Dylan Thomas and the Poetry of Lorca

Gwynne Edwards
Emeritus Professor, University of Aberystwyth

There can be no doubt that the Swansea poet, Vernon Watkins, knew and admired the poetry of the great Spanish poet and playwright, Federico García Lorca. Although Lorca died in 1936, murdered by Nationalists in the first months of the Spanish Civil War, many of his poems were quickly translated into English and would have become known to Watkins in the late 1930s. Watkins was in any case a linguist who possessed a very good knowledge of French and German and who, as his widow, Gwen Watkins, has informed me, had no problem in understanding Spanish, which meant that he could read Lorca's work in its original form.[1] In 1936 a visit to Spain resulted in a mixture of prose pieces and poems, with titles such as 'Street in Seville' and 'Cadiz Bay', in which Watkins recorded his impressions of the south.[2] There is no mention of Lorca in this miscellany, but, given the fact that he was by far the most famous writer in Spain at this time, it is inconceivable that Watkins would not have come into contact with his work.

Seven years later, in 1944, Watkins addressed the English Club at Oxford University and, after his talk, distributed books to members of his audience. A few weeks later, Philip Larkin, one of the recipients, made it his business to return the books and later recalled the incident:

> I gave him his books back ... Then he showed me others: the American anthology of the work of Dylan Thomas called *The World I Breathe*, and some translations of Lorca. When it was time for me to go for my train, he pressed the latter on me, and while we were waiting on the station he reclaimed it for an impromptu reading. 'At five in the afternoon! At five in the afternoon!' he chanted, while a huge engine drew hissingly past.[3]

'At five in the afternoon' is the repeated refrain in Lorca's poem of 1935, 'Lament for Ignacio Sánchez Mejías' ('Llanto por Ignacio Sánchez Mejías'). Which book of English translations of Lorca's poems, then, did Watkins press into Larkin's hands?

In 1937, just one year after Lorca's death and two years after his composition of this poem, *Lament for the Death of a Bullfighter and Other Poems*, in translations by A. L. Lloyd, was published in London, the 'Lament' accompanied by five poems from Lorca's *Gypsy Ballads* (*Romancero gitano*, 1928). In 1939, *Poems by F. García Lorca, with English translation by Stephen Spender and J. L. Gili*, also published in London, contained twenty-nine individual poems, a further two from Lorca's *Poet in New York* (*Poeta en Nueva York*, 1929–30), and seven poetic passages from the plays *Mariana Pineda* (1925), *When Five Years Pass* (*Así que pasen cinco años*, 1931), *Blood Wedding* (*Bodas de sangre*, 1933) and *Yerma* (1934). And in 1943, *Selected Poems of Federico García Lorca*, again published in London, contained twenty-three of the items translated by Spender and Gili which had appeared in the earlier volume.[4] All three collections, we should note, contained the Spanish text alongside the English translation. By this time a number of translations of the poems had also been published in the USA, but available evidence suggests that Watkins was familiar with those published in London.

His familiarity with A. L. Lloyd's translation of 'Lament for the Death of a Bullfighter' is proven by the fact that he referred to it specifically in an unpublished talk entitled 'Poetry in Translation': 'A. L. Lloyd's translation of Lorca's "Lament" is wonderful, not because it is near to the music of the Spanish, which it is not, but because it has all the qualities of a great original poem.'[5] He then proceeded to read to his audience forty-four lines from the poem, all evidence of his admiration for it. As for the Spender/Gili translations, both the 1939 and 1943 editions contained 'Lament', two highly dramatic passages from *Blood Wedding*, a play which Gwen Watkins says that Vernon greatly admired, and the great poem from *Gypsy Ballads*, 'Somnambular Ballad' ('Romance sonámbulo'), which, rather curiously, Spender and Gili entitled 'Somnambule Ballad'. But, more importantly, this collection contains two poems of which Vernon Watkins produced his own translations: 'Ballad of the Little Square' ('Balada de la placeta') from *Book of Poems* (*Libro de poemas*, 1921) and 'Song of the Dark Doves' ('Casida de las palomas oscuras') from the later *Diván of the Tamarit* (*Diván del Tamarit*, 1936), which Spender and Gili entitled 'Song'. Despite their presence in the volume, it is quite possible, of course, that Watkins translated them directly from the original Spanish, though, as we have seen, this was also set alongside the English translation in the Spender/Gili collection. But what exactly was it that attracted Watkins to Lorca's work and led him to translate the two poems in question?

Lorca and Watkins seem to have had much in common, not least the emotional trauma which they experienced during their late teens and early twenties. The Granada in which Lorca grew up was a narrow-minded, strongly Catholic city in which, already aware of his homosexual orientation, he felt both a deep anxiety and a strong sense of being an outsider. Watkins's psychological problems, though different from Lorca's, had even more serious consequences, for fundamental changes in his personal life – from happy final years at Repton Public School to failure to complete his studies at the University of Oxford and a subsequent period of unfulfilling employment as a junior bank clerk in Cardiff – led to severe depression which saw him placed in a nursing institution at the age of twenty-one. Consequently, for both young men, the sense of lost youth became something central to their experience: in Lorca's case, a feeling of childhood innocence gone forever; in that of Watkins, an awareness of happy years at Repton now vanished, as Roland Mathias has noted: 'Whatever academic advantages he had obtained from the School, the vision he carried away was in no sense academic – it was a vision of eternal, unscarred youth.'

While the biographical element underpins the work of both writers in the sense that they lament lost childhood or youth, the more important points of contact are, of course, those that link them as poets. At the age of twenty-one Lorca became a student at the prestigious Residencia de Estudiantes in Madrid, where he was exposed to the avant-garde movements – Cubism, Dadaism, Futurism and the like, and their Spanish counterparts of *creacionismo* and *ultraísmo* – which were then changing the European artistic landscape. Their effect, even though Lorca refused to subscribe to any particular school, was to bring about a rejection of the melancholy, rather Romantic self-absorption evident in his earliest poems in favour of a much sparer and simpler style of poetic expression. But if he was strongly influenced by modern movements in the arts, he also drew his inspiration both from older contemporary Spanish poets, such as Antonio Machado (1975–1939), and from the great Spanish poets of the sixteenth and seventeenth centuries, such as Lope de Vega and Luis de Góngora, in all of whose work popular tradition in the form of ballads and songs figured prominently.[7] In this respect, Lorca and Watkins embraced both Modernism and popular forms in their work – for Watkins too wrote many ballads. Again, both men belonged to the bardic tradition in the sense that they read their work, as well as that of others, to a live audience, even if Lorca's exuberant, declamatory performances were very different from Watkins's stiffer manner. And they were poets too who were deeply concerned with all the various elements – imagery, rhythm, sound, rhyme – which constitute the craft of poetry.

As well as this, and more significantly, Lorca and Watkins sought in their work to transform personal experience into something more universal. After recovering from his nervous breakdown, Watkins succeeded in overcoming what he perceived as temporal chaos in his life by seeking to see the trials and tribulations of daily existence as merely moments in a timeless succession of such experiences, as a pattern which is eternal. In his poetry, he therefore sought to express the here and now of our lives as metaphors for a reality beyond the given moment. He himself observed: 'I could never write a poem dominated by time', an approach emphasised by M. Wynn Thomas: 'Vernon Watkins' vocation as a poet is to anticipate in imagination the restoration of all things that will occur at the end of time ... but he will never be reconciled or subdued to the flux of the temporal order.'[8]

This aspect of Watkins's thinking and writing, reinforcing his studies of French and German at Repton and Oxford, drew him naturally to European poetry, and in particular to Symbolism. He had a sound knowledge of the German poets Hölderlin, Heine and Rilke, as well as of the French poets Baudelaire, Rimbaud, Valéry and Laforgue. And he believed too that by translating such poets – he produced nearly two hundred translations in his lifetime – he not only strengthened his own use of symbolism but also connected directly with mainstream European culture, as the following translation of lines from a poem by Hofmansthal suggests:

> I can never cast off from my eyelids
> Lassitudes of long-forgotten peoples,
> Nor from my astonished soul can banish
> Soundless falls of stars through outer distance.
>
> Many destinies with mine are woven;
> Living plays them all through one another,
> And my part is larger than this slender
> Life's ascending flow or narrow lyre.[9]

When, furthermore, Watkins's own poetry was inspired by a Welsh background, as in, 'The Ballad of the Mari Lwyd', 'Returning to Goleufryn' or 'Ballad of the Equinox', the traditional story or the particular place was also invested with a symbolic and archetypal significance:

Pwlldu – an eternal place!
The black stream under the stones
Carries the bones of the dead.[10]

As in the case of the translation of Hofmansthal's poem, Watkins connects his poetics with the European mainstream.

Lorca's poetry and plays place a similar emphasis on the archetypal. In describing *Gypsy Ballads*, for example, he insisted that, despite the implications of the title, the true protagonist of the collection is Anguish, which may be seen as his own anguish, but is also, beyond that, the anguish of Andalusia through its history and the anguish of all persecuted and marginalised human beings.[12] Similarly, in *Poet in New York*, the denunciation of the bankers' exploitation of the poor and the underprivileged may be Lorca's protest, but through the poetic voice of the poems it also becomes the protest of all just and fair-minded men against the abuse of the unfortunate throughout the civilised world. And if we consider the plays, the action of *Blood Wedding*, *Yerma* and *The House of Bernarda Alba* (*La casa de Bernarda Alba*, 1936) may be located in rural Andalusia, but the characters have generic names – the Bride, the Bridegroom, the Mother, the Father, Male, Female – while physical objects have a symbolic resonance – a horse, a knife, a house – and the unseen powers of fate and death hover over the lives of individuals.

In the case of the early *Book of Poems*, consider the opening lines of the poem entitled 'Countryside' ('Campo'):

The sky is made of ash.
The trees are white,
And the burnt fields
Are blackened embers.
The wound in the West
Is dried blood,
And the faded paper
Of the mountains has been crumpled.[12]

The landscape reflects the poet's individual solitude and sadness, but that landscape is also universal and the poet's solitude is also ours, as in the landscape poems of Verlaine. In short, in the poetry of Lorca and Watkins, the voice of the man becomes the voice of the poet, the seer and the visionary who speaks universal truths.

Watkins produced two versions of Lorca's 'Ballad of the Little Square', the first described as 'translated from Lorca', the second as 'adapted from Lorca'. Of the translation there are four identical versions, one handwritten, the other three typed, all four undated. In each case the paper is yellowing and stained by damp, which may suggest a fairly early date. As for the adaptation, there are three identical versions, again undated, but the much better condition of the paper points to a rather later date, as does the fact that this is an adaptation, which is likely to have been attempted after the translation. At all events, the following is Watkins's translation:

The children sing
In the quiet night.
Clear spring!
Serene fountain!

The Children:
Your divine heart,
What does it seek?

I
A tolling of bells
Lost in the mist.

The Children:
You leave us singing
In the little square.
Clear spring.
Serene fountain!
What do you hold in your hands,
What gift of Spring?

I
A rose of blood
And a Madonna lily.

The Children:
Refresh them in the water
Of the antique song.
Clear spring,
Serene fountain!
What do you feel in your mouth,
Red and thirsting?

I
The savour of the bones
Of my great skull.

The Children:
Drink the peaceful water
Of the antique song.
Clear spring,
Serene fountain!
Why do you go so far
From the little square?

I
I go in search of wise men
And of princesses.

The Children:
Who was it taught you
The path of the poets?

I
The fountain and the water
Of the antique song.

The Children:
Do you go far, very far

From the sea and the earth?

I

It has filled with lights
My heart of silk.
With sound of lost bells,
With lilies and bees.
And I shall go very far,
Far beyond those mountains,
Beyond the seas,
Close to the stars,
To beseech Christ
The Lord to restore to me
My ancient soul of a child,
With the feathered cap
And the sword of wood.

The Children:
Already you leave us singing
In the little square.
Clear spring,
Serene fountain!

The enormous pupils
Of the shrivelled foliage
Bruised by the wind
Weep for the dead leaves.[13]

From a biographical point of view, 'Ballad of the Little Square' springs from Lorca's sense of lost childhood innocence and has a clear basis in reality. The little square of the poem is precisely the kind of square in which he had played as a child in the rural villages of Fuente Vaqueros and Asquerosa, before the family move to Granada when he was eleven years old. Similarly, the game of question and answer in which the 'I' of the poem participates with the children is the kind of game in which, as a child, Lorca would also have taken part. But, this said, 'Ballad of the Little Square' is much more than that. The 'I' of the poem may be Lorca in one sense, but in another is the voice of the poet, or the poetic persona who experiences and expresses that inevitable and difficult transition from childhood to adulthood which is common to us all. The poem therefore works on two levels, of which the deeper, symbolic level is the more important. In this regard, the poem's game of question and answer is scarcely the innocent game which children would play in reality, for the voice which answers their questions speaks only of frightening truths which lie ahead: death – 'The savour of the bones / Of my great skull' – and the futile attempt to cling to childhood – 'My ancient soul of a child / With the feathered cap / And the sword of wood.' In this respect, G. G. Brown has observed of the slightly later collection called *Songs* (1921–24) what is also true of *Book of Poems*: '[They] reveal that Lorca's interest in the folklore of childhood, and in the kind of response children make to verse and song, is an adult and sophisticated one ... It is far from his purpose to reproduce naïve songs of innocence. Themes of frustration, loss and death throw dark shadows over the playfulness of the poems.'[14]

At the same time, a rather different interpretation has been suggested by Gareth Walters. Denying that Lorca's poetry in general can be read 'as a more or less direct reflection of life at a given moment', Walters argues that the poetry of *Book of Poems* and *Songs* should be seen more as an example of Lorca's poetic development, of a sense of 'onwardness', in the context of which 'Ballad of the Little Square' is 'representative of a kind of poetry that Lorca was to cultivate extensively over the next few years. This is readily definable in purely formal terms: highly stylized, frequently symmetrical structures that make generous use of frames and refrains, sparse in manner and often aping folk-song.'[15] Given that the often traumatic events and anguished emotions of Lorca's life are the undoubted spring-board for his poetry and his plays, the suggestion that particular collections of his poems are merely stages in the development of his art rather than meaningful reflections on human experience is clearly untenable. Indeed, if this deeper significance did not exist, Vernon Watkins would hardly have responded to Lorca's poetry in the way that he did.

Watkins may have reacted initially to 'Ballad of the Little Square' in relation to the theme of lost youth, for the grief associated with his departure from Repton School and the friends he had made there – the 'tribe' alluded to in the following poem – continued to haunt him for many years:

> I chose this path, the rock which no man loves
> Familiar to birds, cast by a barren sea.
> Cold on this ridge among the breeding winds,
> Starved in the famine forced by Adam's rib,
> Here I hold my breath, knowing the door of my friends
> Is rock, and I am exiled from their tribe (*CP* 32)

On the other hand, Watkins would also have seen much more in Lorca's poem, for, as we have seen, it contains those eternal themes which lie at the heart of Watkins's own poetry, and the notion of the poet voicing the difficulties which confront us during the journey through life would have greatly appealed to him. In addition, he would have been attracted by Lorca's expression of such issues in the traditional form of the ballad, which Watkins himself used in 'The Ballad of the Mari Lwyd' and the collection *The Death Bell: Poems and Ballads*, in which there are eight ballads, most containing the dialogue between individuals of which Lorca was so fond. And, as well as this, there was the question of the poet's craft, to which both Lorca and Watkins attached such importance.

Lorca's poem consists of lines of seven and sometimes five syllables, and each alternate line, beginning with the second, ends in a word in which, as in the traditional Spanish ballad, the stress falls on the penultimate vowel, which, together with the final unstressed vowel, is the same throughout:

Cantan los niños
en la noche quieta:
¡arroyo claro,
fuente serena! (*OC* 134)

Assonance is a typical Spanish pattern which is not rhyme but which is a kind of equivalent of rhyme whose effect is to create a smooth continuity through the length of the poem. On this particular point Watkins noted in one of his talks on poetry in translation that 'Spanish translates superbly into English, but it is superbly unlike Spanish. For Spanish lyric poetry is full of assonances which cannot be translated.'[16] Consequently, Watkins's translation of 'Ballad of the Little Square' does not attempt to echo the pattern of Lorca's line endings, nor does it employ rhyme as a substitute. But otherwise the translation remains faithful to the Spanish poem, recreating its sprightly rhythm and retaining its meaningful images. Indeed, Watkins's observation on the duty of the poet/translator in general is clearly true of the skill with which he transposed Lorca's poem into English: 'For the first condition of a translation by a poet is that it should read like an original poem. In this sense translation is a creative art like the art of poetry.'[16]

Watkins's adaptation of 'Ballad of the Little Square' differs from the translation of the poem in that the ending of certain lines is changed in order to create a rhyming effect. 'In the quiet night' becomes 'In the night's no-sound'; 'In the little square' 'In the white stone pound'; 'Refresh them in the water / Of the antique song' 'Dip them in the flowing / Of old-lip sound.' There are other changes too, including some alteration of word order. In this respect, the adaptation is more removed from the simple directness of Lorca's original, but Watkins was evidently experimenting and attempting to create a poem which could be 'read like an original poem.' In doing so, he was also connecting, as mentioned earlier, with the broader European poetic tradition through the work of a poet he greatly admired.

The second poem translated by Watkins was, as we have seen, Lorca's 'Casida de las palomas oscuras', which he entitled 'Song of the Dark Doves'. It comes from the collection of late poems, the *Diván del Tamarit*, the word 'diván' deriving from a Persian word meaning a collection of poems, while 'Tamarit' was the name of a house outside Granada which belonged to one of Lorca's uncles. A great admirer of Granada's Arabic heritage, from the beautiful and intricate architecture and decoration of the Alhambra palaces to the many Arabic buildings in the neighbouring Albaicín, Lorca was also, as Andrew Anderson has observed, 'well acquainted with classical Arabic verse and its verse-forms a number of years before he actually decided to use its vocabulary in the context of his own writing'.[18] The poems contained in the *Diván* bear the titles of two kinds of poem written by the classical Arabic poets: the *gacela* and the *casida* (or *qasida*). The *gacela* was a short composition ranging in length from four to fifteen lines and was often of an amorous or erotic nature. The *casida* had a minimum length of thirty lines and was also a poem about love: a lament, the recollection of love, a search for the beloved, a final elegy. But, for all Lorca's love of things Arabic, it would be wrong to assume that in the *Diván* he closely modelled the poems on Arabic verse, for, as Anderson notes, there is no evidence that he was 'attempting to emulate and incorporate the Arabic themes and style in his *Diván* poems'.[19] Indeed, the theme of death, which is central to Lorca's *casida,* was a rare subject in Arabic poetry. In the collection, his intention was not to produce a conscious imitation of classical Arabic verse but to pay homage to it, and the themes and motifs of his poems are again those which we have seen to be the preoccupations of his work in general. Jeremy C. Foster has stated the matter concisely: 'The nine qasidas lay increasing emphasis on the metaphysical problems of life's mystery and death.'[20]

Watkins produced four typed copies of his translation of

Lorca's poem. Three are undated and the fourth has the year 1966 written in ink at the end of the poem. All four copies are identical and may have been typed out over a number of years, though there is no proof of this. As for his source, he may have consulted the Spender/Gili translations of 1939 and 1943, but, as indicated previously, he may also have translated directly from the Spanish original. That the former is a strong possibility is suggested by the fact that, in the fourth line from the end of the poem, Watkins changed Lorca's line 'Through the branches of laurel' to 'Through the branches of cherry', which is to be found in the Spender/Gili version. At all events, this is Watkins's translation:

Through the branches of laurel
Go darkling doves two.
The one was the sun,
The other the moon.
Little neighbours, I said to them,
Where is my tomb?
In my tail, said the sun,
In my throat, said the moon.
And I who was walking
With the earth at my girdle,
Saw two eagles of marble
And a stark naked girl.
The one was the other
And the girl was not either.
Little eagles, I said to them,
Where is my tomb?
In my tail, said the sun,
In my throat, said the moon.
Through the branches of cherry
Two doves I saw like her,
The one was the other
And the two were not either.[21]

From a biographical point of view, the poems in the *Diván del Tamarit* can be seen in the context of Lorca's emotional life in the years immediately preceding. In 1929 he suffered a serious depression, the result in part of the breakdown of relationships with Salvador Dalí and a young Madrid sculptor, Emilio Aladrén, the first possibly homosexual, the second definitely so. The depression led to Lorca leaving Spain for New York, where his anguish expressed itself in the poems of *Poet in New York* and in the violent sexual images of the cinematic *Trip to the Moon*.[22] After his return to Spain in 1930, he completed *The Public* (*El público*), his only overtly homosexual play, which again reveals deep feelings of anguish, and in the following year *When Five Years Pass*, much concerned with the themes of lost childhood, passing time and the horror of death. Indeed, death seems to have been a major preoccupation throughout Lorca's adult life. It led him on numerous occasions to enact his own death and decomposition in the presence of his friends, and to state unequivocally that 'A dead man in Spain is more alive ... than anywhere else in the world.'[23] Lorca's depressions were also quite frequent, even if on other occasions he could be the life and soul of the party. It is hardly surprising, then, that his view of the world should have frequently been pessimistic.

In this particular sense, the speaker in 'Casida' who puts his question to the doves and the eagles can be seen to be Lorca himself. But, beyond that, he is also, of course, the everyman who travels the road of life in search of where his end might be, but receives only ambiguous answers. The frustration experienced by the traveller is also to do with love, for the doves which are traditionally the symbols of love are not white but dark and are soon transformed into the altogether more menacing form of the eagles. In short, the speaker of the poem finds the world around him to be disconcerting and enigmatic and, as the voice who speaks to all of us, suggests that man is lost in a world which has no answers to his questions.

As in the case of 'Ballad of the Little Square', it is likely to have been the metaphysical implications of Lorca's 'Casida' which attracted Watkins to the poem. Like Lorca, he had struggled to find meaning in the chaos of life, and even if he had survived his early traumatic experience in a way that Lorca did not, the realisation that life was indeed mysterious and often baffling remained with him and formed an essential theme in his own poetry. He himself observed: 'I am concerned with paradoxical truths, and my poems are addressed to those who underestimate the subtlety of life and death.'[24] Lorca's 'Casida' matches in every respect Watkins's metaphysical concerns.

Watkins's translation is very fine. Lorca's original poem has the kind of assonance which we have already encountered in 'Ballad of the Little Square', but on this occasion in a 'u' 'a' pattern:

> Por las ramas del laurel
> vi dos palomas osc<u>u</u>r<u>a</u>s.
> La una era el sol,
> la otra la l<u>u</u>n<u>a</u>.

Watkins did not attempt to replicate assonance but introduced instead a number of rhymes or approximations to rhyme: 'moon', 'tomb', 'girdle', 'marble', 'other', 'either', all of which create a pleasing musical effect and also tie individual lines to each other. As far as poetic craft is concerned, Watkins produced a translation which does, as he observed, read 'like an original poem'. Furthermore, here, as in 'Ballad of the Little Square', he identified in thought and spirit with the work of another poet: 'The translator who is a poet is concerned with the whole orbit of the poet's thought during the period of composition; the written text is the track of a secret and more elaborate movement to which he alone, through the affinity of mind, has the key.'[24] It was an affinity which, in the case of the two Lorca translations, placed a Welsh poet in the context of the European cultural tradition and also, in the case of the 'Song of the Two Dark Doves', in the context of Arabic poetry.

Another interesting aspect of Vernon Watkins's engagement with Lorca's poetry is that he shared his knowledge of it with Dylan Thomas. In her account of her husband's friendship with Thomas, Gwen Watkins has noted that Vernon 'loved French and German poetry, and could repeat much by heart. Dylan would listen with interest to his readings of Rilke, Lorca, and other foreign poets.'[26] And she goes on to specify that Watkins introduced Dylan Thomas to Spanish poetry in the summer of 1938: '"I went over to Bishopston," he wrote to Francis [Dufau-Labeyrie] in September, "taking with me Lorca and a book of Welsh translations from Taliesin ... We read a lot of Lorca, which is grand – I found I knew about half of it by heart."'[27] In 1938 the only translations of Lorca published in Great Britain were, as we have seen, those by A. L. Lloyd. Thomas could therefore have become acquainted with 'Lament for the Death of a Bullfighter', given Watkins's admiration for it, as well as with the other poems in the volume: 'The Faithless Wife', 'Preciosa and the Wind', 'The Ballad of the Spanish Civil Guard', 'The Arrest of Antoñito el Camborio', and 'The Martyrdom of Saint Eulalia'. Indeed, a letter written to Rayner Heppenstall on 2 November 1939, points to Thomas's familiarity with 'Lament':

> If to undergo contemporary reality to its most extreme is to join in a war – the evil of which is the war itself – ... then one can only say flippantly that the best poems about death were always written when the poets were alive, that Lorca didn't have to be gored before writing a bullsong ...[28]

Moreover, it is also evident from a letter of 1941, that Thomas knew A. L. Lloyd personally (*CL* 544).

After 1939, Watkins could also have read to Thomas any of the thirty-eight poems and poetic passages from the Spender/Gili volume – Thomas knew Spender quite well – including 'Ballad of the Little Square' and 'Song', even if by that time he had not produced his own translations of them, and also, perhaps, 'Somnambule Ballad', one of Lorca's greatest poems. Furthermore, Gwen Watkins has said that, in addition, Vernon Watkins read to Thomas poems in Spanish, followed by his own on-the-spot translation of them, which means that he could have acquainted Thomas with poems which did not appear in any volume of translations.[29]

There are various other pointers to Thomas's familiarity with Lorca. In 1944, the leftist journal, *Our Time*, published his poem 'Ceremony After a Fire Raid' in a May Day supplement dedicated to the memory of Lorca, and in a letter to Watkins dated 27 July of that year he noted: 'Here is a poem ["Ceremony"] which perhaps you haven't seen. I didn't print the Lorca lines above the poem' (*CL* 580). Again, Thomas would have been further acquainted with Lorca's poetry as a result of his friendship with the South African poet, Roy Campbell. During the Second World War, when Thomas often worked in London for the BBC, Campbell was both one of his drinking partners and his radio producer. He possessed an extremely good knowledge of Spain as well as a deep love of Lorca's poetry, and in 1952 he saw the publication of *Lorca: An Appreciation of His Poetry*, a detailed study in which he included, as examples, his own translations both of complete poems and of parts of poems, together with poetic passages from Lorca's plays.[30] The date of publication preceded Thomas's death by only one year, which suggests that Thomas, frequently on visits to the USA, may not have had time to absorb Campbell's book, but this does not exclude the probability that he and Campbell discussed Lorca well before this. Indeed, he evidently discussed the Spanish poet to the very end, for George Tremlett has drawn attention to the following event which occurred on the eve of Thomas's death:

> [John] CuRoi said that he had met Dylan Thomas previously [that evening], accompanied by their mutual friend the sculptor Dave Slivka when they had talked at length of the Spanish poet Lorca. That was in the White Horse Tavern ...[31]

In short, Thomas's acquaintance with Lorca's work extended over a period of fifteen years.

Like Lorca and Watkins, Lorca and Thomas had much in common. Both were performers, entertaining whatever group they happened to be in with their brilliant conversation and anecdotes. Both were also highly accomplished public performers of their own poetry, as well as of their prose and dramatic works. Lorca, prior to the first performances of his plays, read them to his friends, playing all the parts himself, while in New York in 1953, Thomas gave a solo performance of *Under Milk Wood.* Both men were consummate craftsmen as far as the poetic art was concerned, and both coincided in their emphasis on the themes of childhood, passing time and death. Lorca's lines from 'Ballad of the Little Square' – 'My ancient soul of a child / With the feathered cap / And the sword of wood' – evoke childhood games as do the following from 'Fern Hill' – 'And honoured among wagons I was prince of the apple towns ... And green and golden I was huntsman and herdsman.'[32] As for passing time, Friend's anguished cry in Lorca's *When Five Years Pass* – 'I've no time. No time for anything. Everything's rushing by' (*OC* II: 338) – is no less chilling than Thomas's lines in 'The force that through the green fuse' – 'The lips of time leech to the fountain head: / ... And I am dumb to tell a weather's wind / How time has ticked a heaven round the stars' (*SP* 19). And on the theme of death, Lorca's memorable lines from 'Lament for the Death of a Bullfighter' – 'But now he sleeps endlessly. / Now mosses and grass / Are opening with sure fingers / The flower of the skull' (*OC* I: 621) – is as unsettling as those from Thomas's 'Poem on his Birthday' – 'Under and round him go / Flounders, gulls, on their cold dying trails, / Doing what they are told, / Curlews aloud in the congered waves / Work at their ways to death' (*SP* 106). Many more examples of these coincidences of theme occur in the work of both writers.

In this respect, Robert Havard has compared Lorca's

'Somnabular Ballad', which Vernon Watkins must have read to Thomas, with 'Fern Hill' in terms of both poets' use of the colour green.[33] Havard notes that in Lorca's poem green occurs on twenty-four occasions and on seven in Thomas's poem. In the opening lines of 'Somnambular Ballad' a young woman dreams about her absent lover and the colour green suggests youth and fertility:

> Green how I want you green.
> Green wind, green branches ... (*OC* I: 420)

The positive implications of green are, however, soon set alongside their negative counterpart, for, in Havard's words, 'there is a warning in the cold silver of her eyes that this [the positive aspect of youth and fertility] is only an illusion'.[34] And by the end of the poem, when the young man of her dreams attempts to seek her out, only to discover that she has drowned herself, green is associated with bitterness and, in Lorca's metaphorical language, 'with the traditional symbolism of the green citrus fruits'.[35]

With regard to 'Fern Hill', Havard points out that, as in Lorca's poem, green is suggestive of youth and vitality:

> Now as I was young and easy under the apple boughs
> About the lilting house and happy as the grass was green ...
> (*SP* 87)

The mood continues through much of the poem as the poet recalls the games he once played on the farm when he was 'green and carefree, famous among the barns' (*SP* 87). But by the end of the poem, as in 'Somnambular Ballad', green has acquired more ominous associations, for the child, happy in his games, is oblivious to the fact that the joy and innocence of childhood will inevitably yield to disillusionment and death:

> Oh, as I was young and easy in the mercy of his means,
> Time held me green and dying
> Though I sang in my chains like the sea. (*SP* 89)

Havard does not, however, suggest that 'Somnambular Ballad' had a specific and direct influence on 'Fern Hill'. Indeed, as others have pointed out, Thomas's immediate sources are to be found in English writers, and Thomas himself, in a letter to Oscar Williams in July 1945, when he was in the process of writing the poem, stated the following: 'I've been reading all [D.H.] Lawrence's poems ... and liking them more & more. Do you remember:– "O the green glimmer of apples in the orchard ..."' (*CL* 622). William T. Moynihan has observed that the influences on Thomas's poetry included the Bible, Shakespeare, Marlowe, Blake, Poe, Keats, Yeats, Eliot, Auden, Lawrence, Hopkins, Housman and Hardy.[36] And John Ackerman, suggesting that 'contemporary Anglo-Welsh writing generally has been influenced by religious poets of the seventeenth century', picks out John Donne, George Herbert, Henry Vaughan and Thomas Traherne, citing the following from Traherne's *Centuries of Meditation* as a specific source of inspiration for 'Fern Hill': 'I saw all in the peace of Eden: Heaven and Earth did sing my Creator's praises, and could not make more melody to Adam than to me. All Time was Eternity and a perpetual Sabbath.'[37]

Bearing all this in mind, but acknowledging too that Vernon Watkins familiarized Thomas with Lorca's work, and that Thomas himself discussed it with others, the most likely conclusion is that, although the Spanish poet's influence on him was more general than it was in the case of Watkins, it was nevertheless real enough.

In this context, Tony Conran has noted that 'Dylan Thomas is a modernist in the symbolist tradition. That is, he looks to an international horizon ...'[38] And Vernon Watkins has drawn an illuminating comparison between the nature of his own poetry and that of Thomas: 'His poems spoke to me with the voice of metaphysical truth; if we disagreed, it was on a metaphysical issue, for natural observation in poetry meant nothing to us without the support of metaphysical truth.'[39] In short, much of what has here been said about the poetry of Lorca and Watkins can also be said about that of Lorca and Thomas in relation to the aims and objectives of their poetry. Thomas would clearly have responded to the universal and archetypal resonance of Lorca's work as Watkins read it to him and as Thomas discussed it with Watkins and others. Both poets drew upon particular incidents and personal experiences but then transformed them into something of wider and greater significance. So, in Lorca's highly poetic play, *Blood Wedding*, Beggar Woman describes the deaths of two young men in the following way:

> They'll be here soon: two rushing streams
> Still at last among the great stones.

And the wife of one of the men continues:

> Their eyes broken flowers, and their teeth
> Two fistfuls of frozen snow (*OC* II: 470)

Throughout the play Lorca's metaphors place human beings in the context of the natural world and within a process – running water, growing and dying vegetation, changing seasons – that is continuous and timeless. Of Thomas's 'Poem on his Birthday' – see the lines quoted earlier – John Ackerman has noted that, although the poem was initially inspired by the poet's observation from his window of the estuary at Laugharne and its birdlife, he saw the particular scene and day as 'a "sandgrain" beside the total immensity of time, and the world ... as a graveyard in which everything living moves toward death'.[40] In addition, Ackerman has drawn attention to the 'many similarities, both in theme and expression, between 'Poem on his Birthday' and some of the poems in Vernon Watkins's *The Lady with the Unicorn*'.[41] All three poets, then, shared common ideas, themes and a desire in their work to see the particular in terms of the archetypal and the timeless.

In conclusion, it is fair to say that the relationship between them was somewhat varied. Vernon Watkins knew

Lorca's work at first hand, identified with his view of the world as expressed in his poetry, translated two of his poems and thereby entered into the Spanish poet's thinking. Thomas, given his lack of any foreign language, became familiar with Lorca's poetry through Watkins's discussions and readings of it, as well as, no doubt, through the English translations which he could read for himself and his discussions with other people. He was doubtless impressed by it, but, because he was inevitably at a stage further removed from it than was Watkins, its influence on his own work is likely to have been more general than precise. Even so, all three individuals shared a common interest in the symbolist tradition in poetry and made a similar leap in their work from the particular to the universal and the timeless. In doing so, Watkins and Thomas were able to relate the Welsh character of their poetry, Lorca the Spanish character of his, to a broader and more resonant European poetic tradition.

NOTES

1 Gwen Watkins kindly provided me with this information in a recent telephone conversation.

2 These unpublished items may be found in the National Library of Wales, Aberystwyth, under 'Vernon Watkins: Prose and Verse 1936'.

3 Philip Larkin, *Required Writing*: *Miscellaneous Pieces 1955–1982* (London: Faber and Faber, 1983), p. 41.

4 See Federico García Lorca, *Lament for the Death of a Bullfighter and Other Poems in the Original Spanish,* with English translation by A. L. Lloyd (London and Toronto: William Heinemann Ltd., 1937); *Poems, F. García Lorca*, with English translations by Stephen Spender and J. L. Gili (London: Dolphin, 1939); *Selected Poems of Federico García Lorca*, translated by J. L. Gili and Stephen Spender (London: Hogarth Press, 1943).

5 See 'Poetry in Translation' in 'Vernon Watkins: Talks and Lectures 1947–1967', a collection of unpublished material held in the archive of the National Library of Wales.

6 See Roland Mathias, *Vernon Watkins* (Cardiff: University of

Wales Press, 1974), p. 19.

7 Gareth Walters, *'Canciones' and the Early Poetry of Lorca* (Cardiff: University of Wales Press, 2002), pp. 63–4.

8 See *Vernon Watkins 1906–1967*, ed. Leslie Norris (London: Faber and Faber, 1970), p. 83; M. Wynn Thomas, *Internal Differences: Twentieth-Century Writing in Wales* (Cardiff: University of Wales Press, 1992), p. 34.

9 See Ian Hilton, 'Vernon Watkins as Translator', in *Vernon Watkins 1906–1967*.

10 *The Collected Poems of Vernon Watkins* (Ipswich: Golgonooza Press, 1986), p. 189.

11 See Lorca's lecture 'On the Gypsy Ballads', in *Federico García Lorca: Deep Song and Other Prose*, ed. and trans. Christopher Maurer (London and Boston: Marion Boyars, 1980), p. 105.

12 For the Spanish original, see Federico García Lorca, *Obras completas*, ed. Miguel García Posada, 3 vols. (Barcelona, Valencia: Galaxia Gutenberg, Círculo de Lectores, 1996), I, p. 146. Unless stated otherwise, all the translations into English are my own.

13 The translation and adaptation are to be found in 'Verse Translations 1930s–1966. Autograph and typescript drafts of verse translations by Vernon Watkins from Italian and Spanish', located in the archive of the National Library of Wales, Aberystwyth. For Lorca's original poem, see *Obras completas*, I, pp. 134–36.

14 G. G. Brown, *A Literary History of Spain. The Twentieth Century* (London: Ernest Benn Ltd., 1972), p. 86.

15 Gareth Walters, *'Canciones' and the Early Poetry of Lorca*, pp. 78–96.

16 See 'Poetry in Translation' in 'Vernon Watkins, Talks and Lectures 1947–1967'.

17 Vernon Watkins, *Selected Verse Translations, with an Essay on the Translation of Poetry*, introduced by Michael Hamburger, ed. Ruth Pryor (London: Enitharmon Press, 1977), p. 16.

18 For the Arabic background, see Andrew Anderson, *Lorca's Late Poetry* (Leeds: Francis Cairns, 1990), pp. 17–28.

19 *Lorca's Late Poetry*, p. 24.

20 Jeremy C.Foster, 'A Prodigy of Passion: Lorca's Last Book of Verse', *Queen's Quarterly* 73:2 (1966), p. 25.

21 For Watkins's translation, see 'Verse Translations

1930s–1966'. For Lorca's original poem, see *Obras completas,* I, p. 606.
22 See *Poet in New York*, ed. Christopher Maurer, trans. Greg Simon and Stephen F. White (London: Penguin, 1988); *Trip to the Moon. A Filmscript*, trans. Bernice C. Duncan (Norfolk, Connecticut: New Directions, 1964).
23 In Lorca's lecture, 'Juego y teoría del duende', *Obras completas*, III, p. 156.
24 See Vernon Watkins, *New Selected Poems*, ed. and introduced by Richard Ramsbotham (Manchester: Carcanet, 2006), p. xviii.
25 In Vernon Watkins, *Selected Verse Translations*, p. 15.
26 Gwen Watkins, *Dylan Thomas. Portrait of a Friend* (Talybont: Y Lolfa, 2005), p. 33.
27 Gwen Watkins, ibid., pp. 69–70.
28 See Dylan Thomas, *The Collected Letters*, ed. Paul Ferris (London: Dent, 2000), p. 480.
29 See note 1.
30 Roy Campbell, *Lorca: An Appreciation of his Poetry* (Cambridge: Bowes and Bowes, 1952).
31 George Tremlett, *Dylan Thomas: In the Mercy of his Means* (London: Constable, 1993), p. 174.
32 Dylan Thomas, *Selected Poems*, ed. Walford Davies (London: Penguin, 2000), p. 87.
33 Robert Havard, 'The Symbolic Ambivalence of "Green" in García Lorca and Dylan Thomas', *Modern Language Review*, 67: 4 (1972), pp. 810–19.
34 Havard, ibid., p. 818
35 Ibid. p. 818.
36 William T. Moynihan, *The Craft and Art of Dylan Thomas* (New York: Cornell University Press, 1966).
37 John Ackerman, *Dylan Thomas. His Life and Work*, 3rd ed. (London: MacMillan, 1996), p. 128. Tony Conran, *Frontiers in Anglo-Welsh Poetry* (Cardiff: University of Wales Press, 1977), p. 114. Dylan Thomas, *Letters to Vernon Watkins* (London: Dent, Faber, 1957), pp. 17–18. Ackerman, op.cit., p. 156. Ibid.
38 Tony Conran, *Frontiers in Anglo-Welsh Poetry* (Cardiff: University of Wales Press, 1977), p. 114.
39 Dylan Thomas, *Letters to Vernon Watkins* (London: Dent, Faber, 1957), pp. 17–18.
40 Ackerman, op.cit., p. 156.
41 Ibid.

Defamiliarising Idris Davies: A Reassessment of *Gwalia Deserta* and 'Gwalia My Song'

Alan Vaughan Jones
University of Aberystwyth

The plurality and cultural complexity of literary Modernism continue to occupy critics and literary historians. However, the distinctively Welsh inflections of Modernism have received little sustained critical attention, and have often been overlooked in inherited narratives of Welsh Writing in English. There are indications, however, that the situation is changing. The marginalised voices of Welsh Modernism have begun to re-acquire mainstream currency – the resurgence of interest in the work of Lynette Roberts is the clearest example to date – and canonical examples of Welsh Writing in English are being re-encountered within a Modernist frame.[1] To view twentieth-century anglophone literature from Wales through this critical aperture is to reveal the extent of its involvement in nuanced dialogues with English, American and European cultural movements, and such a view necessitates significant critical realignments. Attuning oneself to a text's Modernist practices and preoccupations often involves experiencing the familiar and the rooted as uncanny and conflicted.

This is certainly the case when examining the work of Idris Davies (1905–1953). The author of the words that form the basis of the folk anthem 'Bells of Rhymney', Davies continues to possess cultural cachet – his name still resonates in south Wales and beyond – but he has been pigeonholed by reductive generalisations ('archetypal poet of the Welsh valleys',[2] 'troubadour of the black valley',[3] 'Poet of Rhymney'[4]), all of which are predicated on cultural, political and aesthetic stereotypes. Moreover, the spokesman-like mantle they confer upon him has inflected critics' readings of his work, so that its 'documentary' poetic has tended to be privileged over the conflicted nature of its discursive constructions of self and history (one recalls Tony Conran's claim that Davies formed part of a transhistorical lineage of bardic 'singers' stretching back to Aneirin[5]). There have been distinguished exceptions to this trend, including Conran himself, of course; nevertheless, there remains a need for further revisionist study.

This discussion of *Gwalia Deserta* (1938) and 'Gwalia My Song' (published 1994) seeks to defamiliarise Idris Davies; it will render him strange and unfamiliar as it attempts to move beyond established orthodoxies associated with his life and work. A conscious departure from readings that locate him as a poet of place, this essay examines the poems' inscriptions of his sense of estrangement from native territory and community, and re-embeds them in the context of literary Modernism. Rather than treating *Gwalia Deserta* as a historical 'document' – a text that is 'best understood', to quote Islwyn Jenkins, 'against the economic, social and cultural background of Rhymney and as a regional work of interpretation'[6] – I encounter it as a complex, multi-layered text 'about' the process of negotiating a sense of national selfhood across geographical, social and cultural frontiers. It is read, in short, as a sophisticated kind of exilic 'self-' or 'life-writing'. This is not to deny that it is a text dealing with the consequences of inter-war depression, since that is precisely what it is at surface level. I wish to suggest, however, that it possesses other strata of signification, and a sophisticated literary and cultural metaconsciousness. 'Gwalia My Song', too, inscribes and dramatises an authorial self; that self differs markedly, however, from the one encountered in *Gwalia Deserta*, and the text's composition was informed by the experience of return as opposed to the experience of exile. Similarities exist between the two poems, and these are discussed where appropriate. My principal foci, however, are the contrasts that distinguish the one from the other.

I begin with *Gwalia Deserta*, the earlier of the two

poems and Davies's first book-length publication. My aim is to read it as a kind of frontier text, and there are several reasons why it is appropriate to do so – one of them being the border background of Davies himself, which haunts the poem even though it is not made manifest.[7] The valley in which he was born and raised was disputed frontier land: divided by the River Rhymney, the counties of Glamorgan and Monmouthshire met along its floor, and Rhymney, Davies's birthplace, actually straddled the boundary itself. In effect, Rhymney was liminally located between two administrative entities – 'partly in Monmouthshire and partly in Glamorgan', as the narrator of 'Collier Boy' (Davies's unfinished, unpublished novel) has it.[8] The debate concerning the cultural status and allegiance of Monmouthshire further complicated matters,[9] and undoubtedly problematised Davies's national and cultural affiliations. Within Rhymney itself, issues of cultural allegiance were no less vexed, and the generation of which Davies was part witnessed unparalleled changes in its socio-cultural landscape.

The most overt form of cultural change was the declining strength of the Welsh language, and the increasing prominence of English. Linguistic plurality had been the norm in the district since the in-migration of Irish and English workers and their families during the nineteenth century; however, it was only in the twentieth century that the decline of the Welsh language became an incontrovertible fact. The 1901 Census recorded that 69 per cent of the population could speak Welsh in the Urban District of Rhymney;[10] by the Census of 1911, however, the proportion had decreased to 56 per cent, though the percentage may have been higher within Rhymney itself (Twyncarno, the upper part of the town, had a particularly strong Welsh identity).

Idris Davies grew up in a household with unambiguously Welsh roots: his mother's family had lived in rural Taliesin in North Ceredigion before moving to

Rhymney in the 1850s, while his father came from a family of crofters who had once possessed land on Rhymney Hill. Welsh was the first language, moreover, of both of Davies's parents – and the only language possessed by Edward Williams, the maternal uncle who lived with the family until his death in 1924. Outside the domestic space, however, the situation was different. The family home (16 Field Street) was located in Middle Rhymney, and the close proximity of an Irish community, Dafydd Johnston suggests, had an impact on the language used on the street during Davies's childhood;[12] it is likely, that is to say, to have made English the lingua franca. English, moreover, was the language of Davies's elementary education and (initially at least) of his literary education. Most of his instruction at infant and junior school was conducted in English, and the evening classes that awakened his interest in literature in the 1920s discussed canonical English texts by such authors as Keats and Robert Louis Stevenson (the English bias was offset slightly by his unbroken attendance of a Welsh class[13]). It would seem, therefore, that a fissure – a linguistic 'frontier', one might say – had opened up between the language of the home and the language of Davies's intellectual development.

This cultural-linguistic polarity was certainly in play during the composition of *Gwalia Deserta* (and, for that matter, the composition of 'Gwalia My Song'); indeed, it is dramatised textually as a juxtaposition of discursive registers. There are echoes aplenty of the 'English' writers instrumental to Davies's literary awakening, and their 'voices' are processed and re-inflected, as will be seen, to form Davies's highly literary constructions of 'Gwalia'. Yet there are lingering echoes, too, of the Welsh cultural tradition on the other side of the 'frontier'.[14] Such echoes are markers of the cultural legacy of his childhood – a legacy that had to be negotiated for the rest of his life.

Over time, Davies's position in relation to his native borderland became ever more marginal. Nevertheless, frontiers of one form or another continued to figure in his biographical trajectory, both in the years leading up to 1938 and subsequently. After seven years at the coal-face it became impossible, after 1926, for Davies to find work underground; he was briefly employed as a surface worker in 1927, but devoted his time thereafter to a rigorous programme of self-education, which culminated in a voluntary departure for England in 1930. He attended courses at Loughborough College and Nottingham University and, after qualifying as a teacher in August 1932, secured a post with London County Council, his employers for the next fifteen years. This period was punctuated by returns to south Wales, including a two-year stay in the Rhondda Valley – a period I shall return to later. However, he did not return permanently until June 1947, when a Rhymney Valley councillor found him a teaching post near his place of birth.[15] For seventeen years, then, Davies's experience of the south Wales valleys was fragmentary and discontinuous. Physical absence was accompanied, moreover, by a progressive estrangement from south Wales's working-class culture – an estrangement that was well advanced by the time Davies wrote *Gwalia Deserta*. Self-tuition, academic studies and immersion in London's metropolitan, cosmopolitan culture impelled a process of social and cultural realignment, and this was underscored by the switch from a proletarian to a middle-class occupation. Social and cultural boundaries had clearly been crossed since his years at the coal-face, and this trajectory obviously complicated his attempts to 'write' working-class south Wales.

As the foregoing details suggest, *Gwalia Deserta* could never have been a poem of place in a straightforward sense; it is rather an attempt to negotiate the distance that Davies's physical, social and cultural border crossings had placed between himself and proletarian south Wales. One strategy for getting a purchase on its complexity is to locate the text within the conceptual category of exilic 'self-' or 'life-writing'. Exile, to quote a phrase from Edward Said's reflections on the subject, is 'a discontinuous state of being',[16] and the poem may be considered exilic because it uses the episodic effect of the sequence to enact that discontinuity. *Gwalia Deserta*, to borrow Conran's highly apt metaphor, is a literary 'mosaic' assembled from textual 'tesserae',[17] and those tesserae are separated by literal and figurative gaps. A number were even published as stand-alone poems before the sequence appeared in the latter part of 1938.[18] *Gwalia Deserta*, then, is a fractured artwork, and its modernist fragmentation a self-conscious reflection of an episodic experience and recollection of south Wales.

Another reason for reading this poem as an exilic text is that it constitutes a re-imagining of the margin from the metropolis. Written in London and published by Dent, *Gwalia Deserta* exemplifies the operation of the Welsh imagination on a Wales–London axis. Moreover, metropolitan encounters with victims of south Wales's economic depression may have had a role in motivating the composition of the sequence. This is certainly what was implied by Islwyn Jenkins in 1958:

> Groups of singing unemployed Welsh miners begging in the indifferent London streets contrasted with the Rhymney visit and promise of Edward VIII immediately prior to his exile. Poetic imagination quickened and soon *Gwalia Deserta* ... was sent to the publishers.[19]

Jenkins's contention is that the disparity between the sight of destitute miners in the metropolis and the King's call, on his visit to south Wales, for something to be done to alleviate its suffering stimulated Davies to write *Gwalia Deserta*. However, it is arguable that the appeal of these incidents to Davies's '[p]oetic imagination' is also linked to the uncanny disjunction within each of them. In his recent book on the subject, Nicholas Royle remarks that the uncanny 'is a peculiar commingling of the familiar and unfamiliar'[20] (he is echoing Sigmund Freud's famous essay on the topic, which highlights the slippage of meaning that has 'extended das Heimliche ["homely"] into its opposite, das Unheimliche'[21]). That 'peculiar commingling', Royle explains, 'can take the form of something familiar unexpectedly arising in a strange and unfamiliar context, or of something strange and unfamiliar unexpectedly arising in a familiar context'[22] – a perfect summary of the two events that are taken to have inspired *Gwalia Deserta*.

The foregoing discussion established that the category of the uncanny or 'unhomely' can cast new light on *Gwalia Deserta*'s conception. Tony Brown's recent work on Glyn Jones and R.S. Thomas has shown, however, that the concept can also be applied in a broader context to yield new insights into the psycho-cultural predicament of the Welsh writer in English.[23] One need not look far to see the broader relevance of ideas of uncanniness and/or unhomeliness to studies of Idris Davies: we have observed already – though not in that conceptual context – that the education he pursued from 1927 on effectively 'unhomed' him from his natal culture. However, it is beyond the scope of this study to offer detailed examination of the uncanny aspects of Davies's life and work, since the subject in truth warrants a separate essay. As a consequence, the uncanny is not used here as a thoroughgoing interpretative paradigm. It will instead be deployed as a local lens through which specific aspects of the poems under discussion can be usefully apprehended – and apprehended anew.

Gwalia Deserta's status as a metropolitan composition and its performance of exilic dislocation encourage us to read it as an exilic text. However, my categorisation of the poem as exilic 'self-' or 'life-writing' implies that it can also be fruitfully read within an autobiographical frame. This would at first seem a strange proposition but there are reasons that make it valid, one of which is the fluid and protean (and therefore broad and expansive) nature of the critical discourse of life-writing. Much as the uncanny is a liminal discourse because it effaces distinctions between familiar and unfamiliar, inside and outside and (according to Freud) imagination and reality,[24] the category of life-writing has always possessed an energising undecidability; indeed, Linda Anderson (following Candace Lang) observes that 'if the writer is always, in the broadest sense, implicated in the work, any writing may be judged to be autobiographical, depending on how one reads it'.[25] Theorists of autobiography in the 1960s and 1970s attempted to delimit the genre with definitions and strict entry criteria, but the question of where to locate autobiography (literally, 'self-life-writing') on the continuum between fiction and non-fiction – together with the issue of how autobiographical intent could be established – remained contentious topics. '[I]n recent years', writes Timothy Dow Adams, 'scholars working with the genre have almost universally come to the realization that whatever else it is, autobiography is not simply nonfiction'; the innate fictiveness of the autobiographical act has become a truism.[26] At the same time, moreover – and as Adams duly explains – 'the forms in which autobiography manifested itself started to expand',[27] so that a variety of non-fictional subgenres now fell within the category of autobiographical writing. The present, more expansive conception of what has never, in fact, been a circumscribed and straightforward genre legitimises our re-encounter with *Gwalia Deserta* (and 'Gwalia My Song', too) as 'confessional' performances of a dislocated selfhood.

The proliferation of 'self-' or 'life-writing' in Davies's published and unpublished oeuvre also encourages us to read *Gwalia Deserta* in that context. The frequency with which he returns to the matter of self and life is striking: there are creative verse autobiographies ('I Was Born in Rhymney', 'Young Man from Rhymney'), aborted manuscript drafts of an autobiographical novel ('Collier Boy'), an unpublished memoir ('Keats and After') and 'authentic' and fictionalised diaries. In addition, reminiscences of childhood were the mainspring of several of Davies's wartime radio broadcasts, especially 'War' (1940), 'A Chapter of Boyhood, 1914–18' (1940) and 'Memories of Childhood' (1945).

The theoretical contentions outlined above are borne out by close reading of *Gwalia Deserta* itself. Such an examination also facilitates understanding of the nature of what one might usefully call Davies's 'folk' Modernism – his culture- and community-specific inflection of High Modernist poetic praxis – and confirms that his poem is a highly sophisticated, allusive text that draws into its orbit Shakespearean, Romantic, late-nineteenth century and contemporary literary voices. Additionally, it shows how Davies knowingly inscribes the difficulties of 'writing' south Wales. One of the textual fissures that disclose those difficulties is the title of the sequence itself, although it has attracted remarkably little critical attention given its resonance, layeredness and instability. A rare exception to the rule is Jim Perrin's recent reappraisal of *Gwalia Deserta*, which contains an intriguing parenthetical aside:

> *Gwalia Deserta* (and consider for a moment the oddity of that title – are we talking Doughty here, and Wales as a desert, or is this the deserted land, ruined and waste?) is a poetic sequence describing the plight of a community in a particular landscape at a given point in history.[28]

Perrin is clearly aware that the poem's title is an unstable signifier; he is unsure whether to read it as an echo of Charles Montagu Doughty's *Travels in Arabia Deserta* (1888), or as an echo of the contemporary (1930s) rhetoric that constructed south Wales as economic desert or waste land. The observation opens up an interesting line of enquiry, but is pursued no further; an opportunity to explore the complex resonances of 'Gwalia' and 'Deserta' is therefore missed. Those resonances certainly merit closer scrutiny, since they are local reflections of the predicament underlying the entire sequence – namely, how an exile should write his native territory, self, and past.

Davies's fraught application of the motif of 'Gwalia' is certainly expressive of that predicament.[29] A name for Wales with romantic, sentimental connotations, the 'Gwalia' in the title sits uneasily with 'Deserta', which invokes a grimmer image of Wales as economic desert or deserted land – an image that had currency, as noted above, in the years of the Depression.[30] Consequently, one might think of the title as a site of disturbance where the idyllic, Victorian 'Gwalia' is shadowed and undercut by a trace of a far less romantic, contemporary construction. 'Deserta', too, is a resonant phrase, and is generally taken as an echo of Wales's abandonment by successive governments and economic emigrants in the 1920s and 1930s. Faced with protracted mass unemployment, men and women left Wales in their thousands to find work in England or further afield, both as part of official schemes and on a more informal basis; the net result, as Kenneth Morgan reminds us, was that around 430,000 people moved out of Wales between 1921 and 1940, the majority permanently.[31] The 'Deserta' in *Gwalia Deserta* undoubtedly refers to this exodus from Wales, but no-one has observed that the word reflects ironically on Davies himself (he left south Wales, we remember, to enrol at Loughborough College in the autumn of 1930, and had resided in London for almost six years at the time of *Gwalia Deserta*'s publication). In naming his sequence *Gwalia Deserta*, then, Davies was inscribing a trace of his own departure from 'Gwalia' onto the text – an act that demonstrates awareness of his own complicity in the 'neglect' of the south Wales valleys.

The tension between the 'Gwalia' of old and the twentieth-century reality that I have discerned in the poem's title is one that penetrates deeply into its textual space. We encounter it again in the final four lines of section XXXV:

> And on a peak in Gwalia, I babble in the night:
> The cargoes steam from Cardiff, and Cardiff streets are bright,
> The trains flash down the valleys, the land is fresh with light,
> The horny hands have honour, and Love alone has might.
>
> (*CPID* 20)

On a first reading, the opening line of that passage seems unexceptional. Closer examination, however, reveals it to be a juxtaposition invested with Modernist irony. Since it conveys a specific perception of a speech act, 'babble' is not a word Davies would have used without careful consideration; he probably had an example of usage in mind, and I suggest he found it in Shakespeare's *King Henry V* – a text that was added to his personal library in November 1934.[32] Mistress Quickly's account of Falstaff's death in Act Two, Scene Three of that play states that he 'babbled of green fields' (II.3.14),[33] and Davies's allusion summons the green fields of Falstaff's boyhood or of Psalm 23 to ironic effect. Industrialisation, as Davies was well aware, had turned the green remembered hills of childhood into waste land, and the echo of Psalm 23's green pastures is also ironically apt. It is impossible to invoke those biblical pastures without invoking their antithesis (the 'valley of the shadow of death'), and the south Wales valleys of the 1920s and 1930s were certainly valleys of death. As Steven Thompson observes in a recent discussion of mortality in inter-war south Wales, standardised death rates for the period 1921–39 show that 'mortality was generally greater in the major administrative districts of south Wales than the England and Wales average throughout the interwar period'.[34]

That allusion to *King Henry V* represents only one stratum of significance, since Davies, I suggest, is simultaneously referencing another canonical text – John Keats's sonnet, 'On First Looking into Chapman's Homer'. In locating his dramatic speaker 'on a peak in Gwalia', Davies is glancing knowingly at that poem's image of Cortez and his men standing 'Silent, upon a peak in Darien';[35] however, in the process, he is playing on the differences between the landscapes of which those peaks are part. In Keats's sonnet, the peak in Darien affords 'stout Cortez' a majestic view of the Pacific; by contrast, the view from stout Davies's Welsh Darien (his Penydarien, one might say) is dominated by landmarks of industrialisation, and elicits babble rather than rapt silence from the speaker observing it. As is well known, the Conquistadors' imperial depredations are the shadow-narrative of Keats's poem,[36] and Davies's allusion to it, I suggest, encodes a comment on the colonial exploitation of his south Wales (the rhetoric of plunder and pillage used in connection with industrialists throughout his oeuvre corroborates such a reading).

The Idris Davies I am refocusing here is a writer with an acute awareness of his own praxis and an ability to turn allusions to account, with an effect that one might term ironic Cymrification. However, critics have been reluctant to entertain the possibility that Davies could operate at this sophisticated level: they have either dismissed him condescendingly as a 'simple' writer, or adopted a compromise position – one that acknowledges the work's nuances and allusions, but fails to credit his ability consciously to modulate their resonance. I would maintain that Davies's allusions and juxtapositions are knowing because they are 'live', resonating suggestively and ironically in their new context. He could draw on – and manipulate – a considerable repository of cultural knowledge in the manner of the most famous literary Modernists.

Gwalia Deserta's echoes of other poets corroborate that contention, since a fracturing of the unitary authorial voice into different discourses embodies the discontinuity that Peter Nicholls regards as 'a founding principle of modernist poetics'.[37] The technique served Davies's own project by offering another means of dramatising the difficulty of writing an 'authentic' account of proletarian south Wales, particularly when geographical, social and cultural distance separated him from that territory and way of life. The fragments of familiar literary voices heard in *Gwalia Deserta* acquire a certain strangeness when deployed in a Welsh context, and the irony is that these uncanny vocalities are mainly derived from 'English' literary texts – texts that contributed to Davies's estrangement from the culture and society of south Wales.

The most pervasive of those vocalities is that of A.E. Housman, whose poetic sequence *A Shropshire Lad* (1896) is knowingly echoed in the language, metre and literary devices adopted by Davies. Critical readings of *Gwalia Deserta* often refer to its 'Housmanesque' four-line stanzas with their rhyming second and fourth lines (*Gwalia Deserta* XXV, XXXII and XXXVI are notable examples), but the schema's ubiquity in English literature and religious hymns means it might not necessarily have been appropriated from Housman. The metrical congruity between *A Shropshire Lad* XXXIV and *Gwalia Deserta* XXXIV is perhaps a more suggestive correspondence, but the accent of Housman is at its most audible when Davies deploys the ludic irony that is integral to Housman's distinctive poetic voice. This irony is very much apparent in *Gwalia Deserta* V, whose account of Jude, an aspiring collier-poet, is concluded in a playfully ambiguous way:

> Not for always shall he grope
> In the galleries of grime –
> 'Tis sure he shall be shouldered,
> And need nor pick nor rhyme.
> (*CPID* 4)

The grim pun on 'shouldered' is a typically Housmanesque conceit. Indeed, Tony Conran has shown that it is a borrowing from *A Shropshire Lad* XIX, where the victorious runner is carried 'shoulder-high' in triumph and, shortly afterwards, in his coffin.[38] Davies has effectively ventriloquised Housman, and the presence of an example of Housman's scholarly irony underscores the literariness of *Gwalia Deserta* V's portrait of a south Welsh collier (his name, we remember, is a nod to Thomas Hardy's *Jude the Obscure* (1896) – a book Davies was reading around the time of *Gwalia Deserta*'s composition.[39])

Such ironies, allusions, juxtapositions and ventriloquisations demonstrate very clearly that *Gwalia Deserta* is a highly complex, sophisticated, self-aware text. The same might be said of the poetic sequence known as 'Gwalia My Song'. This late, overlooked composition engages yet again with the people, culture and history of south Wales, but constitutes a more focused and ambitious attempt at tracing the 'dark history' of the industrial waste-land (*CPID* 215) than *Gwalia Deserta*, *The Angry Summer* (published 1943) or the long, six-part poem, 'Tonypandy' (published 1945). 'Gwalia My Song' revisits some of the major themes of Davies's oeuvre – there is much discussion, for instance, of the evils of industrial capitalism – but new preoccupations also come to the fore, most notably a concern that south Welsh culture was becoming vulgar and debased. The poem grew out of revisions made to a typescript of 'The Valleys of My Fathers' – an earlier sequence still unpublished in its entirety[40] – and most of these revisions appear to have been made between August and December 1945, when Davies was lodging at Thane Villas in North London. However, he was still revising sections of the poem in the early 1950s, and alterations made after June 1947 were probably composed in Rhymney. 'Gwalia My Song', then, took shape over several drafts and many years, and was written on both sides of the border. A complete text was not published until 1994, when Dafydd Johnston's *Complete Poems* printed a version that utilised what were deemed to be 'the final revision[s] of each section'.[41] This long-standing problem of access has precluded extensive critical discussion of 'Gwalia My Song', so that Nigel Jenkins has been moved to comment that the sequence has been 'shamefully neglected'.[42] The reading offered here is to be taken as a gesture towards its future reclamation.

Although this discussion is principally concerned with the contrasts between *Gwalia Deserta* and 'Gwalia My Song', there are similarities of form and technique that should be acknowledged. In terms of form – and as Johnston observes – 'Gwalia My Song' is 'much closer ... to *Gwalia Deserta* than to either "Tonypandy" or *The Angry Summer*, having exactly the same number of sections (36), very loosely connected by theme, lacking the tighter unity of event and character which the other two sequences have'.[43] 'Gwalia My Song' also possesses the fragmentary quality discerned in

Gwalia Deserta: many of its sections carry separate titles and some were composed prior to 1945, were re-workings of earlier material or were published in Davies's lifetime as separate texts.[44] Furthermore, 'Gwalia My Song' recycles many of the techniques (some of them Modernist) deployed in *Gwalia Deserta*: polyvocality is certainly in evidence, the sequence form is retained and the incongruous, ironic juxtapositions are also carried over. Similarly, there are more appropriations of literary voices, such as those of Blake, Shakespeare, Housman and T. S. Eliot.

Those similarities are significant, but should not obscure the fact that the two poems are ultimately different kinds of text: *Gwalia Deserta* was written after Davies had spent many years living in England, whereas 'Gwalia My Song' was inflected by a lengthy return to wartime south Wales and – perhaps – by Davies's permanent return to Rhymney in 1947. In November 1942, Davies was instructed by London County Council to accompany evacuees to Treherbert in the Rhondda – a posting that lasted until December 1944. Though he made friends in the Rhondda, the return was not an experience he savoured, as his friend Glyn Jones explained in a letter to Tony Conran:

> What irked him [Idris Davies] about the Rhondda was what appeared to him the Philistinism of the people – the myth of the cultured working-class community died for him – no choirs, no regard for literature, no art-galleries or the desire for them. The club-and-bingo mentality had for him begun.[45]

As Jones attests, the experience of living and working in the Rhondda was profoundly disappointing for the prodigal son, and Islwyn Jenkins's 'Writers of Wales' monograph suggests it compelled Davies 'to reconsider his political and poetic ideals'.[46] The vibrant working-class culture that had surrounded him in pre-war Rhymney seemed absent from wartime Rhondda, and Davies concluded that it had been vulgarised (he told Glyn Jones at the end of 1944 that he had encountered 'about the narrowest and most vulgar people I have met anywhere' in the Rhondda[47]). Life in south Wales was certainly transformed by the Depression and the Second World War; however, we should remember that Davies, too, had changed. In London, he had gradually become accustomed to a cosmopolitan culture, and his response to the Rhondda threw the true extent of his *embourgeoisement* into relief. I will concentrate here on two sections of 'Gwalia My Song', and suggest that they are self-aware inscriptions of the disillusionment – and hyperconsciousness of estrangement – characterising Davies's returns to industrialised south Wales.

'In a Rhondda Valley Bus' – section four – certainly gives voice to the disillusionment referred to above. It does so, moreover, by alluding to (and re-inflecting) section XXIX of Davies's own *Gwalia Deserta* – a self-reflexive poetic manoeuvre. In this fragment of 'Gwalia My Song', the passengers on a late-night bus express a weakened faith in politicians and the political system, or embody the decline of once-powerful political ideas (witness the strangely bourgeois 'quiet Socialist in his Sunday best', who is '[t]oo timid to hold his nose' [*CPID* 216]). One disillusioned figure holds a particular fascination for the poet/speaker:

> And who's that dreamer brooding on fragments of his dreams,
> Those easy dreams of summer days and summer hills,
> With all the world so simple beneath the skylark's song.
> Bleaker the summers have grown of late,
> The anger not so righteous ...
>
> (*CPID* 216)

Though Davies's oeuvre contains numerous dreamers, he seems to be invoking the dreamer of *Gwalia Deserta* XXIX in that excerpt from section four of 'Gwalia My Song'. Certainly, there are suggestive parallels between the two texts. The 'summer days and summer hills' in the passage quoted above echo the 'summer hills' where the dreamer roams in *Gwalia Deserta* XXIX (*CPID* 16), and when we notice that singing larks also appear in both texts, the similarities start to seem deliberate rather than coincidental. By far the most interesting connection between the two is 'Gwalia My Song' section four's ironic comment on the righteous indignation of the dreamer of *Gwalia Deserta* XXIX. In the earlier text, we are told that the dreamer's spirit has been 'fired' by 'the just anger of the blood' (*CPID* 16); the speaker of section four of 'Gwalia My Song', as though in response, declares that the same anger is 'not so righteous'.

This worrying of the carcase of an old song (*Gwalia Deserta* XXIX) confirms Davies's status as a self-reflexive writer, and it re-inflects that 'old song' by undercutting its romantic idealism. In that fragment of Davies's 1938 sequence, the dreamer is high above the mining town, and in the dusk of a summer evening a grandiose, socialist-utopian vision is conceived – a vision 'of shining lands, and love unhampered / By the callous economics of a world / Whose god is Mammon' (*CPID* 16). In section four of 'Gwalia My Song', we re-encounter this dreamer after seven years, during which much has changed: we find him in a bus rather than on a mountain, brooding over fragments of shattered dreams. The dreamer's collapse, moreover, is considered part of a wider moral, spiritual and cultural crisis. In this section of 'Gwalia My Song', the Rhondda is disturbingly surreal terrain – a place where the vulgar 'shine', a place where youthful dreams are gnawed at by rats, and a place where the boor marks the death of cultured society by 'lower[ing] the flags of life' (*CPID* 216).

The despair that issued in those nightmarish images is also apparent where section four of 'Gwalia My Song' borrows from T.S. Eliot's 'Choruses from "The Rock"'(1934).[48] As Johnston suggests, the 'broken-down parson' – a figure who serves as a reminder 'of the wilderness between the Word and the word' (*CPID* 216) – evokes the '[k]nowledge of words, and ignorance of the Word' mentioned in section I of Eliot's text (*CP* 161),[49] and the note of despondency is plain. Similarly negative connotations are attached to Davies's reference to crumbling 'cornerstones' (*CPID* 216), which invokes the comparison made in section II of 'Choruses from "The Rock"' between the 'ruined house' of a secular society and the 'household of God', whose 'cornerstone' is Christ himself (*CP* 166). Davies was drawn to these particular elements of Eliot's text because their pessimistic characterisation of 1930s society dovetailed with his responses to 1940s and 1950s south Wales. He removes Eliot's imagery from its original ideological context, and uses it to fashion a bleak assessment of the Rhondda Valley.

Davies's re-encounter with the dreamer of *Gwalia Deserta* XXIX dramatises his cultural disillusionment and the shift in his ideological make-up. Having lived through the Second World War, Davies revisits a figure from the poem he wrote in 1938 – a figure that might well be a self-portrait – and re-inflects that figure's representation to suit his changed post-war sensibility. His ploy initiates a dialogic exchange between inscriptions of early and late authorial selves – one that is essentially uncanny. Figments of different authorial selves – or encounters with them – are often seen in Davies's work, and they certainly exemplify the Modernist inflections of his writing (one thinks in particular of the 'familiar compound ghost' of Eliot's 'Little Gidding' in *Four Quartets* – a book Davies bought at Whitsun 1945.[50])

If Davies's oeuvre is populated by Eliotic 'ghosts', it is fair to say that Eliot himself was a guiding spirit instrumental to Davies's literary success. As Eliot recalled in a letter to Islwyn Jenkins, it was he who sent Davies to Dent after Faber turned him away in the 1930s,[51] and when Dent rejected *The Angry Summer*, Eliot accepted it for Faber. From that moment on, Davies was a 'Faber Poet', and his author–editor relationship with Eliot was maintained until his death in 1953.[52] Even after his own death in 1965, Eliot has continued to exert a powerful influence over Davies's reception; his endorsement of Davies's work as 'the best poetic document I know about a particular epoch in a particular place' has been reproduced time and again in critical literature.[53] The irony is that endless repetition of this statement has impeded appraisal of Eliot's resonant presence in Davies's work, and – more importantly – has obscured the layeredness and Modernist effects of Davies's poetry by grounding him in circumscribed particularity and in a tradition of 'folk' poetry.

Section twenty-four of 'Gwalia My Song' is the best example of the text's engagement with Eliot; even its title – 'Crossing the Waste Land' – points to a dialogue with Eliot's most famous work. Davies maps *The Waste Land*'s vision of social, cultural and spiritual crisis onto the landscape of industrialised south Wales, and the product, I suggest, is another uncanny construction of Davies's 'Gwalia'. In other words, 'Crossing the Waste Land' is a text where familiar fragments of Eliot appear unexpectedly in a Welsh context, and Davies uses those fragments to inscribe his dislocated, disillusioned post-war self. From the beginning of 'Crossing the Waste Land', it is clear that Davies is marshalling Eliot's lament on the state of Western civilisation after the First World War to get a purchase on 1940s and 1950s south Wales; two very different cultural spaces are collapsed together. The vacant land on the outskirts of Aberglo – land explicitly associated with Eliot's waste land – is dead, littered with the detritus of modern living, like the 'Sweet Thames' in Eliot's poem (the phrase, we remember, is an ironic recycling of Spenser's 'Prothalamion'[54]). Social and cultural life, too, is impoverished, and its traditional guiding influence – religion – is largely ineffectual. The sole trace of high culture in Aberglo's listless society is a contralto singing in the Miners' Welfare Hall, but the crowd listening to her Italian songs is 'dim' and 'dumb' (*CPID* 226). Eventually, thunder and rain come to derelict Aberglo in a passage replete with echoes of section V of *The Waste Land*, 'What the Thunder Said':

> And then the thunder came, and the rains,
> O the rains came, and great was the downpour

On churches and chapels and collieries and cabbages,
And there was weeping in the furnace-ruins by the river,
And ghostly laughter in the gloom
Behind the smashed windows of the derelict Goshen,
And then there was silence, silence,
And the prayer that passeth all comprehending
And the dream of desolation
And the desire of doom.

(*CPID* 226)

Allusions are enactments of the uncanny, being echoes of familiar texts heard in unfamiliar contexts. The above passage is, and is not, T.S. Eliot. Its reference to 'derelict Goshen', for example, recalls the roofless chapel used by Eliot to symbolise the decay of the Christian Church, but it locates Eliot's vision of decay in a specifically south Welsh context, since Goshen was a chapel in Rhymney that had been destroyed by fire.[55] Another interesting example of the passage's *unheimlichkeit* is its handling of the symbolism of water. In Eliot's poem, water and rain are synonymous with rebirth and revitalisation, but rain never actually falls on the Waste Land; restoration of fertility and vitality to the modern world is for Eliot a possibility, not a certainty. The situation is ironically reversed in 'Crossing the Waste Land', where Aberglo does not lack water; the problem is that the water is revitalising neither its streets nor its inhabitants.

Both of the examples cited above show that Davies adapts *The Waste Land*'s symbolism to delineate the social and cultural space of post-war south Wales. It should be emphasised, however, that this section of 'Gwalia My Song' also engages with the interplay between Eliot's poem and its paratext, the 'Notes on the Waste Land'. When Davies refers in 'Crossing the Waste Land' to 'the prayer that passeth all comprehending' (*CPID* 226), he has in mind 'The Peace which passeth understanding' – the biblical 'equivalent' offered in Eliot's 'Notes' for the Sanskrit word 'Shantih', which is repeated at the end of *The Waste Land*.[56] Christopher Ricks implies that the presence of

'Shantih' in Eliot's poem is an integral part of its critique of Western culture:

> The inaccessibility, except to merely schooled memory, of 'Shantih' is Eliot's piercing point. 'The Peace which passeth understanding' has passed from our memory; 'Shantih' can never be part of our memory.[57]

'Schooled memory' neatly encapsulates the structures of *embourgeoisement* that went into the retrospective construction of Davies's south Wales. Ricks's contention is that 'Shantih' has been used instead of its 'equivalent' because that 'equivalent' no longer resonates in Western culture – it 'can no longer effect within our culture what "Shantih" can effect within its culture',[58] as he puts it. Idris Davies, I suggest, understood what Eliot had done here; he was a careful reader of Eliot's work, and an avid consumer of critical debate on it.[59] He saw that Eliot was gesturing at the cultural amnesia affecting Western civilisation after the First World War, and believed amnesia of a similar kind was affecting 1940s and 1950s south Wales. In 'Crossing the Waste Land', the moribund 'equivalent' of 'Shantih' ('The Peace which passeth understanding') is once again implicated in a cultural argument; indeed, it is the same argument rehearsed by Eliot. Davies, however, makes Eliot's point through deliberate, ironic parody of that famous fragment of Philippians, as his literary manuscripts confirm. In the typescript of 'The Valleys of My Fathers' that was reshaped to produce 'Gwalia My Song', the prototype of 'Crossing the Waste Land' contains a reference to 'the peace that passeth all understanding'; Davies, however, altered it to read 'the prayer that passeth all comprehending'.[60] The revision deflects the language of scripture into new ironic, demotic territory – Davies's point being that society at large was failing to recognise and vitally respond to a phrase integral to Christian devotion and practical Christianity alike. It is an implicit criticism, too, of the way the indigenous language was swiftly passing beyond understanding/

comprehending – and it is interesting to note that Davies became a supporter, towards the end of his life, of the campaign to establish a Welsh-medium school in the Rhymney Valley.[61] In short, Davies recycles the textual material that resonated with Eliot to inscribe his concerns about south Wales's cultural health in the 1940s and 1950s.

This essay has attempted to re-inflect the received image of Idris Davies in a reading of *Gwalia Deserta* and 'Gwalia My Song' that departs from established critical orthodoxies. It has sought to reveal that the poems are highly sophisticated, self-aware texts that deploy High Modernist irony, juxtaposition, uncanny allusions and traces of multiple subjectivities to inscribe or dramatise fraught negotiations with native language, culture and society. *Gwalia Deserta*, I have suggested, is an exilic, autobiographical frontier text: it is a discursive, highly literary construction of south Wales, and constitutes Davies's attempt to write across cultural, chronological, geographical and class frontiers from London. 'Gwalia My Song', by contrast, was informed by lengthy returns to south Wales, and the sections examined here suggest that Davies's experience of 1940s and 1950s south Wales was characterised by disillusionment and feelings of dislocation or estrangement. High Modernist techniques are again deployed to articulate these feelings, but the accent of Modernism is now stronger (the appropriations of Eliot being a contributory factor). Future studies might read *The Angry Summer* along similar lines; the poem's plenitude of vocalities and musicalities, together with its fragmentation into different authorial personae, certainly lend themselves to such an interpretation.

One point remains to be made, and it concerns T.S. Eliot. In this essay and the notes that follow, I have endeavoured to give a sense of the important role Eliot played in Davies's literary career, and to offer a preliminary outline of the dynamics of their author–editor relationship. Eliot emerges from their correspondence as a careful, supportive editor with a personal interest in his author, and his wider interest in Welsh writing is reflected in the work he accepted for publication (Faber's poetry list, we remember, placed Idris Davies alongside David Jones, Vernon Watkins and Lynette Roberts, and it was Faber who published Keidrych Rhys's important anthology, *Modern Welsh Poetry*, in 1944). It has recently been argued that any examination of Welsh Modernist literature needs to consider Eliot's role in publishing and encouraging Welsh authors,[62] and the role of Eliot and Faber and Faber in the development of twentieth-century anglophone Welsh writing undoubtedly merits more detailed treatment. Further work in this area would contribute to the rewriting of broader narratives of literary history – narratives that have overlooked Idris Davies, and Welsh Modernism more generally, for too long.

NOTES

This essay is a revised version of material delivered at the Twentieth Annual Conference of the Association for Welsh Writing in English (April 2008), and the postgraduate symposium 'Reappraising Welsh Modernism' (November 2008); I am grateful to all who attended those events for observations and suggestions. I would also like to acknowledge support received from the Arts and Humanities Research Council.

1 For a recent example see Chris Wigginton, *Modernism from the Margins: The 1930s Poetry of Louis MacNeice and Dylan Thomas* (Cardiff: University of Wales Press, 2007).

2 See the back cover of *The Collected Poems of Idris Davies*, ed. by Islwyn Jenkins (Llandysul: Gomerian Press, 1972).

3 The epithet is a translation of the title of David Raymond's article on Davies in *Y Cymro* (17 April 1953) p. 6.

4 Islwyn Jenkins, 'Idris Davies: Poet of Rhymney', *Anglo-Welsh Review*, 9, no. 23 (1958) pp. 13–21.

5 'As Aneirin in the sixth century celebrated the defeat of his people at Catraeth, so Idris Davies celebrated the grandeur and despair of working-class resistance to capitalism in Britain between the wars and the all but crushing defeat of the Welsh proletariat.' See *The Cost of Strangeness: Essays on the English Poets of Wales* (Llandysul: Gomer, 1982) p. 154.

6 Islwyn Jenkins, *Idris Davies*, 'Writers of Wales' Series (Cardiff: University of Wales Press on behalf of the Welsh Arts Council, 1972) p. 18. Subsequent references are abbreviated to *ID*.

7 John Powell Ward observes that 'Idris Davies, T.H. Jones, Eiluned Lewis, Roland Mathias, Ernest Rhys and Hilda Vaughan have all had some border connection, although clearly they belong further into the homeland both geographically and by identification.' See Chapter Three, 'Borderers and Borderline Cases' in *A Guide to Welsh Literature VII: Welsh Writing in English*, ed. by M. Wynn Thomas (Cardiff: University of Wales Press, 2003) pp. 91–119 [118].

8 National Library of Wales, Aberystwyth (hereinafter NLW), MS 22409C, fol. 8r.

9 For further details on Monmouthshire's tortuous history see John Davies, *A History of Wales*, rev. edn (London: Penguin, 2007) esp. p. 230.

10 Siân Rhiannon Williams, *Oes y Byd i'r Iaith Gymraeg: Y Gymraeg yn ardal ddiwydiannol Sir Fynwy yn y bedwaredd ganrif ar bymtheg* (Caerdydd: Gwasg Prifysgol Cymru, 1992) p. 123.

11 Ibid. p. 124.

12 Dafydd Johnston, 'Idris Davies a'r Gymraeg', in *DiFfinio Dwy Lenyddiaeth Cymru*, ed. by M. Wynn Thomas (Caerdydd: Gwasg Prifysgol Cymru, 1995) pp. 96–119 [97].

13 Islwyn Jenkins, *Idris Davies of Rhymney: A Personal Memoir* (Llandysul: Gomer, 1986) p. 58. Subsequent references are abbreviated to *IDR*.

14 For comments on the possible influence of Welsh-language prosody on Davies's verse, see *ID* pp. 24–25 and *IDR* p. 121 (the former suggests that Davies 'does not consciously conform [to the rules of Welsh prosody], but his accidental conformities, exact or otherwise, are evidence of his enduring Welshness'). Davies's Welsh cultural inheritance is also echoed in the sequences through their (often ironic) biblical references, and their occasional use of hymn-like stanzas. It is also worthy of note that section twenty-one of 'Gwalia My Song' ('The Cynic') appears to be echoing a hymn by Ann Griffiths (its reference to '[t]he eye that once saw God behind the hawthorn' suggests an allusion to 'Rhyfedda fyth, Briodas ferch', whose second verse begins with the words 'Wele'n Sefyll rhwng y myrtwydd').

15 *IDR* p. 202.

16 Edward W. Said, 'Reflections on Exile', in *Reflections on Exile and Other Literary and Cultural Essays* (London: Granta, 2000) pp. 173–86 [177].

17 M. Wynn Thomas and Tony Brown make reference to Conran's reading of the lyrics of *The Angry Summer* as '*tesserae* in a dramatic mosaic' in their co-written essay, 'The Problems of Belonging'. See Thomas (ed.), *Welsh Writing in English*, pp. 165–202 [186].

18 *Gwalia Deserta* VII was published as 'Dai' in the *Left Review* (January 1937, p. 866), while a slightly different version of section XIV appeared as 'Near Rhymney' in *Wales*, no. 4 (March 1938, p. 152). Section XXXIV was published separately on two occasions: it first appeared as 'Rhymney to Merthyr' in the *Merthyr Express* (18 January 1936), and was published again two months later in the *Western Mail* (18 March 1936). The thirty-sixth and final section of the sequence first saw print in the *Daily Herald* in 1938, and was somewhat confusingly given the title 'Gwalia Deserta'. These details are included in the notes to *Gwalia Deserta* in *The Complete Poems of Idris Davies*, ed. Dafydd Johnston (Cardiff: University of Wales Press, 1994) pp. 277–80. Subsequent references to this edition are abbreviated to *CPID*.

19 'Idris Davies: Poet of Rhymney' p. 15.

20 Nicholas Royle, *The Uncanny* (Manchester: Manchester University Press, 2003) p. 1.

21 Sigmund Freud, 'The "Uncanny"', in *Art and Literature: Jensen's 'Gradiva', Leonardo Da Vinci and Other Works*, The Penguin Freud Library, 14 (Harmondsworth: Penguin, 1990) pp. 339–76 [363]. The parenthetical insertion appears in the original.

22 Royle, *The Uncanny* p. 1.

23 Tony Brown, 'Glyn Jones and the "Uncanny"', *Almanac: The Yearbook of Welsh Writing in English*, 12 (2007–8) pp. 89–114; *R.S. Thomas*, 'Writers of Wales' Series (Cardiff: University of Wales Press, 2006).

24 Freud, 'The "Uncanny"' p. 367.

25 Linda Anderson, *Autobiography* (London: Routledge, 2001) p. 1.

26 Timothy Dow Adams, *Light Writing & Life Writing: Photography in Autobiography* (Chapel Hill and London: University of North Carolina Press, 2000) p. xi.

27 Ibid.

28 Jim Perrin, 'The Achievement of *Gwalia Deserta*', *Poetry Wales*, 39.2 (Autumn 2003) pp. 42–6 [45].

29 Perrin refers in passing to 'the complex motif of "Gwalia" itself', but does not elaborate on the remark. See 'The Achievement of *Gwalia Deserta*' p. 45.

30 The etymology and usage of 'Gwalia' are discussed by an entry in *The New Companion to the Literature of Wales*, ed. Meic Stephens (Cardiff: University of Wales Press, 1998) p. 291. It observes that the term 'has been used with piquant effect by some modern writers, as in the title of the poem which is the subject of the next entry [*Gwalia Deserta*]'.

31 Kenneth O. Morgan, *Rebirth of a Nation: A History of Modern Wales* (Oxford: Oxford University Press; Cardiff: University of Wales Press, 1981, rpr. 2002) p. 231.

32 See the 'Field Notes' on the contents of Idris Davies's personal library, which were compiled by Islwyn and Jean Jenkins between 1954 and 1955; and now form part of NLW ex 947. The notes are incomplete as not all books were available for listing, but the data compiled constitutes an important resource for studies of Davies's work.

33 *King Henry V*, ed. Andrew Gurr, updated edn (Cambridge: Cambridge University Press, 2005) p. 114.

34 See Steven Thompson, *Unemployment, Poverty and Health in Interwar South Wales*, Studies in Welsh History, 25 (Cardiff: University of Wales Press, 2006) pp. 182–3.

35 L. 14 in *John Keats: The Complete Poems*, ed. with an introduction by John Barnard, 3rd edn (London: Penguin, 1988, rpr. 2003) p. 72.

36 See Nicholas Roe, *John Keats and the Culture of Dissent* (Oxford: Clarendon Press, 1998) p. 56.

37 Peter Nicholls, 'The poetics of modernism', in *The Cambridge Companion to Modernist Poetry*, ed. by Alex Davis and Lee M. Jenkins (Cambridge: Cambridge University Press, 2007) pp. 51–67 [58].

38 See Conran, *Frontiers in Anglo-Welsh Poetry* (Cardiff: University of Wales Press, 1997) p. 48.

39 The link with Hardy's novel is also made by Conran; see *Frontiers in Anglo-Welsh Poetry* p. 48. With regard to Davies's encounter with the text, he states in 'Keats and After' that he began reading Hardy's novels when he was

approximately twenty-three, adding that 'perhaps it was fortunate that I did not read "Jude the Obscure" till about ten years later'. See NLW MS 22410C, fols 209v–210r.

40 Nine sections were selected for publication in *Poetry Wales*, 16.4 (1981) – an Idris Davies Special Issue.

41 *CPID* p. 309.

42 Nigel Jenkins, 'O What Can You Give Me?', *Poetry Wales*, 40.4 (Spring 2005) pp. 48–52 [52].

43 *CPID* pp. lxviii–lxix.

44 As Johnston points out, '[s]ection 34 was originally composed in 1931, and section 32 in 1935' (*CPID* p. lxxix). He also observes that '[s]ections 19 and 30 are adapted from the prose-poem "Land of My Mothers", published in 1937'. (Ibid.) Sections 9 ('Come to Our Revival Meeting'), 28 ('A Carol for the Coalfield'), 30 ('Land of My Mothers') and 32 ('Midnight') appeared as separate texts in Davies's *Selected Poems* (1953) – a book Faber published less than a month before his death (*CPID* p. 289).

45 Quoted in *The Cost of Strangeness* p. 150.

46 *ID* p. 35.

47 Quoted in Glyn Jones, 'Some Letters of Idris Davies', *Poetry Wales*, 16.4 (1981) pp. 76–84 [79].

48 *Complete Poems 1909–1962* (London: Faber and Faber, 1974) pp. 161–85. Subsequent references are abbreviated to *CP*.

49 *CPID* p. 310.

50 See the 'Field Notes' in NLW ex 947.

51 NLW MS 23539E, fol. 23r; letter dated 22 April 1955.

52 Insights into the nature of their author–editor relationship are provided by two letters from Eliot to Davies in NLW MS 22415C, and by transcriptions of others (one addressed to Davies's mother) contained in the 'Field Notes'. The first letter from Eliot in NLW MS 22415C (fol. 30r) is dated 25 June 1944: it advises Davies on which poems to exclude from *Tonypandy and Other Poems* (published 1945), mentions the importance of the ordering of the collection, and suggests that the word 'pansy' be changed to 'violet' in 'The Lay Preacher Ponders'. (The latter is illustrative of Eliot's careful editing, and of his sensitivity to the resonances of words: 'pansy', he remarks ruefully, 'always provokes a snigger nowadays, but one has to take the associations of words as one finds them'.) The enclosure of an article from the *Partisan Review* referring to Davies's *The Angry Summer* also reveals '[s]omething of T.S.

Eliot's encouragement and concern as Faber publisher', as Islwyn Jenkins comments (*IDR* 149). The second letter (fol. 39r) is dated 7 August 1944, and queries whether Davies had intended to include 'The Sacred Road' in the collection (Davies, it seems, had not listed the poem in his table of contents, and Eliot had returned it). One of the letters transcribed in the 'Field Notes' is a letter from Eliot to Davies dated 24 May 1944; it refers to poems returned to Davies for revision, and Eliot suggests that Davies substitute poems taken out for others given the collection's short length. Advice is offered, too, on a specific textual issue (Davies's use of the phrase 'a moleskin trousers'), but Eliot also glances off to discuss matters of more personal interest, such as his friend George Every; the letter ends with the hope that the two will be able to talk if Davies returns once again to London (this meeting never took place). Another of the transcribed texts is a letter of condolence written by Eliot to Davies's mother, and dated 21 April 1953; it is a testament to the close personal interest Eliot took in his author. A third transcription duplicates fol. 30r of NLW MS 22415C. Mention should also be made, finally, of the Christmas card from Eliot contained in NLW MS 22415C (fols 60–61). Drawn and lithographed by Barnett Freedman 'for the directors and members of Messrs Faber and Faber to send to their friends' (fol. 61v), the card is yet another proof of the positive nature of Davies's relationship with his editor.

53 NLW MS 23539E, fol. 23r.

54 *CP* p. 82, note to l. 176.

55 E.E. Edwards, *Echoes of Rhymney*, 2nd edn (Risca: Starling Press, 1974) p. 61.

56 *CP* p. 86, note to l. 433.

57 Quoted in *T.S. Eliot, The Waste Land: A Reader's Guide to Essential Criticism*, ed. by Nick Selby (Basingstoke: Palgrave Macmillan, 1999) p. 148.

58 Ibid. p. 147.

59 The 'Field Notes' in NLW ex 947 confirm this. They record that Davies's personal copy of *The Waste Land and Other Poems* (inscribed 'November 1940 Bishop's Stortford') was annotated with quotations from Geoffrey Bullough and T.E. Hulme, excerpts from Eliot's 1929 essay on Dante, and what were thought to be Davies's own comments. Similarly, his copy of *Four Quartets* contained, amongst other papers, newspaper

cuttings concerning Eliot and his work, and a letter from Eliot himself dated 1944 (no further details concerning this letter are recorded). Davies also possessed copies of *The Poetry of T.S. Eliot* by H.R. Williamson (dated 'Summer 1934'), and of Raymond Preston's *Four Quartets Rehearsed: A Commentary on T.S. Eliot's Cycle of Poems* (inscribed 'Rhymney 1946.')

60 NLW MS 10810D, fol. 264r.

61 For further details see 'Successful struggle', *Western Mail* (24 February 1987) p. 13. The piece is a letter written to the editor by Nora Isaac.

62 The observation was made by Patrick McGuinness in 'Lynette Roberts, modernist?', a paper delivered at 'Reappraising Welsh Modernism'. This postgraduate symposium was held at the National Library of Wales, Aberystwyth on 14 November 2008.

Hugh MacDiarmid & Keidrych Rhys:

The Arrow from Wales

Hugh Manson
Independent scholar

Hugh MacDiarmid corresponded briefly with Welsh writers from 1937 to 1939 at the time when Keidrych Rhys, Dylan Thomas and Nigel Heseltine edited at different times the eleven issues of *Wales*, 1937–1940, Gwyn Jones was editing Vol. 1 Nos 1–6 and Vol. 2 Nos 1–4 of *Welsh Review* (from February to November 1939) and MacDiarmid was editing the five quarterly issues of the first series of *The Voice of Scotland* (between June 1938 and August 1939). MacDiarmid received letters from the Welsh writers mentioned and also from Glyn Jones[1] and T. E. Nicholas.[2] He also published poems by Rhys and Thomas in *The Voice of Scotland* Vol. 1 No. 3 and by Nicholas, in Welsh, in Vol. 1 No. 4. At the same time, MacDiarmid's poems 'On Reading Professor Ifor Williams's "Canu Aneurin" in Difficult Days', 'Poetry Like the Hawthorn' and 'Diamond Body' were published in *Wales* 8/9 and 11 and *Welsh Review* Vol. 2 No. 4 respectively.

MacDiarmid's first contact was with Keidrych Rhys and recent research in the National Library of Scotland and Edinburgh University Library Special Collections shows that this contact left a number of traces in MacDiarmid's creative and polemical writing. Rhys's first, rather disconnected, letter (preserved in part), dated 1 September 1937,[3] shows that MacDiarmid had written to him, no doubt on the occasion of the publication of the first issue of *Wales* (stamped August 11 in the National Library of Wales) which Rhys might have sent him. Did the missing page or pages contain Rhys's arrangement of Glyn Jones's words from a story in *The Blue Bed* (stamped 2 February in the National Library of Scotland) which MacDiarmid may have incorporated into his poem 'Perfect' first published in *The Islands of Scotland* in June 1939, and which has caused so much controversy?[4] In his letter to *The Times Literary Supplement*, 6 May 1965, Rhys wrote, 'Except for the one added line of his own, and the omission of inverted commas, and the title "Perfect", Mr Hugh MacDiarmid's line arrangement happens to coincide with mine.' Rhys added that he had discussed this arrangement 'with a few friends and correspondents'.

MacDiarmid made extensive use of another closely-written four-page letter from Rhys, dated 1 April 1939,[5] both in his article 'The English Literary Left' in *The Voice of Scotland*[6] and in his autobiography, *Lucky Poet*.[7] Here he gave parts of this letter verbatim, sometimes in his own words, sometimes acknowledging 'a friend' or 'a correspondent'. The letter consisted of a series of wild and sometimes homophobic attacks, particularly on left-wing writers in London. MacDiarmid's repetition of the (false) attack on Edgell Rickword, 'but even he was in the Black-and-Tans',[8] resulted in the withdrawal from sale of *Lucky Poet* until two lines were rewritten.[9] MacDiarmid had included the same attack in 'The English Literary Left.'[10] MacDiarmid adapted another attack in 'The English Literary Left:' 'In Wales, there is now the *Welsh Review*, which is wealthy and financed by the crowd of Welsh bureaucrats and coalowners, who hope to send all the young Welsh literati to sleep by dealing out fivers.'[11] In a letter to MacDiarmid, dated 31 August 1939, Gwyn Jones noted that he had allowed himself to be completely deceived by his 'correspondent'.[12] On 5 September MacDiarmid wrote an unreserved apology and said that he had at once sent off a retraction to his printer for the next issue.[13] However, *The Voice* did not appear again until the second series commenced in 1945; MacDiarmid did not repeat the attack in *Lucky Poet*. Jones acknowledged the apology in another letter on 12 September and published MacDiarmid's poem 'Diamond Body' in *Welsh Review* Vol. 2 No. 4.[14]

MacDiarmid dedicated two poems to Keidrych Rhys. The earlier perhaps pays tribute to the encouragement Rhys had given Welsh writers as the founder of the journal, *Wales*. It was rediscovered in the National Library of Scotland in 2003 and published in *The Revolutionary Art of the Future* by Carcanet that year:

ALL THE WELSH WRITERS IN GREAT BRITAIN TODAY
To Keidrych Rhys

Thanks to you, all the Welsh writers in Britain today
Have become like the salmon in the River Wye
When that quiet stream suddenly begins to rage
And moorhen nests, and rubbish, and tree-trunks whirl by.

Heedless of any lure, the salmon are at once
Possessed with a sort of mania to rush upstream
Toward the Radnor cloudburst that has caused
This fortuitous flooding. So today all these writers seem.[15]
(?1939)

The second poem was 'The Arrow from Wales' and was dedicated 'To my friend Keidrych Rhys, on the cessation of his magazine *Wales* – one of the early casualties of the Second Imperialist War, April 1940.'[16] This poem has been in the public domain for over fifty years and forms part of *In Memoriam James Joyce* (1955) where MacDiarmid says 'The reference here is to the author's friend, Dylan Thomas.'[17] MacDiarmid had not been able to publish the poem in 1940 and simply removed the dedication to Keidrych Rhys and re-dedicated it to Thomas on his death.

The poem extends to fifty-four lines, beginning

I rejoiced when from Wales once again
Came the ffff-putt of a triple-feathered arrow
Which looked as if it had never moved.

As published, it differs only in four details from the manuscript. It has an exclamation mark after 'beautiful' (l.

7), 'my bowman' for 'that Rhys' (l. 33), a comma after 'Cuchulainn' (l. 37) and a full stop instead of '- - -' at the end of l. 49.

The source of the first three lines is unexpected. MacDiarmid had read *The Sword in the Stone* by T. H. White, published in 1938, a tale of the fantastic adventures of Kay, the proper son, and Wart, the not proper son, of Sir Ector of the Castle of the Forest Sauvage, set on the Welsh border. The author imagines the Castle in its heyday: 'and perhaps from Wales there will come the ffff-putt of a triple-feathered arrow which looks as if it had never moved'.[18] This quality of an arrow had been described earlier. When Wart had been shot at, he went behind a tree: 'As he did this, another arrow came whirr and tock, but this one buried all except its feathers in the grass, and stayed there still, as if it had never moved.'[19]

The main part of MacDiarmid's source occurs later in *The Sword in the Stone*.[20] His transformation of this source has been well described by Alan Riach in *Hugh MacDiarmid's Epic Poetry*.[21] Archery was part of Kay and Wart's programme on Thursday afternoons. The archers were allowed to shoot one last arrow straight up into the air: 'It was partly a gesture of farewell, partly of triumph, and it was beautiful. They did it now as a salute to their first prey.'[22] (They had shot a rabbit.) However, Wart's arrow was seized by a crow which 'flew away, heavy and hoisting, / With the arrow in its beak.' (ll. 23–24) MacDiarmid concludes:

But the crow cannot quench the light
With its outstretched wings forever
Nor break the law of gravity
Nor swallow the arrow.
We shall get it back. Never fear!

And how I shall rejoice when the War is over
And there comes from Wales once again
The fff-putt of a triple-feathered arrow
Which looks as if it had never moved! (ll. 46–54)

The reference to 'the War' was to the Second World War, which MacDiarmid sometimes called the Second Imperialist War, and this was consistent with a dedication to Keidrych Rhys but anachronistic with the dedication to Dylan Thomas. Therefore Rhys remains 'The Arrow from Wales' in all but name.

NOTES

(MSS are quoted by permission of the National Library of Scotland and of Mr Dorian Grieve for the MacDiarmid Estate)

1 Two letters [June 1939], Edinburgh University Library MS2951.10 fols 12-13 and 9 October 1939, National Library of Scotland Accession 7361/10 respectively.

2 18 October 1938, NLS Acc 7361/9 unfoliated.

3 NLS Acc 7361/8 unfoliated.

4 The most recent discussion of this controversy is outlined in Meic Stephens' article, 'Sad case of a "perfect" Welsh skull in a Scottish cupboard', in *New Welsh Review* 23, Winter 1993–94, pp. 37–42.

5 EUL MS2970 folder T-Z of 'Various Publishers' unfoliated. This letter will appear in *Dear Grieve: Letters to Hugh MacDiarmid* in 2009.

6 *The Voice of Scotland*, Vol. 2 No. 1, June–August 1939, pp. 1–6, reprinted in *Hugh MacDiarmid, The Raucle Tongue: Hitherto Uncollected Prose* III, edited by Angus Calder, Glen Murray and Alan Riach (Manchester: Carcanet, 1998), pp. 30–36.

7 Hugh MacDiarmid, *Lucky Poet* (London: Methuen, 1943), pp. 171–3.

8 Ibid. p. 172.

9 'Edgell Rickword is about the only person with some idea of Nationalism but even he was in the Black-and-Tans' became 'Hardly one of the English literati, has any idea of Nationalism or does not aid and abet Imperialism in one way or another.'

10 *The Voice of Scotland*, Vol. 2 No. 1, p. 5; *The Raucle Tongue* III, p. 36.

11 *The Raucle Tongue* III, p. 35.

12 31 August 1939, EUL MS2970 folder T–Z of 'Various

Publishers' unfoliated.

13 National Library of Wales, Gwyn Jones 1/10/3–4.

14 As 12.

15 Hugh MacDiarmid, *The Revolutionary Art of the Future: Rediscovered Poems*, edited with an introduction by John Manson, Dorian Grieve and Alan Riach (Manchester: Carcanet, 2003), p. 38.

16 NLS MS27024 fols 64–6 recto and verso in pencil.

17 Hugh MacDiarmid, *In Memoriam James Joyce* (Glasgow: William MacLellan, 1955), p. 9. Hugh MacDiarmid, *Complete Poems*, edited by Michael Grieve and W. R. Aitken, Vol. 11 (London: Martin Brian and O'Keeffe, 1978), p. 828.

18 T.H. White, *The Sword in the Stone* (London and Glasgow: Collins, 1976), p. 49.

19 Ibid. p. 21.

20 Ibid. pp. 65–66. Alan Riach, *Hugh MacDiarmid's Epic Poetry* (Edinburgh: Edinburgh University Press, 1991), pp. 103–6. *The Sword in the Stone*, p. 65.

The Burial of T. J. Llewelyn Prichard:

An Addendum to a Note Concerning the Finding of a Prichard Manuscript[1]

Sam Adams
Independent scholar

The *Dictionary of Welsh Biography* is inaccurate about some of the key facts relating to T. J. Llewelyn Prichard, most notably those concerning his death.[2] It states, 'He was alive on 24 Nov. 1875, the date of one of his letters printed in *Cymru Fu*, II, v, 80.' The quoted reference is to an essay in a series published in that journal under the general title 'Men Whom I Have Known', by Charles Wilkins. This one incorporates the complete text of a letter from Prichard asking the unnamed addressee to forward fourteen copies of his latest book, *Heroines of Welsh History*, to the postmistress at Neath, where he evidently planned his next door-to-door selling expedition. In the magazine (actually the number for July–December *1889*), the letter is dated '24th Nov. *1857*'.

The author of the entry was Sir William Llewelyn Davies, the National Librarian and Associate Editor of the *Dictionary*. Perhaps it was a case of Homer nodding. In any event, the errors meant that it took a long time to find the date and circumstances of Prichard's death, though Wilkins's brief essay gives the clues that 'he was literally burned to death' in 'a hovel, near Swansea', and that there was 'a paragraph in *The Cambrian*'.[3]

We owe more than that to Wilkins. The same essay provides the only description of Prichard to have so far come to light:

> My earliest recollection of Llewelyn Prichard was in finding him sitting near me in a dramatic entertainment at Merthyr, and listening to a long string of remembrances of old players and old authors. It was as if a nightly habitué

> of by-gone Sadler's Wells had come to life, familiar with the stage and its annals from Shakespeare and Ben Jonson down to the days of Beaumont, Fletcher, Dryden, and Sheridan, and able to give varied quotations from celebrated players as well as from all the poets, from Savage and Churchill to Cowper, Southey, and Crabbe, and a host beside. He was gaunt and grey, with thin features and lustrous eyes, a false nose – having lost his natural one in a fencing match – and he spoke with an earnest snuffle – I say this kindly – from which most people would quickly have turned away. There was a measured prosiness, too, about his conversation, which grated in ordinary ears, and a young man in love, or an older one with business or social cares, would have regarded him as a bore and a 'button-holder'[4]

How did Wilkins come into possession of Prichard's letter to whoever held the stock of *Heroines of Welsh History*, from which he hoped to obtain a further fourteen copies? That is easily answered. Charles Wilkins (1831–1913) was born in Stonehouse, Gloucestershire, and came to Merthyr Tydfil when his father, William Wilkins, entered business there as a bookseller. In 1851, when his father was appointed postmaster of the town, Charles was given the job of clerk. What would be more natural than that Prichard, meeting the young post office employee at 'a dramatic entertainment', should hand him the letter for posting? We might then conjecture that he did not, at the same time, also hand over the £2 2s for the 'Post Office order' that should have accompanied the letter – and there was no point in sending off the one without the other. A less likely scenario would have Wilkins simply pocketing both letter and cash.[5] In any event, the letter was not sent and Wilkins hung on to it, so that when, more than thirty years later, he wrote about Prichard for *Cymry Fu*, he was able to quote it in full.

Later in his letter Prichard refers to a dispute with Mr Jefferies, who 'undertook to pay the carriage of my books to you – but continually omits to do so.' The name appears listed among the joint 'publishers' of the book, thus:

LONDON
W. and F. G. Cash, 5, Bishopsgate Street, (Without.)
Bristol: C. T. Jefferies, Canynge's House, Redcliff Street.
Swansea: William Morris, Stamp Office, High Street.

But this was a stratagem, designed to persuade prospective buyers that the book had the imprimatur of a London publisher. The letter, in which Prichard declares 'I shall never publish again, except on the terms of selling the copyright to a London publisher', shows that he had funded the publication of *Heroines* himself, albeit perhaps by loans; we shall never know. We cannot tell either whether W. and F. G. Cash knew they had been nominated in this way. It is, however, worthwhile pausing for a moment to consider why Prichard chose them.

Welsh Minstrelsy (1824), the book that brought Prichard back to Wales on his first selling tour after long years of exile in London, was printed by John Cox in Aberystwyth. Yet the title page names John and H. L. Hunt, of Tavistock Street, Covent Garden, London, as publishers. In 1813, the brothers John and Henry Leigh Hunt, printer and editor respectively of *The Examiner*, a weekly newspaper, had each been fined £500 and imprisoned for two years for (in the judge's words) 'publishing a scandalous and defamatory libel upon His Royal Highness the Prince Regent'. The Hunts represented liberal idealism, and Prichard deliberately chose to align himself with them. W. and F. G. Cash did not share the Hunts' notoriety with the establishment, but they too were publishers at the leading edge of liberal thought. Among works bearing their imprint were anti-slavery pamphlets, the *Transactions of the Central Relief Committee of the Society of Friends during the Famine in Ireland, in 1846 and 1847* (1852) and William G. Allen's *The American Prejudice Against Colour* (1853). That *Heroines* might attract the interest and financial investment of a London publisher was wishful thinking, but this choice, too, clearly reveals Prichard's ambition as a writer and his political sympathies.

It is clear from further remarks in Wilkins's essay that C. T. Jefferies, in Bristol, printed *Heroines*.[6] If we ponder the intended recipient of Prichard's letter, our best guess must surely be the third member of the triumvirate on the title page: William Morris of the Stamp Office in Swansea High Street. To him, then, Jefferies would despatch copies of the book ordered by Prichard, and he in turn would forward them to a predetermined post office, where they would be collected by the author for another bout of door-to-door selling. How effective a salesman he was with his 'earnest snuffle', the 'measured prosiness ... about his conversation, which would have grated on ordinary ears'[7] and buttonholding tendency is hardly in doubt.

On the other hand, by living, or barely living, from hand to mouth, Prichard might have gone on in this way for a considerable time. Perhaps the selling was brought to a halt only by age and infirmity: he was about sixty-four when he wrote the letter and had only recently suffered a 'very long illness ... which kept me an invalid, after being confined indoors and mostly in bed the whole of last summer'.[8] Or, possibly, the transfer of copies of *Heroines* from Bristol had been compromised because Jefferies (as the letter tells us) usually neglected to pay the carriage of the books to Swansea, as he had undertaken to do. Whether Prichard was to blame or not, it would not have enhanced his standing with William Morris.

Morris, businessman, with an entrée to social and cultural affairs in Swansea and a finger in several pies, became a member (probably chairman) of the committee assembled to succour Prichard when he was discovered in November 1861, starving, in dreadful squalor, at Major Roteley's Cottage, World's End.[9] And it was Morris who acquired Prichard's manuscripts and copyrights 'by a properly constructed deed of sale',[10] as part of a deal to set him up comfortably at last, with new furniture, a woman to call in and see the cottage was cleaned and a fire lit, and at least five shillings weekly 'as out-door relief' granted by the Board of Guardians of Swansea Union Workhouse.

There should have been more money. On 29 November 1861, *The Cambrian* added to its report of the changes that had been wrought to Prichard's circumstances the welcome news that 'contributions from various parts [to the subscription fund for the writer it had instigated] are rolling in rather freely'. Little more than six weeks later, on 17 January, 1862, the paper carried the testimony of Esther Bird, the woman who had been attending to his daily needs, at the inquest on his death. He had suffered severe burns from falling into his own fire. She said, 'He had plenty of everything. On Wednesday last the deceased told me he had received £5 from a cousin of his who is a clergyman ... I believe Mr. George redeemed some things with part of the money.' After the jury had returned the verdict of accidental death

> Mr Yorath made a few observations with the view of showing that the deceased had been properly cared for, and the private subscriptions which had poured in from all quarters were quite sufficient to keep him in comfort and to provide him with every necessary. It was also stated that there were quite sufficient funds in hand to bury the deceased in a respectable and decent manner.'[11]

Where then was he buried? *The Dictionary of Welsh Biography*, quoting from *Cyfaill yr Aelwyd*, 1887 (113), says he was buried in Tabernacle graveyard, Swansea.[12] That, too, is inaccurate. There might have been a Tabernacle Chapel in High Street, but if there was, it no longer exists.[13] In any case, the official record of burials in Swansea[14] shows that T. J. Llewelyn Prichard was interred on 17 January 1862 at Dan-y-Graig Cemetery, Port Tennant, overlooking the docks and Swansea Bay. But if you are the sort of literary pilgrim who likes to visit the graves of writers and ponder upon their headstones, this is one you might as well, indeed, 'pass by'. There is no headstone. Prichard was buried in what is officially termed a 'Board Grave', that is, a common grave, a pauper's grave. He was the first to occupy a particular plot, Section L, number 179, but others followed him, including a Mr J. Evans in 1865, and, in due course, a Mr F. Woolacot, a Mr Alphonso Corsi and a stillborn baby. Until recently, it was at least possible to identify the plot by its cast-iron marker, but (along with all the others indicating Board Graves in Section L) it has been stolen by scrap metal thieves. If you make your way to that part of the cemetery, you will now see quite a broad expanse of well-kept lawn, beneath which Prichard lies with unnumbered nameless others.

Where did the money go that should have obtained for him a 'respectable and decent' burial? Some, and I cannot exclude myself, might be tempted to put William Morris in the frame, but the proper answer is we do not know, and we never shall. To the very end, Prichard's story remains unsatisfactory, and haunting.

NOTES

1 Sam Adams, 'T. J. Llewelyn Prichard: A Manuscript Found', *Welsh Writing in English* [*WWE*], Vol. 9, 2004, pp. 157–169.

2 *The Dictionary of Welsh Biography Down to 1940*, 1959, p. 796.

3 *Cymru Fu*, Vol. II. Part V, July–Dec. 1889, p. 80. *The Cambrian*, the first English language newspaper to be published in Wales ran from 1804 until 1930. It carried a good deal more than a paragraph on Prichard's death. The 'hovel', Major Roteley's Cottage, was in Thomas Street, World's End, not far from the heart of Swansea.

4 The letter is extensively quoted in Sam Adams, *Thomas Jeffery Llewelyn Prichard*, Writers of Wales Series (Cardiff: University of Wales Press, 2000), p. 94.

5 Wilkins (Catwg) eventually succeeded his father as postmaster, but also wrote prolifically for weekly newspapers and became a historian of note. His 'History of the Literature of Gwent and Morganwg' won the National Eisteddfod essay prize in 1880.

6 Furthermore, there was a second volume in manuscript (Wilkins, p. 80) that has simply disappeared – no great loss,

as readers of the first volume will agree.

7 Wilkins, p. 80.

8 Wilkins, p. 81.

9 Adams, *WWE*, pp. 158–9.

10 Ibid., p. 162.

11 *Slater's Directory* for Swansea, 1858–59 (now digitised), shows William Yorath kept the Bird-in-Hand at 217 High Street, Swansea; The Stamp Office where William Morris was 'sub-distributor' was at 228 High Street. They were almost certainly acquainted. Morris also knew Major Roteley, whose cottage was occupied by Prichard, because both were members of the Swansea Association for the Prosecution of Felons (Adams, *WWE*, pp. 160–161).

12 *Cyfaill yr Aelwyd: Cylchgrawn Misol at Wasanaeth Oriau Hamddenol y Cymry*, edited by Beriah Gwynfe Evans and published in Llanelli, had a regular 'notes and queries' ('Holiadur') section. In Volume 7, page 113 this includes an answer by Cadrawd (Thomas Christopher Evans, 1846–1918) to an earlier enquiry about Prichard, in which, perhaps for the first time, the error about the date of the writer's death appears, together with that regarding his burial: 'Bu farw rhywle tua'r flwyddyn 1874, neu 1875, a chladdwyd ef yn mynwent y Tabernacle, lle y dylai cofnodiad o'r amgylchiad fod yn nghadw.' Perhaps Sir William Llewelyn Davies, seeking to reconcile Cadrawd's testimony with that of Charles Wilkins for his entry in the *Dictionary of Welsh Biography*, chose to trust the former, and therefore assumed Wilkins had stumbled in dating Prichard's letter 1857, rather than 1875.

13 The City and County of Swansea Archive Service has no record of a Tabernacle Chapel, nor is there any reference to a chapel of that name in *The Cambrian* index.

14 Information supplied by the department responsible for cemeteries, City and County of Swansea.

Welsh Writing in English: A Bibliography of Criticism 2008

compiled by Catherine Phelps
Cardiff University

This bibliography covers books, contributions to books, periodical articles, review-articles, reviews of listed critical writing and selected theses. Readers aware of relevant material published in 2008, which has been omitted, are kindly asked to forward details to the editor, Katie Gramich, Almanac – Welsh Writing in English, School of English Communication and Philosophy, Cardiff University, CF10 3EU.

GENERAL CRITICISM

Adams, Sam. Letter from Wales. *PN Review* 34.4 (March/April 2008) 6–7. ISSN 0144 7076. (Focuses on The Library of Wales, specifically its anthology *Poetry 1900-2000*)

Adams, Sam. Letter from Wales. *PN Review* 35.2 (November/December 2008) 7–10. ISSN 0144 7076. (A piece on Zoë Skoulding and her fellow feminist literary critics, and a discussion of 'alternative' Welsh poetry.)

Ballin, Malcolm. The Welshness of William Emrys Williams: strands from a biography. *Almanac – A Yearbook of Welsh Writing in English: Critical Essays* Vol. 13 (2008–2009) 81–108. (A discussion of Sander Meredeen's biography that focuses on the importance of Williams's Welsh identity and its impact on the British cultural establishment.)

Barnie, John. What the Raven told the Eagle. *Poetry Wales* 43:3 (Winter 2008) 11–15. ISSN 0332 2202. (On climate change and extinction in Welsh nature poetry.)

Bohata, Kirsti. A Female Tradition. *New Welsh Review* 80 (Summer 2008) 25–33. ISSN 0954 2116. (Discusses new publications that offer a feminist perspective of the Welsh writing in English canon.)

Brockway, Anthony. The Last Word. *New Welsh Review* 82 (Winter 2008) 91–95. ISSN 0954 2116. (Anthony Brockway argues the case for a place in the Welsh canon for native science fiction.)

Curtis, Tony. After the First Death ... Literature and Wales in the Second World War. *Literatures of War*. Eve Patten and Richard Pine (editors.) Newcastle upon Tyne: Cambridge Scholars, 2008. ISBN 978-1-84718-637-9.

Gramich, Katie (editor). *Almanac – A Yearbook of Welsh Writing in English: Critical Essays* Vol. 13 (2008–2009). ISBN 978-1-90576-275-0.
Contents: 'Yeats Said That': R.S. Thomas and W.B. Yeats, by Damian Walford Davies, pp. 1–26 – 'He was thinking in Welsh now, though he spoke in English': Negotiating identity in the language of Hilda Vaughan's novels, by Lucy Thomas, pp. 27–54 – Tales of the *Boneddigion*: Nigel Heseltine's Gentry Context, by Rob Gossedge, pp. 55–80 – The Welshness of William Emrys Williams: strands from a biography, by Malcolm Ballin, pp. 81–108 – The *London Kelt* 1895–1914: Performing Welshness, Imagining Wales, by Tomos Owen, pp. 109–125 – 'Passionate and simple': R.S. Thomas and Irish Writing, by Sam Perry, pp. 126–161 – 'Magnifique, n'est-ce pas?': Representations of Wales and the world in Islwyn Ffowc Elis's *Wythnos Yng Nghymru Fydd*, by Craig Owen Jones, pp. 162–189 – International elements in early *Poetry Wales*: A Response to Malcolm Ballin, by Matthew Jarvis, pp. 190–201 – 'Welsh Writing in English': A Bibliography of Criticism 2007, by Laura Wainwright, pp. 202–232.

Gregson, Ian. *Poetry 1900–2000*: One hundred poets from Wales. *Poetry Wales* 44:1 (Summer 2008) 9–11. ISSN 0332 2202. (Review-article of *Poetry 1900–2000* edited by Meic Stephens and which stresses the importance and the need for such an anthology.)

Jarvis, Matthew. An absent art? 'Alternative' poetry since The Second Flowering. *Poetry Wales* 44:1 (Summer 2008) 8–14. ISSN 0332 2202. (Through the examination of a variety of Welsh 'alternative' poets, argues that this genre of poetry has flourished since the 1970s.)

Jarvis, Matthew. International Elements in Poetry Wales: A Response to Malcolm Ballin. *Almanac – A Yearbook of Welsh Writing in English: Critical Essays* Vol. 13 (2008–2009) 191–201.

Jarvis, Matthew. Voices of Renewal: Anglophone Welsh Poetry in the 1960s. *Poetry Wales* 44: 2 (Autumn 2008) 22–27. ISSN 0332 2202.

Jarvis, Matthew. *Welsh Environments in Contemporary Poetry: Writing Wales in English*. Cardiff: University of Wales Press, 2008. ISBN 978-0-70832-152-2. Contents: Conifers, pp. 3–5 – A Digression on Writing and Environment, pp. 6–14 – The 1960s Generation and R.S. Thomas to 1968, 15–32 – Gillian Clarke: Beyond an Environment of the Senses, pp. 35–53 – Ruth Bidgood: Reinhabiting Mid Wales, pp. 54–72 – Robert Minhinnick: From Pen-y-Fai to Iraq, pp. 73–87 – Mike Jenkins: Locating the Depredations of Power, pp. 88–106 – Christine Evans: Creating Sacred Space, pp. 107–124 – Ian Davidson: 'the form and function of the world', pp. 125–139 – Afterword: 'a landscape with everything in it', pp. 140–143.

Jarvis, Robin. Madoc in Scotland: a transatlantic perspective on 'Stepping Westward'. *European Romantic Review* 19:2 (April 2008) 149–156. ISSN 1740 4657 (A reading of Wordsworth's 'Stepping Westward' which is contrasted with Southey's 'Madoc').

Kerrigan, John. *Archipelagic English: Literature, History and Politics 1603–1707*. Oxford: Oxford University Press, 2008. (An exploration of the formation of British identity viewed from the peripheries of Britain as opposed to its metropolitan centre. This includes a chapter dedicated to Morgan Llwyd, Katherine Philips and Henry Vaughan.)

Owen, Tomos. The *London Kelt* 1895–1914: Performing Welshness, Imagining Wales. *Almanac – A Yearbook of Welsh Writing in English: Critical Essays* Vol. 13 (2008–2009) 109–125. (An examination of newspapers and periodicals produced for the Welsh in exile, specifically the *London Kelt* and its role in the construction of Welsh identity.)

Prescott, Sarah. *Eighteenth Century Writing from Wales: Bards and Britons*. Cardiff: University of Wales Press, 2008. ISBN 978-0-70832-053-2. (An investigation of eighteenth-century literature from and about Wales, and which centre on contemporaneous ideas around national identity.)

Riach, Alan. One Hundred Welsh Poets. *New Welsh Review* 80 (Summer 2008) 17–23. ISSN 0954 2116. (Review-article of Meic Stephens' anthology, *Poetry 1900–2000*.)

The Welsh Academy Encyclopaedia of Wales. John Davies, Nigel Jenkins, Menna Baines and Peredur I. Lynch (editors.) Cardiff: University of Wales Press, 2008. (An invaluable resource that has a number of entries on a wide-range of authors, as well as sections on genre.)

INDIVIDUAL AUTHORS

Dannie Abse

Broughton, Sarah. 'We tell ourselves stories in order to live.' *New Welsh Review* 82 (Winter 2008) 31–37. ISSN 0954 2116. (Review-article that discusses both Dannie Abse's *The Presence* and Joan Didion's *The Year of Magical Thinking*.)

Ruth Bidgood

Jarvis, Matthew. Ruth Bidgood: Reinhabiting Mid Wales. *Welsh Environments in Contemporary Poetry: Writing Wales in English*. Cardiff: University of Wales Press, 2008.

Gillian Clarke

Gramich, Katie. Sounding the Depths. *New Welsh Review* 82 (Winter 2008) 18–27. ISSN 0954 2116. (Review-article which looks at the blending of nature writing and memoir in Gillian Clarke's *At the Source* and Christine Evans's *Bardsey*.)

Jarvis, Matthew. Gillian Clarke: Beyond an Environment of the Senses. *Welsh Environments in Contemporary Poetry: Writing Wales in English*. Cardiff: University of Wales Press, 2008.

John Cowper Powys

Ballin, Malcom. Morine Krissdóttir, Descents of memory: the life of John Cowper Powys. *Powys Journal* 18 (2008) 136–41. ISSN 0962 7057. (Review-article.)

Fawkner, H. W. World without christening: domestic life and iniquity in the twenty-sixth chapter of *A Glastonbury Romance*. *Powys Journal* 18 (2008) 67–84. ISSN 0962 7057.

Fisher, Roy. On JCP's letters (with two letters from JCP to Fisher). *Powys Journal* 18 (2008) 30-7. ISSN 0962 7057.

Marie-Laverrou, Florence. 'Encroaching fields' in *Weymouth Sands*. *Powys Journal* 18 (2008) 85–104. ISSN 0962 7057.

Nash, Katherine Saunders. John Cowper Powys's *'great new art'*: intermental influence in the lecture career. *Powys Journal* 18 (2008) 38-66. ISSN 0962 7057.

Ian Davidson

Jarvis, Matthew. Ian Davidson: 'the form and function of the world.' *Welsh Environments in Contemporary Poetry: Writing*

Wales in English. Cardiff: University of Wales Press, 2008.

Russell T. Davies

Charles, Alec. War Without End?: Utopia, the Family, and the Post-9/11 World in Russell T. Davies's Doctor Who. *Science Fiction Studies* 35:3 (November 2008) 450–465. ISSN 0091 7729.

Amy Dillwyn

Owen, Tomos. 'Never Again Stop the Way of a Welshman': Rioting and Rebellion in Amy Dillwyn's *The Rebecca Rioter. Riots in Literature.* David Bell and Gerald Porter (editors). Cambridge: Cambridge Scholar, 2008. ISBN 978-1-84718-582-2

Menna Elfyn

Ap Hywel, Elin. The Song and not the Singer: The importance of *And ... Poetry Wales* 44: 1 (Summer 2008) 47–49 ISSN 0332 2202 (Review-article of Menna Elfyn's *Perfect Blemish: New and Selected Poems 1997–2007.*)

Miguélez-Carballeira, Helena. In Conversation: María do Cebreiro and Menna Elfyn. *Poetry Wales* 44: 2 (Autumn 2008) 10–14. ISSN 0332 2202. (An interview which considers the implications of translating poetry.)

Islwyn Ffowc Elis

Jones, Craig Owen. 'Magnifique, n'est-ce pas?': Representations of Wales and the world in Islwyn Ffowc Elis's *Wythnos Yng Nghymru Fydd. Almanac – A Yearbook of Welsh Writing in English: Critical Essays* Vol. 13 (2008–2009) 162–190.

Christine Evans

Gramich, Katie. Sounding the Depths. *New Welsh Review* 82 (Winter 2008) 18–27. ISSN 0954 2116. (Review-article which looks at the blending of nature writing and memoir in new works by Gillian Clarke and Christine Evans.)

Alan Garner

Wood, Naomi. The Cultural Geography of Fantasy Britain. *Children's Literature: Annual of the Modern Language Association Division on Children's Literature and the Children's Literature Association* 36 (2008) 251–256 ISSN 0092 8208 (Review-article of Charles Butler's study of Susan Cooper, Alan Garner, Penelope Lively and Diana Wynne Jones.)

Ian Gregson

Hill, Greg. So What's New? *Planet* 187 (February/March 2008) 60–64. ISSN 0048 4288. (Review-article of Ian Gregson's study of Welsh writing in English, *The New Poetry in Wales*.)

McGuiness, Patrick. Creative Disturbance. *Planet* 190 (August/September 2008) 39–45. ISSN 0048 4288. (Interview.)

Niall Griffiths

Peddie, Ian. Warmth and Light and Sky: Niall Griffiths in Conversation. *Critical Survey* 20:3 (September 2008) 119–127. ISSN 0011 1570.

Dafydd ap Gwilym

Johnston, Dafydd. Semantic Ambiguity in Dafydd ap Gwilym's 'Trafferth mewn Tafarn'. *Cambrian Medieval Studies* 56 (Winter 2008) 59–74. ISSN 1353 0089.

Felicia Hemans

Boutin, Aimée. Transnational Migrations: Reading Amable Tastu with Felicia Hemans. *Romance Studies* 26:3 (July 2008) 210–220. ISSN 0263 9904.

Ryan, Brandy. 'Echo and Reply': The Elegies of Felicia Hemans, Letitia Landon and Elizabeth Barrett. *Victorian Poetry* 46:3 (Autumn 2008) 249–277. ISSN 0042 5206.

George Herbert

Canning, Patricia. 'The Bodie and the Letters Both': 'Blending' the Rules of Early Modern Religion. *Language and Literature: Journal of the Poetics and Linguistics Association* 17:3 (August 2008) 187–203. ISSN 0963 9470.

Cruikshank, Frances. The Speaking Picture: Visions and Images in the Poetry of John Donne and George Herbert. *The Reformation Unsettled: British Literature and the Question of Religious Identity, 1560–1660.* Jan Frans van Dijkhuizen (editor). Belgium: Brepols, 2008. ISBN 978-2-50352-624-9.

Orvis, David L. 'Thy Glorious Household-Stuffe': Doctrinal (Re)Inscription in George Herbert's Church Furnishing Poems. *The Sacred and Profane in English Renaissance Literature.* Mary A. Papazian (editor). Newark: University of Delaware Press, 2008. ISBN 978-0-87413-025-6.

Pierce, Robert B. Richard Wilbur and George Herbert. *Modern Philology* 106:1 (August 2008) 83–100. ISSN 0026 8232.

Pursglove, Glyn. 'Not with *leaf* only, but with some *fruit* also'. *Scintilla* 12 (2008) 34–52. ISSN 1368 5023.

Reece, Spencer. In Praise of George Herbert. *American Poetry Review* 37-2 (March-April 2008) 32–34. ISSN 0360 3709.

Sullivan, Ceri. *The Rhetoric of the Conscience in Donne, Herbert and Vaughan.* Oxford: Oxford University Press, 2008. ISBN 978-019954-784-5.

Van Dijkhuizen. In Thy Passion Slain: Donne, Herbert and the Theology of Pain. *The Reformation Unsettled: British*

Literature and the Question of Religious Identity, 1560-1660. Jan Frans van Dijkhuizen (editor). Belgium: Brepols, 2008. ISBN 978-2-50352-624-9.

Wolberg, Kristine A. *'All Possible Art': George Herbert's The Country Parson*. Madison, NJ: airleigh Dickinson University Press, 2008. ISBN 978-0-83864-170-5.

Nigel Heseltine

Gossedge, Rob. Tales of the *Boneddigion*: Nigel Heseltine's Gentry Context. *Almanac – A Yearbook of Welsh Writing in English: Critical Essays* Vol. 13 (2008–2009) 55–80.

Richard Hughes

Sands-O'Connor, Karen. High Winds and Broken Bridges: The Gothic and the West Indies in Twentieth-Century British Children's Literature. *The Gothic in Children's Literature: Haunting the Borders*. Anna Jackson, Karen Coates and Roderick McGillis (editors). New York: Routledge, 2008. ISBN 978-0-41596-036-6.

David Jones

Bouyssou, Roland. The Sacrificial Victim in David Jones's *In Parenthesis*. *Ecstasy and Understanding: Religious Awareness in English Poetry from the Late Victorian to the Modern Period*. Adrian Grafe (editor). London: Continuum, 2008. ISBN 978-0-82649-864-9.

Phillips, Ivan. Penmen and brushmen: the remediation of word and image in the work of Wyndham Lewis and David Jones. *Word and Image* 24:1 (January–March 2008) 103–14. ISSN 0266 6286.

Thorpe, Adam. Book of a Lifetime: The Anathemata by David Jones. *The Independent* (13 June 2008).

Alun Lewis

Caldwell, Roger. Accidental War Poets. *PN Review* 34:4 (March–April 2008) 61–3. ISSN 0144 7076. (Review-article of Isaac Rosenberg's unpublished letters, *Poetry out of My Own Heart* and Alun Lewis's *A Cypress Walk – Letters to 'Freida'*.)

Thomas, M. Wynn. The Outsider. *The Guardian* (9 February 2008). (Review-article)

Gwyneth Lewis

Szabo, Daniel. Feminine Irony in the Religious Poetry of Gwyneth Lewis. *E-rea* 6:1 (2008). ISSN 1638 1718.

The Mabinogion and related materials

Evans, Andrew J., John Nettleship and Steven Perry. Linn Liuan/Llyn Lyw: The Wondrous Lake of the Historia Brittonum's de Mirabilibus Brittaniae and Culhwch ac Olwen. *Folklore* 119:3 (2008) 295–318. ISSN 0015 587X.

Field, P.J.C. Arthur's Battles. *Arthuriana* 18:4 (Winter 2008) 3–32. ISSN 1078 6279.

Knight, Stephen. From Myrrdin to Merlin and Back Again. *Transactions of the Honourable Society of Cymmrodorion 2007* Vol 14 (2008) 5–20. ISSN 0959 3632. (On the changing representations of Merlin from his first appearance in sixth-century Welsh poetry to the present day.)

Simpson, Roger. Arthurian Pageants in Twentieth-Century Britain. *Arthuriana* 18:1 (Spring 2008) 63–87. ISSN 1078 6279.

Roland Mathias

Adams, Sam, Letter from Wales. *PN Review* 34.3 (January/February 2008) 6–9. ISSN 0144 7076. (Obituary.)

Robert Minhinnick

Jarvis, Matthew. Robert Minhinnick: From Pen-y-Fai to Iraq. *Welsh Environments in Contemporary Poetry: Writing Wales in English*. Cardiff: University of Wales Press, 2008.

Iolo Morganwg

Jones, David Ceri. Fictional Selves in the Life and writing of Edward Williams ('Iolo Morganwg', 1747–1826). *The Welsh History Review* 24:1 (June 2008) 29–51. ISSN 0083 792X.

Jan Morris

Fenwick, Gillian. *Traveling* (sic) *Genius*. South Carolina: University of South Carolina Press, 2008. ISBN 978-1-57003-747-4.

Pascale Petit

Brigley, Zoë. Confessing the Secrets of Others: Pascale Petit's Poetic Employment of Latin American Cultures and the Mexican Artist, Frida Kahlo. *Journal of International Women's Studies* 9:2 (March 2008) 20–28. ISSN 1539 8706.

Katherine Philips

Stanton, Kamille Stone. 'Capable of Being Kings': The Influence of the Cult of King Charles I on the Early Modern Women's Literary Canon. *New Perspectives on the Eighteenth Century* 5:1 (Spring 2008) 20–29. ISSN 1544 9009.

Lynette Roberts

Rumens, Carol. Poem of the Week. *The Guardian* (3 March 2008).

Dylan Thomas

Lycett, Andrew. The Reluctant Propagandist. *The Guardian* (21 June 2008).

Thomas, Colin. Green Mountain Black Mountain. *Planet* 187 (February/March 2008) 20–25. ISSN 0048 4288. (A discussion of Dylan Thomas's wartime propaganda films)

Edward Thomas

Freeman, Nick. Edward Thomas, Swinburne, and Richard Jefferies: 'The Dead Oak Tree Bough'. *English Literature in Transition (1880–1920)* 51:2 (2008) 164–183. ISSN 0013 8339.

Longley, Edna (editor). *The Annotated Collected Poems/ Edward Thomas*. Tarset: Bloodaxe, 2008. ISBN 978-1-85224-746-1.

McDonald, Peter. Edward Thomas, *The Annotated Collected Poems*. *Times Literary Supplement* 5512 (21 November 2008) 3–5. (Review-article.)

Perry, Sam. 'In Search of Something Chance Would Never Bring': The Poetry of R.S. Thomas and Edward Thomas. *Review of English Studies: The Leading Journal of English Literature and the English Language* 59:241 (September 2008) 582-603. ISSN 0034 6551.

R.S. Thomas

Brown, Tony. 'Love's Depths': R.S. Thomas's Poems to his Wife. *Renascence* 60.2 (Winter 2008) 132-60. ISSN 0034 4346.

Dafydd, Fflur. 'There were Fathoms in her too': R.S. Thomas and Women. *Renascence* 60.2 (Winter 2008) 118–131. ISSN 0034 4346.

Davis, William V. 'The Lame Feet of Salvation': A Reading

of R.S. Thomas and Robinson Jeffers. *Renascence* 60.2 (Winter 2008) 162–179. ISSN 0034 4346.

Jarvis, Matthew. The 1960s Generation and R.S. Thomas to 1968. *Welsh Environments in Contemporary Poetry: Writing Wales in English*. Cardiff: University of Wales Press, 2008.

Perry, Sam. 'In Search of Something Chance Would Never Bring': The Poetry of R.S. Thomas and Edward Thomas. *Review of English Studies: The Leading Journal of English Literature and the English Language* 59:241 (September 2008) 582–603. ISSN 0034 6551.

Perry, Sam. 'Passionate and Simple': R.S. Thomas and Irish Writing. *Almanac – A Yearbook of Welsh Writing in English: Critical Essays* Vol. 13 (2008–2009) 126–161.

Szabo, Daniel. 'For the Failure of Language There Is No Redress': R. S. Thomas, Poetry and Prayer. *Ecstasy and Understanding: Religious Awareness in English Poetry from the Late Victorian to the Modern Period.* Adrian Grafe (editor). London: Continuum, 2008. ISBN 978-0-82649-864-9.

Thomas, M. Wynn. 'The Fantastic Side of God': R.S. Thomas and Jorge Luis Borges. *Renascence* 60.2 (Winter 2008) 178–196. ISSN 0034 4346.

Walford Davies, Damian. 'Yeats Said That': R.S. Thomas and W.B. Yeats. *Almanac – A Yearbook of Welsh Writing in English: Critical Essays* Vol. 13 (2008–2009) 1–26.

Westover, Daniel Kirk. Stylistic Destinations: The Prosodies of R.S. Thomas 1936–2000. PhD thesis, University of Wales [Bangor], 2008.

Henry Vaughan

Major, Philip. Urne-Buriall and the Interregnum Royalist. *'A Man Very Well Studyed': New Contexts for Thomas Browne*. Kathryn Murphy and Richard Todd (editors.)

Leiden: Brill Academic Publishers, 2008. ISBN 978-9-00417-173-2.

Monta, Susannah. Vaughan's *Life of Paulinus*: recharting the Royalist journey. *Renaissance tropologies: the cultural imagination of early modern England.* Jeanne Shami (editor.) Pittsburgh: Duquesne University Press, 2008. ISBN 978-0-82070-409-8

Pursglove, Glyn. 'Not with *leaf* only, but with some *fruit* also'. *Scintilla* 12 (2008) 34–52. ISSN 1368 5023.

Rudrum, Alan. Bring Peace Back to Life: The Anglican Irenicism of Lancelot Andrewes, Henry Vaughan and Rowan Williams. *Scintilla* 12 (2008) 111–120. ISSN 1368 5023.

Sullivan, Ceri. *The Rhetoric of the Conscience in Donne, Herbert and Vaughan.* Oxford: Oxford University Press, 2008. ISBN 978-0-19954-784-5.

West, William N. Less Well-Wrought Urns: Henry Vaughan and the Decay of the Poetic Monument. *ELH* 75:1 (Spring 2008) 197–218. ISSN 0013 8304.

Wilcher, Robert. Henry Vaughan, Jeremy Taylor, Edward Sparke, and the Preservation of the Anglican Communion. *Scintilla* 12 (2008) 141–159. ISSN 1368 5023.

Hilda Vaughan

Thomas, Lucy. 'He was thinking in Welsh now, though he spoke in English': Negotiating identity in the language of Hilda Vaughan's novels. *Almanac – A Yearbook of Welsh Writing in English: Critical Essays* Vol. 13 (2008–2009) 27–54.

Sarah Waters

Bishton, Joanne. Kissing Women: The Fiction of Sarah Waters. *American, British, and Canadian Studies* 10 (July 2008) 91–105. ISSN 1841 964X

Kapla, Cora. *Fingersmith*'s coda: feminism and Victorian Studies. *Journal of Victorian Culture* 13:1 (2008) 42–55. ISSN 1355 5502.

MacPherson, Pauline. 'Fictions can change. It's only the facts that can trap us': Images of female sexuality from Oranges to Velvet. *Women: A Cultural Review* 19:3 (November 2008) 261–274. ISSN 1470 1367.

Mundler, Helen Esther. Seeming and Being: The Play of Alterity in *Affinity* by Sarah Waters. *Résonances* 9 (February 2008) 103–115. ISSN 1245 2262.

Preston, Peter. Victorianism in Recent Victorian Fiction. *History, Politics, Identity: Reading Literature in a Changing World*. Marija Knezevic and Aleksandra Nikcevic-Batricevic (editors.) Newcastle upon Tyne: Cambridge Scholars, 2008. ISBN 978-1-84718-509-9.

Raymond Williams

Dix, Hywel. *After Raymond Williams: Cultural Materialism and the Break-up of Britain*. Cardiff: University of Wales Press, 2008. ISBN 978-0-70832-153-9.

Eagleton, Terry. Performance and Identity. *New Welsh Review* 82 (Winter 2008) 8–16. ISSN 0954 2116. (Review-article of Dai Smith's *A Warrior's Tale*.)

Inglis, Fred. Raymond Williams: A Warrior's Tale by Dai Smith. *The Independent* (20 June 2008). (Review-article)

Thomas, Ned. It is Never the Native Who Returns. *Planet* 190 (August/September 2008) 11–16. ISSN 0048 4288. (Review-article of Dai Smith's *A Warrior's Tale*.)

Rowan Williams

Barker, Sebastian. 'Red Kites Against a Dark Blue Sky': On the Aesthetic of Art in the Theology of Rowan Williams. *Scintilla* 12 (2008) 121–130. ISSN 1368 5023.

Rudrum, Alan. Bring Peace Back to Life: The Anglican Irenicism of Lancelot Andrewes, Henry Vaughan and Rowan Williams. *Scintilla* 12 (2008) 111–120. ISSN 1368 5023.

Tonkin, Boyd. A song of praise for the poet in peril. *The Independent* (25 July 2008). (Review-article)

Diana Wynne Jones

Wood, Naomi. The Cultural Geography of Fantasy Britain. *Children's Literature: Annual of the Modern Language Association Division on Children's Literature and the Children's Literature Association* 36 (2008) 251–256. ISSN 0092 8208 (Review-article on Charles Butler's study of Susan Cooper, Alan Garner, Penelope Lively and Diana Wynne Jones.)

NOTES ON CONTRIBUTORS

Sam Adams is the author of *Thomas Jeffery Llewelyn Prichard* in the Writers of Wales series and is the editor of Roland Mathias's collected poems and collected short stories.

Malcolm Ballin is a Research Associate in the School of English at Cardiff University. His book *Irish Periodical Culture* was published by Palgrave Macmillan in 2008. He is now working on a new book about periodicals and the public sphere in Wales.

Gwynne Edwards was until fairly recently Professor of Spanish at Aberystwyth University, where he specialized in Spanish theatre and cinema. He has published thirteen academic books and more than forty articles, as well as ten volumes of play translations, many of which have had professional productions in major UK venues.

Steve Hendon is a PhD student at the School of English, Communication and Philosophy, Cardiff University. He is working on a thesis that compares the writings of Joseph Conrad and Alun Lewis, particularly in the context of postcolonial approaches to issues of identity and Welsh Writing in English.

John Manson edited the first Penguin *Hugh MacDiarmid: Selected Poems* (with David Craig) in 1970, and *Hugh MacDiarmid: The Revolutionary Art of the Future*, sub-titled 'Rediscovered Poems' (with Dorian Grieve and Alan Riach), Manchester, 2003. He has published essays on MacDiarmid and other Scottish authors in various journals and is at present editing *Dear Grieve: Letters to Hugh MacDiarmid*.

Catherine Phelps is currently working on her PhD thesis on contemporary Welsh Crime Fiction at Cardiff University.

She has a forthcoming publication on genre in Alison Taylor's *Simeon's Bride* and is editing a collection of essays on crime fiction in capital cities.

Gwyneth Tyson Roberts is an independent scholar. Her publications include *The Language of the Blue Books: the perfect instrument of empire* (UWP, 1998).

Alyce von Rothkirch holds a PhD on Welsh Drama in English from Swansea University. She currently works at the Department of Adult Continuing Education at Swansea University. Her research focuses on Welsh writing in English and Detective Fiction.

Alan Vaughan Jones is a PhD student at Aberystwyth University. He is writing his thesis on the works of Idris Davies and Alun Lewis.

John Powell Ward's latest academic book is *The Spell of the Song: Letters, Meaning, and English Poetry* (Fairleigh-Dickinson University Press, USA, 2004); his latest collection of poetry is *The Last Green Year* (Cinnamon Press, 2009); his *Selected and New Poems* appeared from Seren in 2004.

Acknowledgements

almanac – welsh writing in english: a yearbook of critical essays is published with the financial support of the Welsh Books Council; the editor also gratefully acknowledges the support of the Association for Welsh Writing in English. We are as ever indebted to those scholars who have found time in busy schedules to act as readers of papers submitted for publication; their advice and guidance are indispensable.

Information for Contributors

Correspondence and contributions for publication should be addressed to the editor: Dr Katie Gramich, School of English, Communication and Philosophy, Cardiff University, Humanities Building, Colum Drive, Cardiff, CF10 3EU (email: GramichK @cf.ac.uk). The *almanac* publishes essays on literary topics, not on purely Welsh historical matters. While its primary concern is the study of Welsh writing in English, papers on Welsh-language authors, written in English, will be considered; the Yearbook will also consider papers which relate the two literatures of Wales or discuss the literatures of Wales in international, comparative contexts. Papers should not normally exceed 8,000 words in length.

Manuscripts (two copies) should be typed on one side of the page, double spaced, and produced according to the current MHRA Style Guide. Include a computer disk with the hard copies, and note the word-processing programme used. All contributions will be refereed. While a decision will be made as expeditiously as possible, allow three months for a decision. Contributors of published papers receive two complimentary copies of the issue in which their paper appears. The *almanac* web page, which includes information on past issues, is at:

http://www.cardiff.ac.uk/encap/journals/periodic/welshwrit.html

LIBRARY OF WALES

SERIES EDITOR: DAI SMITH

1	Ron Berry	*So Long, Hector Bebb*
2	Raymond Williams	*Border Country*
3	Gwyn Thomas	*The Dark Philosophers*
4	Lewis Jones	*Cwmardy & We Live*
5	Margiad Evans	*Country Dance*
6	Emyr Humphreys	*A Man's Estate*
7	Alun Richards	*Home to an Empty House*
8	Alun Lewis	*In the Green Tree*
9	Dannie Abse	*Ash on a Young Man's Sleeve*
10	Ed. Meic Stephens	*Poetry 1900-2000*
11	Ed. Gareth Williams	*Sport: an anthology*
12	Rhys Davies	*The Withered Root*
13	Dorothy Edwards	*Rhapsody*
14	Jeremy Brooks	*Jampot Smith*
15	George Ewart Evans	*The Voices of the Children*
16	Bernice Rubens	*I Sent a Letter to My Love*
17	Howell Davies	*Congratulate the Devil*
18	Geraint Goodwin	*The Heyday in the Blood*
19	Gwyn Thomas	*The Alone to the Alone*
20	Stuart Evans	*The Caves of Alienation*
21	Brenda Chamberlain	*A Rope of Vines*
22	Jack Jones	*Black Parade*
23	Alun Richards	*Dai Country*
24	Glyn Jones	*The Valley, the City, the Village*
25	Arthur Machen	*The Great God Pan*
26	Arthur Machen	*The Hill of Dreams*
27	Hilda Vaughan	*The Battle to the Weak*
28	Margiad Evans	*Turf or Stone*

WWW.LIBRARYOFWALES.ORG

LIBRARY OF WALES
titles are available to buy online at: gwales.com
Llyfrau ar-lein
Books on-line